ENCYCLOPEDIA OF
Animals

ENCYCLOPEDIA OF
Animals

KAREN McGHEE • GEORGE McKAY PH.D

NATIONAL GEOGRAPHIC

WASHINGTON, D.C.

Conceived and produced by Weldon Owen Pty Ltd

61 Victoria Street, McMahons Point

Sydney, NSW 2060, Australia

First published in North America in 2007 by the

National Geographic Society

1145 17th Street N.W.

Washington, D.C. 20036-4688

For information about special discounts for bulk purchases,
please contact National Geographic Books Special Sales:
ngspecsales@ngs.org

Chief Executive Officer John Owen

President Terry Newell

Publisher Sheena Coupe

Creative Director Sue Burk

Vice President International Sales Stuart Laurence

Administrator International Sales Kristine Ravn

Project Editor Jessica Cox

Project Designer Domenika Markovtzev

Editor Clara Finlay

Designers Kathryn Morgan, Juliana Titin

Editorial Coordinator Irene Mickaiel

Author Karen McGhee

Consultant Editor Dr. George McKay

Consultants Lucéia Bonora, Dr. Mark Hutchinson,
           Dr. Stephen Hutchinson, Dr. Noel Tait

Index Puddingburn Publishing Services

Production Director Chris Hemesath

Production Manager Louise Mitchell

Production Coordinator Monique Layt

Hardcover Edition:
ISBN-10: 0-7922-5936-X
ISBN-13: 978-0-7922-5936-7

Library Edition:
ISBN-10: 0-7922-5937-8
ISBN-13: 978-0-7922-5937-4

Direct Mail Expanded Edition:
ISBN-10: 0-7922-7458-X
ISBN-13: 978-0-7922-7458-2

Deluxe Direct Mail Expanded Edition:
ISBN-10: 0-7922-7460-1
ISBN-13: 978-0-7922-7460-5

Color reproduction by Colourscan Overseas Co Pte Ltd

Printed in China by SNP Leefung Printers Ltd

A Weldon Owen production

Contents

7 ORDERS • 19 FAMILIES • 83 GENERA • 295 SPECIES

Marsupials

All marsupials are born in an extremely immature state. Their gestation time can be as few as 9 days for the eastern quoll or as many as 38 days for the eastern gray kangaroo. They weigh only a few milligrams when they are born. Young marsupials then usually develop in a pouch or fold of skin, feeding on their mother's milk. This method of reproducing and raising young is the main difference between marsupials and placental mammals. Marsupials were once widespread across the Americas and Europe, as well as in Australia. Today, only 70 species of marsupials still survive in the Americas—opossums, shrew-opossums, and the monito del monte.

Monito del monte (colocolo)
Dromiciops gliroides
It uses bamboo leaves, moss, and twigs to build a round nest, where it may hibernate in winter.

Common opossum
Didelphis marsupialis
After living in her pouch for two months, young are carried on mother's back until they are three to four months old.

Little water opossum
Lutreolina crassicaudata
This opossum's thick tail has a hairless tip.

Ecuadorean shrew-opossum
Caenolestes fuliginosus

Patagonian opossum
Lestodelphys halli

Robinson's mouse opossum
Marmosa robinsoni
Opposable thumbs on all four paws help grip thin branches and vines.

Southern short-tailed opossum
Monodelphis dimidiata

Yapok (water opossum)
Chironectes minimus
The only aquatic marsupial, the yapok has webbed toes and oily fur.

Marsupials

Some marsupials occur in the Americas, but most are native only to Australia and New Guinea. They have been introduced to the islands of New Zealand, Hawaii, and Britain.

STARTING OUT

A newborn is little more than an embryo when it emerges from its mother's cloaca.

Using strong front legs, it crawls upward through its mother's hair toward her pouch.

The newborn attaches firmly to a teat in the pouch for weeks or months of rapid growth.

Possums and kangaroos

Possums and kangaroos belong to a large order of marsupials called diprotodonts that also includes wombats and the koala. Diprotodonts all have two large, protruding incisor teeth on the lower jaw. They are found only in the Australasian region. Most are grass- or leaf-eaters, but some possums eat insects or nectar. Very few species in this group are diurnal, or active during daylight hours, preferring to feed at twilight or at night. The largest living member of the group is also the largest marsupial—the male red kangaroo can reach heights of 4½ feet (1.5 m) and weights of 190 pounds (85 kg). Most kangaroos and wallabies move by hopping on well-developed back legs, although the tree kangaroos of northern Australia and New Guinea climb trees. Possums are mostly tree dwellers.

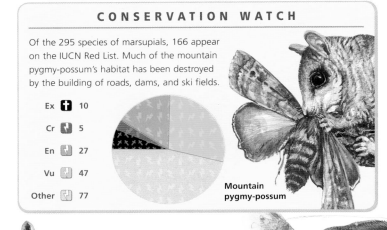

CONSERVATION WATCH

Of the 295 species of marsupials, 166 appear on the IUCN Red List. Much of the mountain pygmy-possum's habitat has been destroyed by the building of roads, dams, and ski fields.

Ex	✝	10
Cr		5
En		27
Vu		47
Other		77

Mountain pygmy-possum

Yellow-footed rock wallaby
Petrogale xanthopus
Back feet have roughened soles for clinging to rocks.

Common wombat
Vombatus ursinus

Goodfellow's tree kangaroo
Dendrolagus goodfellowi
Has strong front legs for climbing trees

BOXING KANGAROOS

Male red kangaroos attempt to dominate others during the breeding season.

Front legs deliver scratches to the face and upper body.

The strong tail is used for balance.

Powerful back legs kick the opponent.

Red kangaroo
Macropus rufus
This marsupial is active mainly at twilight or nighttime.

Western gray kangaroo
Macropus fuliginosus
These kangaroos often form social groups, called mobs, which usually consist of related family members.

Rufous bettong
Aepyprymnus rufescens

Common ringtail possum
Pseudocheirus peregrinus

Herbert River ringtail possum
Pseudochirulus herbertensis
This possum rarely leaves the safety of the trees for the ground.

Koala
Phascolarctos cinereus
Their diet of eucalyptus leaves is low in nutrients, but high in toxins. Koalas need to sleep 20 hours a day.

Striped possum
Dactylopsila trivirgata

Leadbeater's possum
Gymnobelideus leadbeateri
One of the most isolated marsupials: Its range is only 1,350 square miles (3,500 km²).

Musky rat-kangaroo
Hypsiprymnodon moschatus

Brushtail possum
Trichosurus vulpecula
This possum was once hunted for its fur; it is now a protected species in Australia.

Sugar glider
Petaurus breviceps
Each back foot has an opposable big toe.

Spotted cuscus
Spilocuscus maculatus

Feathertail glider
Acrobates pygmaeus
The feather-like fur on its tail acts as a rudder when gliding. A gliding membrane extends from knee.

Mountain pygmy-possum
Burramys parvus

Scaly-tailed possum
Wyulda squamicaudata

SIMILAR SOLUTIONS

Like the aye-aye of Madagascar, the Australian striped possum has a long, narrow finger for hooking grubs out of tree holes.

STRIPED POSSUM

AYE-AYE

Bandicoots and quolls

Some marsupials, including the catlike quolls and the Tasmanian devil, are meat-eaters. The dog-size thylacine was the largest member of this order. It was hunted into extinction in the early 1900s. These marsupials have different teeth from those of the plant-eating kangaroos and possums, because they capture other animals, tear flesh, and gnaw bone. The smaller dunnarts, phascogales, and antechinuses hunt mostly insects. In a separate order are the omnivorous bandicoots, which eat both plants and animals. They are often solitary creatures. Some species dig pits in their search for food. Marsupial moles burrow just underground for invertebrates. Unlike true moles, they leave no tunnels.

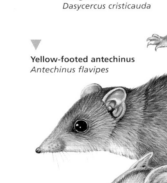

Spotted-tailed quoll
Dasyurus maculatus
This quoll lives in trees, where it hunts small animals. It also scavenges dead flesh.

Mulgara
Dasycercus cristicauda

Yellow-footed antechinus
Antechinus flavipes

Thylacine (Tasmanian tiger)
Thylacinus cynocephalus
The Tasmanian tiger has 13 to 19 dark stripes along its back. Its stiff tail is thick at the base but tapers to a point.

Tasmanian devil
Sarcophilus harrisii
Its strong jaw and heavy molar teeth can crush bones.

Fat-tailed dunnart
Sminthopsis crassicaudata
Stores fat in its tail

Bilby
Macrotis lagotis
The bilby has a long, pointed snout and a two-colored, bushy tail.

Numbat
Myrmecobius fasciatus
Its sticky tongue extends as far as 4 inches (10 cm) from its mouth. Females have no external pouch.

Southern brown bandicoot
Isoodon obesulus

Southern marsupial mole
Notoryctes typhlops
Does not have external ears; its silky, shimmering fur is stained by iron-rich soil.

Striped bandicoot
Microperoryctes longicauda

2 ORDERS • 5 FAMILIES • 14 GENERA • 36 SPECIES

Anteaters and Pangolins

Anteaters, armadillos, and sloths are an order of placental mammals with small brains and few, or no, teeth. They have extra backbone joints that strengthen the lower back and hips. This is especially useful for diggers like anteaters and armadillos. Anteaters are toothless insect-eaters with a preference for termites, which they lap up with a long, sticky tongue. Armadillos also have sticky tongues for picking up insects, but most eat plants. They are powerful diggers and swimmers with a protective shell of large bony scales that extends over their backs. Sloths are known for their extremely sluggish movements, caused by their low-energy diet of leaves. Pangolins form their own order. They resemble armadillos with their armor of overlapping horny plates. Their tongue can be longer than the combined length of their head and body.

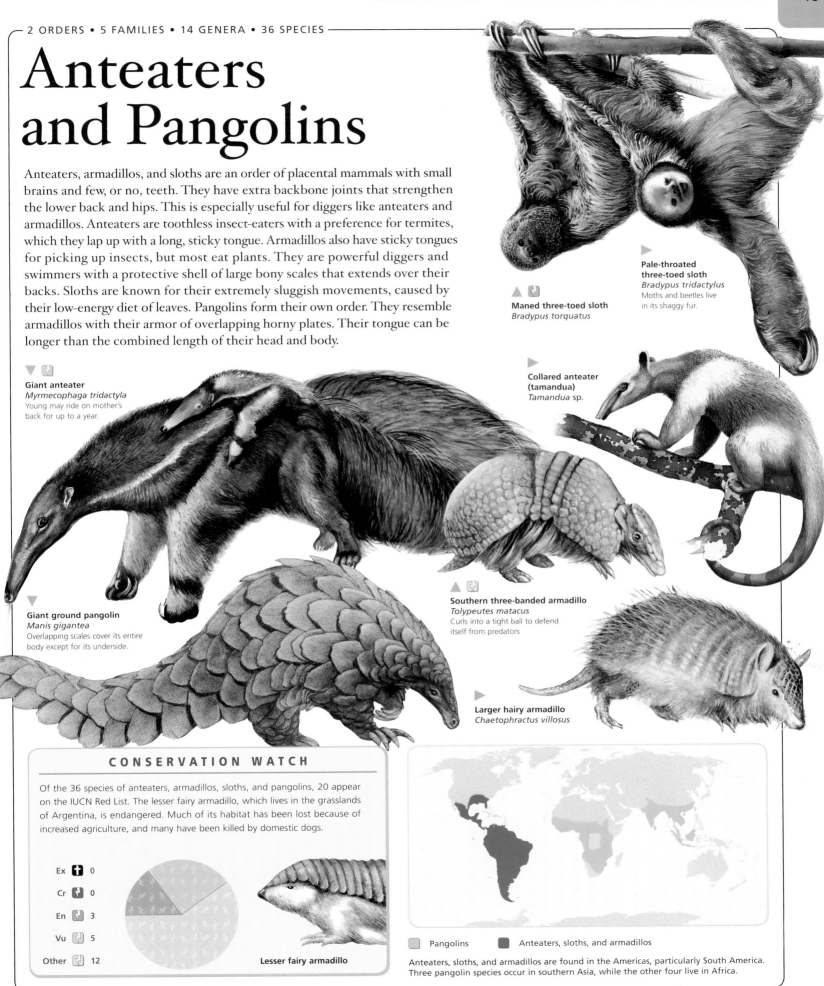

Pale-throated three-toed sloth
Bradypus tridactylus
Moths and beetles live in its shaggy fur.

Maned three-toed sloth
Bradypus torquatus

Giant anteater
Myrmecophaga tridactyla
Young may ride on mother's back for up to a year.

Collared anteater (tamandua)
Tamandua sp.

Giant ground pangolin
Manis gigantea
Overlapping scales cover its entire body except for its underside.

Southern three-banded armadillo
Tolypeutes matacus
Curls into a tight ball to defend itself from predators

Larger hairy armadillo
Chaetophractus villosus

CONSERVATION WATCH

Of the 36 species of anteaters, armadillos, sloths, and pangolins, 20 appear on the IUCN Red List. The lesser fairy armadillo, which lives in the grasslands of Argentina, is endangered. Much of its habitat has been lost because of increased agriculture, and many have been killed by domestic dogs.

Ex	0
Cr	0
En	3
Vu	5
Other	12

Lesser fairy armadillo

Pangolins ☐   Anteaters, sloths, and armadillos ☐

Anteaters, sloths, and armadillos are found in the Americas, particularly South America. Three pangolin species occur in southern Asia, while the other four live in Africa.

1 ORDER • 7 FAMILIES • 68 GENERA • 428 SPECIES

Insect-eating Mammals

Many of the earliest mammals were probably insect-eaters, or insectivores. Modern insect-eating mammals feed almost exclusively on insects and other small invertebrates. Some will also eat plants and even small fish and lizards, if they get the chance. The order includes shrews, tenrecs, hedgehogs, and moles. Insectivores have small, smooth brains and simple teeth that are primitive compared to those of other mammal groups. They are small, shy creatures, active only at night. While most live at ground level, some shrews and moles prefer the water. Most of them are small with long snouts and well-developed senses of smell and touch. Their vision is often poor—burrowing moles, in particular, can see little through their tiny eyes. Hedgehogs and some tenrecs have spines along their upper bodies to protect them from predators.

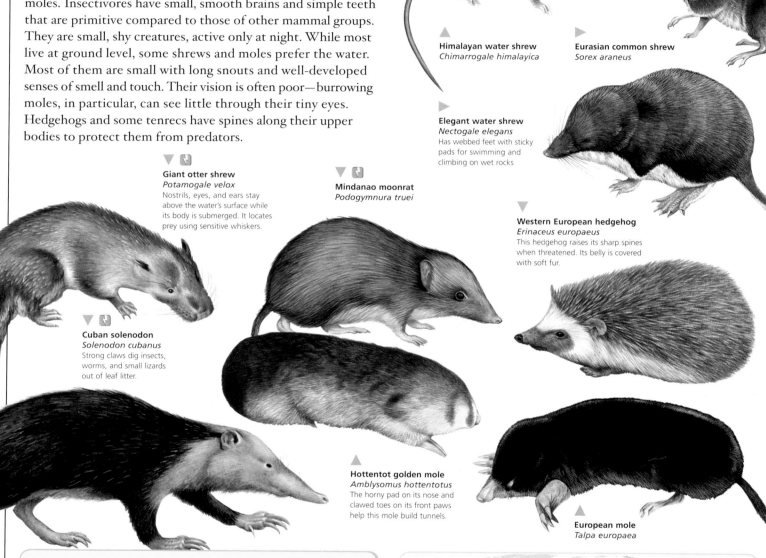

Himalayan water shrew
Chimarrogale himalayica

Eurasian common shrew
Sorex araneus

Elegant water shrew
Nectogale elegans
Has webbed feet with sticky pads for swimming and climbing on wet rocks

Giant otter shrew
Potamogale velox
Nostrils, eyes, and ears stay above the water's surface while its body is submerged. It locates prey using sensitive whiskers.

Mindanao moonrat
Podogymnura truei

Western European hedgehog
Erinaceus europaeus
This hedgehog raises its sharp spines when threatened. Its belly is covered with soft fur.

Cuban solenodon
Solenodon cubanus
Strong claws dig insects, worms, and small lizards out of leaf litter.

Hottentot golden mole
Amblysomus hottentotus
The horny pad on its nose and clawed toes on its front paws help this mole build tunnels.

European mole
Talpa europaea

CONSERVATION WATCH

Of the 428 species of insectivores, 173 appear on the IUCN Red List. This figure includes one of the world's rarest animals, South Africa's giant golden mole. The Ruwenzori otter shrew lives in rivers and streams around the Congo Basin in Africa. It is endangered because these streams are becoming polluted by waste and sewage as more humans settle in the area.

Ex	✝	5
Cr		22
En		48
Vu		54
Other		44

Ruwenzori otter shrew

Insect-eating mammals

Hedgehogs, moonrats, moles, desmans, and shrews can be found throughout much of the world. Solenodons, tenrecs, and otter shrews live in more limited ranges.

2 ORDERS • 2 FAMILIES • 6 GENERA • 21 SPECIES

Flying Lemurs and Tree Shrews

There are just two living species of flying lemurs. Also known as colugos, both are leaf-eating tree dwellers that are active at night. They are small animals, with adults reaching as much as 4½ pounds (2 kg) in weight. Flying lemurs have a thin, but tough, membrane of skin that stretches between their front and back legs. They do not fly, but glide as far as 300 feet (91 m) between trees. Grace in the air does not equal grace on the ground, however; flying lemurs are clumsy and helpless walkers. Most of the 19 tree shrew species live in trees, scampering up and down in their search for small animals and fruit. They are active, territorial, and noisy creatures that look a little like squirrels. Although they are not related to squirrels, tree shrews have the same ability to hold food in their front paws while sitting up on their haunches.

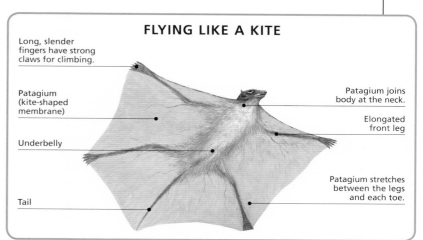

FLYING LIKE A KITE

Long, slender fingers have strong claws for climbing.

Patagium (kite-shaped membrane)

Underbelly

Tail

Patagium joins body at the neck.

Elongated front leg

Patagium stretches between the legs and each toe.

Common tree shrew
Tupaia glis

Malayan flying lemur
Cynocephalus variegatus

Pen-tailed tree shrew
Ptilocercus lowii
This is the only tree shrew that is active at night. Its scaly, plumed tail twitches constantly.

Large tree shrew
Tupaia tana
The large tree shrew uses its long snout to root through leaf litter for insects and seeds.

CONSERVATION WATCH

Of the 21 species of flying lemurs and tree shrews, 8 appear on the IUCN Red List. The vulnerable Philippine flying lemur is considered to be a pest by farmers and is hunted for its meat. Logging also threatens its rain forest habitat.

Ex	✝	0
Cr		0
En		2
Vu		5
Other		1

Philippine flying lemur

☐ Tree shrews   ☐ Flying lemurs and tree shrews

Flying lemurs and tree shrews are found only in the tropical forests of southern and Southeast Asia. Most tree shrews live on the Indonesian island of Borneo.

1 ORDER • 18 FAMILIES • 177 GENERA • 993 SPECIES

Bats

Bats are the only mammals that can truly fly. They probably evolved from tree-dwelling ancestors that moved between high branches, first by leaping and later by gliding. Their wings are more flexible than those of birds, allowing more agility in flight. Bats form the second largest order of mammals; the group contains one-quarter of all mammal species. The smallest is the tiny Thai hog-nosed bat, also called the bumblebee bat. Its skull measures less than ½ inch (10 cm) across and its wingspan is 6 inches (15 cm). The largest bat is the Malayan flying fox, with a wingspan of almost 80 inches (2 m). There are two kinds of bats: the fruit bats, or flying foxes, and the microbats, most of which eat insects. Both groups of bats are usually social animals that live in colonies. Females may form special nursery colonies, where they roost and raise their young away from males and nonpregnant females.

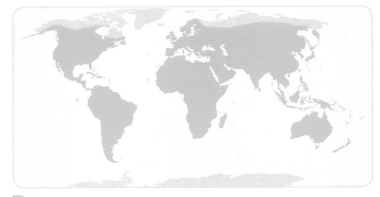

☐ Bats

Bats occur in all regions of the world except for the polar regions and a few isolated islands. They are most common in warmer areas, especially the tropics.

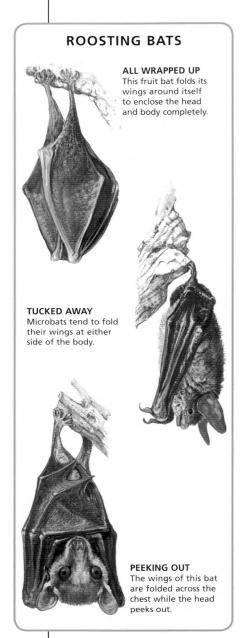

ROOSTING BATS

ALL WRAPPED UP
This fruit bat folds its wings around itself to enclose the head and body completely.

TUCKED AWAY
Microbats tend to fold their wings at either side of the body.

PEEKING OUT
The wings of this bat are folded across the chest while the head peeks out.

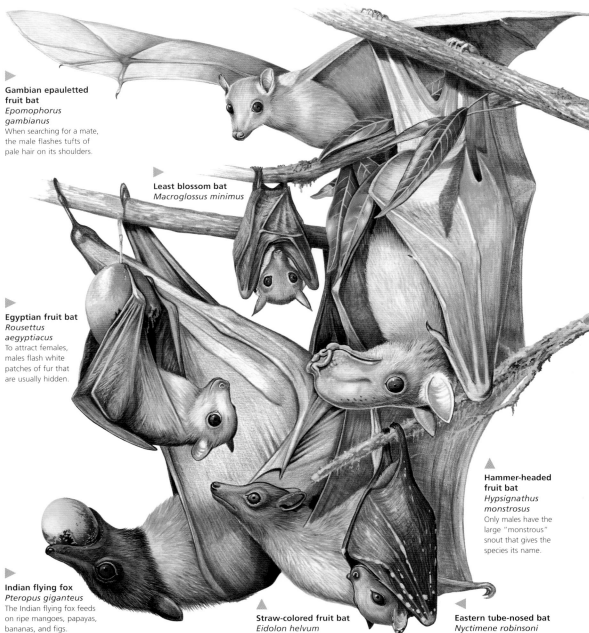

Gambian epauletted fruit bat
Epomophorus gambianus
When searching for a mate, the male flashes tufts of pale hair on its shoulders.

Least blossom bat
Macroglossus minimus

Egyptian fruit bat
Rousettus aegyptiacus
To attract females, males flash white patches of fur that are usually hidden.

Indian flying fox
Pteropus giganteus
The Indian flying fox feeds on ripe mangoes, papayas, bananas, and figs.

Hammer-headed fruit bat
Hypsignathus monstrosus
Only males have the large "monstrous" snout that gives the species its name.

Straw-colored fruit bat
Eidolon helvum

Eastern tube-nosed bat
Nyctimene robinsoni

SIGHT AND SOUND

ECHOLOCATION

Fruit bats rely on vision to get around. Microbats "see" by using a radar-like sense called echolocation. This enables many species to hunt in the dark. They send out high-pitched sounds, then assess what surrounds them by judging the echoes that bounce back off solid objects, such as insect bodies.

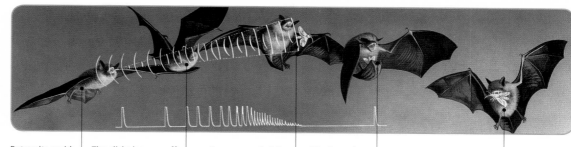

Bat emits rapid, high-pitched clicks of sound.

The clicks bounce off prey, revealing its location to the bat.

Frequency of clicks increases as it nears, pinpointing prey.

The bat seizes prey in its back claws.

The prey is then transferred to the bat's mouth.

MAKING SONAR

Ear detects reflected sound.

Nose emits clicks of sound.

Ear detects reflected sound.

Mouth emits clicks of sound.

TRIDENT BAT

WHISKERED BAT

EARS AND NOSES

LONG-EARED BAT
Ears with flaps may improve echolocation.

TENT-BUILDING BAT
Leaf-shaped nose helps detect prey's echoes.

LESSER BARE-BACKED FRUIT BAT
Nostrils sniff out food.

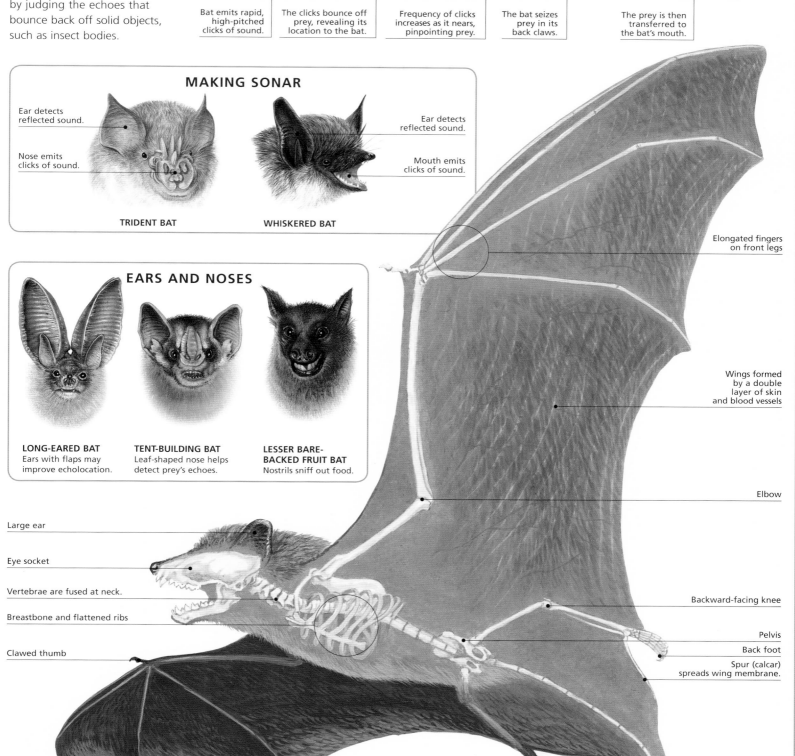

Elongated fingers on front legs

Wings formed by a double layer of skin and blood vessels

Elbow

Backward-facing knee

Pelvis

Back foot

Spur (calcar) spreads wing membrane.

Large ear

Eye socket

Vertebrae are fused at neck.

Breastbone and flattened ribs

Clawed thumb

Tail

Microbats

The majority of bats are microbats. All use echolocation to find and capture their food. Most species eat flying insects that they pursue and capture on the wing at night. However, some of the larger species are meat-eaters, hunting small vertebrates such as fish, frogs, birds, lizards, and rodents. Others eat fruit, nectar, or flowers. Three species survive by lapping up fresh blood. As their name suggests, microbats tend to be smaller than fruit bats, with most reaching a body length of less than 6 inches (15 cm) when fully grown. Because they rely on echolocation, their eyes are usually small and ears more developed. The faces of some microbats are adorned with noseleaves, leaf-shaped flaps of skin and tissue that may help them find food.

Wrinkle-faced bat
Centurio senex
This bat has strange-looking folds of skin around its face.

Diadem leaf-nosed bat
Hipposideros diadema

Pocketed free-tailed bat
Nyctinomops femorosaccus
Its thick tail extends beyond the wing membrane.

Common vampire bat
Desmodus rotundus
Modified thumbs and back legs let it move on all fours as it hunts.

American false vampire bat
Vampyrum spectrum

HONDURAN WHITE BATS

These small Central American fruit-eaters cut large leaves with their teeth in such a way that the leaves flop over to form protective "tents." Small colonies of as many as six bats shelter from heavy tropical downpours in these tents. When the sun shines through the rain forest leaves, the bats' soft white fur reflects the green light. This makes them appear almost invisible. At least 14 other bat species make leaf tents.

Veins of heliconia leaf are nibbled along the stem, making it flop over.

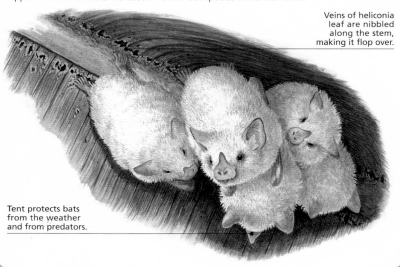

Tent protects bats from the weather and from predators.

Greater bulldog bat
Noctilio leporinus
Long back legs with huge feet and strong claws snatch fish from the water. Cheek pouches store chewed fish so it can continue fishing.

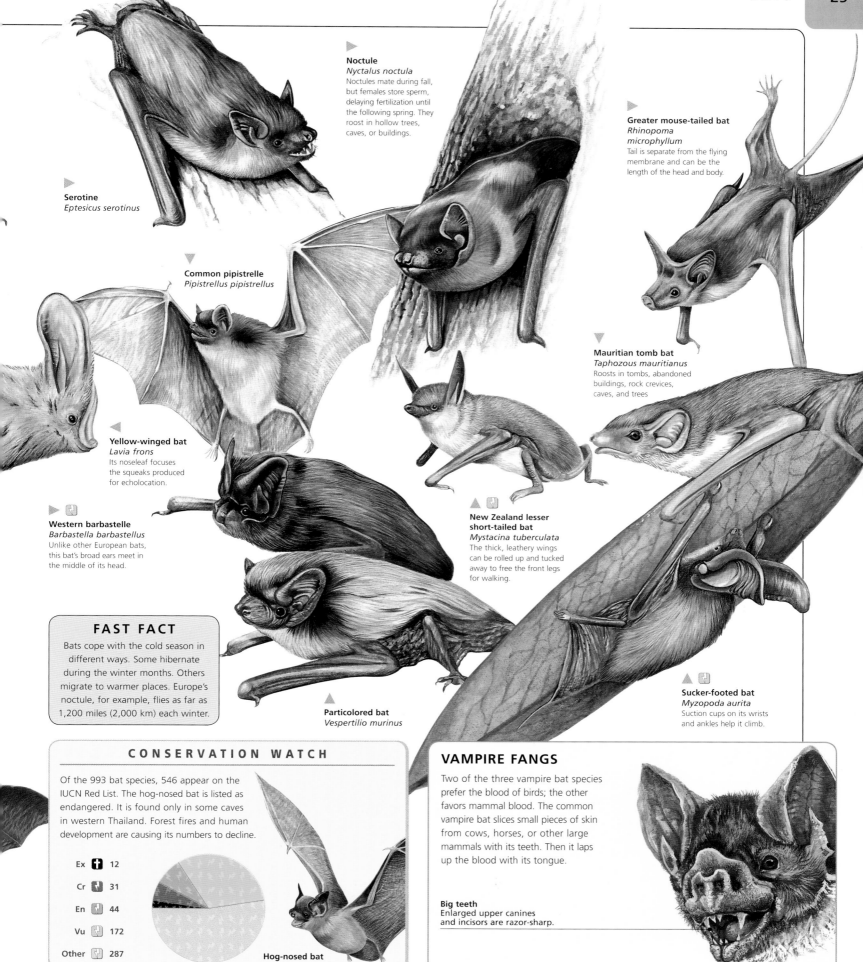

Noctule
Nyctalus noctula
Noctules mate during fall, but females store sperm, delaying fertilization until the following spring. They roost in hollow trees, caves, or buildings.

Serotine
Eptesicus serotinus

Greater mouse-tailed bat
Rhinopoma microphyllum
Tail is separate from the flying membrane and can be the length of the head and body.

Common pipistrelle
Pipistrellus pipistrellus

Mauritian tomb bat
Taphozous mauritianus
Roosts in tombs, abandoned buildings, rock crevices, caves, and trees

Yellow-winged bat
Lavia frons
Its noseleaf focuses the squeaks produced for echolocation.

Western barbastelle
Barbastella barbastellus
Unlike other European bats, this bat's broad ears meet in the middle of its head.

New Zealand lesser short-tailed bat
Mystacina tuberculata
The thick, leathery wings can be rolled up and tucked away to free the front legs for walking.

Sucker-footed bat
Myzopoda aurita
Suction cups on its wrists and ankles help it climb.

Particolored bat
Vespertilio murinus

FAST FACT

Bats cope with the cold season in different ways. Some hibernate during the winter months. Others migrate to warmer places. Europe's noctule, for example, flies as far as 1,200 miles (2,000 km) each winter.

CONSERVATION WATCH

Of the 993 bat species, 546 appear on the IUCN Red List. The hog-nosed bat is listed as endangered. It is found only in some caves in western Thailand. Forest fires and human development are causing its numbers to decline.

Ex		12
Cr		31
En		44
Vu		172
Other		287

Hog-nosed bat

VAMPIRE FANGS

Two of the three vampire bat species prefer the blood of birds; the other favors mammal blood. The common vampire bat slices small pieces of skin from cows, horses, or other large mammals with its teeth. Then it laps up the blood with its tongue.

Big teeth
Enlarged upper canines and incisors are razor-sharp.

1 ORDER • 13 FAMILIES • 60 GENERA • 295 SPECIES

Primates

Gorillas live in family troops in eastern, central, and west-central Africa. Baby gorillas suckle for as long as 18 months and stay with their mothers for about three years.

Primates are intelligent mammals that live mostly in trees. Their forward-facing eyes let them see in three dimensions and judge distances. Their thumbs are opposable—they can reach around to touch the tips of the other fingers—which lets them hold objects. There are two main groups of primates: lower primates, or prosimians, and higher primates, or monkeys and apes.

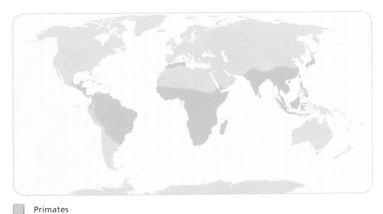

Primates

Most primates live in rain forests, mainly in the tropical and subtropical regions of Africa, Asia, and South America. Only a few live in temperate areas.

PRIMATE FEATURES

UPRIGHT SKELETON
Apes sometimes sit and walk upright. Their arms, which are longer than their legs, help with balance as they walk.

Large brain and skull

Broad rib cage

Extended arms

Flexible wrists

TARSIER
Disklike pads help when climbing trees.

AYE-AYE
Long third digit pulls grubs from holes.

GORILLA
Broad, flat feet (left) support heavy body.

Lower primates

Lemurs, bushbabies, and tarsiers are lower primates, also known as prosimians. They have moist, doglike noses and faces covered with hair. Prosimians rely on smell—from their urine, feces, or scent glands—to mark territory and identify others. Most are small, nocturnal tree dwellers. They have large eyes to help them see in the dark, but they do not have full-color vision. Prosimians eat mostly insects, but some will also gather fruit, leaves, flowers, nectar, and plant gums. The name lemur comes from the Latin word for "ghost," which suits their haunting stares and eerie cries. Bushbabies get their name from the childlike wails they make in the middle of the night. Tarsiers are named for the long tarsus bones in their feet.

CONSERVATION WATCH

Of the 63 species of prosimians, 49 appear on the IUCN Red List. The endangered aye-aye is threatened by the destruction of its forest home.

Ex 0
Cr 3
En 9
Vu 11
Other 26

Aye-aye

Spectral tarsier
Tarsius spectrum
Its huge eyes are larger than its stomach.

Angwantibo (golden potto)
Arctocebus calabarensis

Demidoff's galago
Galagoides demidoff

Aye-aye
Daubentonia madagascariensis
The aye-aye uses echolocation to find grubs.

Slender loris
Loris tardigradus
Enjoys play and wrestling sessions at dawn and dusk

Eastern needle-clawed bushbaby
Euoticus inustus
Enlarged front teeth on lower jaw, called a dental comb, are used to scrape sap off tree bark.

Diadem sifaka
Propithecus diadema

Indri
Indri indri
The indri has large, black, tufted ears and a short tail.

Weasel sportive lemur
Lepilemur mustelinus
Makes giant leaps on its strong back legs

Ruffed lemur
Varecia variegata

New World monkeys

There are two groups of monkeys—the New World and the Old World monkeys. New World monkeys are found in the tropical rain forests of Central and South America and as far north as Mexico. They include the spider, howler, and squirrel monkeys, as well as the tamarins, marmosets, and uakaris. All have broad, flat noses; nostrils that face sideways; and a distinctive arrangement of teeth. Many have a prehensile tail, which works like an extra limb. Most New World monkeys are diurnal and spend their lives in trees eating leaves, fruit, nuts, and other parts of plants. Some will also eat insects or small animals, such as lizards or baby birds. New World monkeys can live alone, in small bands or mating pairs, harems, family groups, or in troops of as many as 500 members.

Common woolly monkey
Lagothrix lagotricha

Long-haired spider monkey
Ateles belzebuth
Thumbless fingers work together like a hook for swinging.

Woolly spider monkey
Brachyteles arachnoide
Likes to eat leaves while hanging only by its tail

Black howler
Alouatta caraya
Produces deep growls so loud they can be heard more than 2 miles (3 km) away

White-faced saki
Pithecia pithecia
Long back legs let it leap 30 feet (9 m) between trees.

Mantled howler
Alouatta palliata

Geoffroy's tamarin
Saguinus geoffroyi
Twins are common, and males help to care for and carry the babies of the whole troop.

Golden lion tamarin
Leontopithecus rosalia
Sleeps in tree holes, such as abandoned woodpecker nests

Black-headed uakari
Cacajao melanocephalus

EXPERT SWINGERS

Spider monkeys rely on their prehensile tails for swooping through the treetops. The tail grasps tree branches like an extra arm or leg and helps spider monkey babies stay on their swinging mothers.

Pygmy marmoset
Callithrix pygmaea

▶ **Northern night monkey**
Aotus trivirgatus
Large eyes help this monkey see at night.

▶ **Common squirrel monkey**
Saimiri sciureus
Females give birth in the rainy season, when there is more food.

▶ **Dusky titi**
Callicebus moloch
Adults form strong, lifelong bonds with just one mate.

NEW AND OLD DIFFERENCES

NEW WORLD
Woolly monkey

OLD WORLD
Vervet monkey

Nostrils are close together and point downward.

Most have a grasping, prehensile tail that works like an extra limb.

Thumbs on both limbs are highly opposable—they help grasp and hold objects.

Broad flat noses with sideways-facing nostrils

Tail, if present, is not prehensile.

Thumbs, when present, are not highly opposable to other fingers.

▲ **Common marmoset**
Callithrix jacchus

▲ **Brown capuchin**
Cebus apella

Old World monkeys

Old World monkeys are found only in Africa and Asia, aside from the Barbary ape, which was introduced to Gibraltar in Europe. All Old World monkeys have protruding nostrils that face downward. While these monkeys lack prehensile tails—a few lack tails entirely—they have strong hands with opposable thumbs that let them pick up objects precisely. Some have thick pads of bare skin called ischial callosities on their bottoms. Most species live in trees, but many forage on the ground. Old World monkeys are divided into two groups. The first group, including baboons, has cheek pouches in which they store their food while they are out in the open, so they can eat in safety. The second group, including colobuses, has a three-chambered stomach, which helps them fully digest their diet of plants.

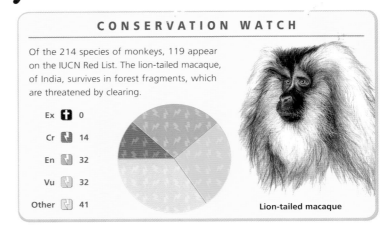

CONSERVATION WATCH

Of the 214 species of monkeys, 119 appear on the IUCN Red List. The lion-tailed macaque, of India, survives in forest fragments, which are threatened by clearing.

Ex	✝	0
Cr		14
En		32
Vu		32
Other		41

Lion-tailed macaque

Gelada
Theropithecus gelada

Hamadryas baboon (savanna baboon)
Papio hamadryas
As many as 750 animals sleep collectively for protection from predators. Bands of 100 animals travel and forage together.

Sykes's monkey (blue monkey)
Cercopithecus mitis
Coat is usually red-brown or gray-brown, but is sometimes blue.

Proboscis monkey
Nasalis larvatus
Big nose on males helps make their calls louder.

Barbary ape
Macaca sylvanus
Unusual among macaques because males help to raise young.

Allen's swamp monkey
Allenopithecus nigroviridis

Red colobus
Procolobus badius

Chinese snub-nosed monkey
Rhinopithecus roxellana
Lives in mountains more than 14,500 feet (4,400 m) above sea level

Douc langur
Pygathrix nemaeus

Bear macaque (stump-tailed macaque)
Macaca arctoides
Bear macaques go bald as they get old.

Hanuman langur
Semnopithecus entellus
Considered sacred in India; lives in troops of 20 or 30, often with a single male

White-cheeked mangabey
Lophocebus albigena
These monkeys make a high-pitched chuckle when alarmed.

Vervet monkey
Chlorocebus aethiops

Redtail monkey
Cercopithecus ascanius
Greet each other before playing or grooming by rubbing noses

King colobus
Colobus polykomos
Babies are white for the first few months of life.

Mandrill
Mandrillus sphinx

GRASS-EATING GELADAS

Geladas are the lawn mowers of the primate world—they eat almost nothing but grass. They live only in Ethiopia, in eastern Africa, in groups of as many as 400. Fatty padding on their bottoms allows them to sit eating for long periods each day. Their thumbs and index fingers work together like pairs of tweezers, picking at single blades of grass. Females also spend a lot of time grooming each other and ignoring the males. Both sexes have a hairless, hourglass-shaped skin patch on the chest. This is always bright red in adult males and is meant to be attractive to females while scaring off other males. This patch only turns red in females when they are ready to mate.

Apes

Apes are the most intelligent primates. They are social animals that spend years looking after their young. While they have similar teeth and noses to Old World monkeys, apes have many different features. They can sit or stand upright, and have shorter spines, barrel chests, and no tail. Their arms are longer than their legs, and their shoulders and wrists are highly mobile. There are two families of apes. The chimpanzee, bonobo, and gorillas of Africa, and the orangutan of Asia are the great apes. The gibbons of Asia are the lesser apes. The two evolved into separate groups about 20 million years ago. The great apes are our closest relatives. They can solve problems with logic and recognize themselves in a mirror. Chimpanzees and orangutans use tools; gorillas have been taught sign language.

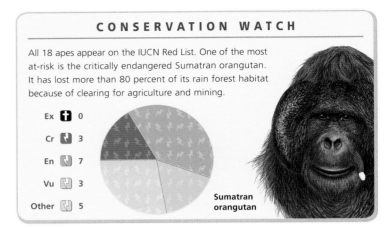

CONSERVATION WATCH

All 18 apes appear on the IUCN Red List. One of the most at-risk is the critically endangered Sumatran orangutan. It has lost more than 80 percent of its rain forest habitat because of clearing for agriculture and mining.

Ex	0
Cr	3
En	7
Vu	3
Other	5

Sumatran orangutan

Chimpanzee
Pan troglodytes
Chimpanzees sometimes hunt monkeys in packs.

Bonobo
Pan paniscus
Young bonobos play games similar to "blind man's bluff."

Mountain gorilla
Gorilla beringei
Under stress, males produce a strong smell from glands in their armpits.

GORILLA SOCIETY

Gorillas live in eastern, central, and west-central Africa. They form family groups that consist of mainly females and their young. At the head of each family group is one large adult male, known as a silverback because of his silvery-white coat markings. He uses his size and aggression to protect his family and will stand upright, slap his chest, and roar to warn other adult male gorillas or predators to stay away.

Western gorilla
Gorilla gorilla

▶ Kloss's gibbon
Hylobates klossii
Its long hands form
hooks for grasping
branches.

▲ Lar gibbon
Hylobates lar

▼ Orangutan
Pongo pygmaeus

▶ Hoolock
Hylobates hoolock
Like humans,
young hoolocks
stay with their
parents until
after adolescence.

◀ Siamang
Hylobates syndactylus
This is the largest gibbon.
When fully inflated, its throat
sac is bigger than its head;
this makes its calls louder.

▶ Black gibbon
Hylobates concolor
The black gibbon is born
with a shiny coat that stays
black in males but turns
golden in females.

FAST FACT
Gibbons tend to avoid open
water. They drink by scooping water
in a cupped hand while hanging
from a tree. Sometimes they rub
their furry hands on wet leaves and
suck the water from their fur.

GIBBON SONGS

Gibbons make long, loud calls, or songs. Each species
of gibbon has its own songs. They often sing for half an
hour first thing in the morning to identify their territory.
Male and female pairs may sing complex duets. Such
"love songs" probably make these pair bonds stronger.

SKULL COMPARISON

LEMUR SKULL
Lower primate

GORILLA SKULL
Higher primate

HUMAN SKULL
Higher primate

1 ORDER • 11 FAMILIES • 131 GENERA • 278 SPECIES

Carnivores

Brown bears that live in the coastal regions of North America will wait at waterfalls to catch salmon. Salmon hurdle the falls on their way upstream to breed.

Many animals eat meat, but the group of mammals called carnivores (or "meat-eaters") have features designed for hunting and eating other animals. Carnivores have two pairs of sharp-edged carnassial, or slicing, teeth. Their digestive system breaks down food quickly. Most carnivores eat meat; many eat both animals and plants; and some eat no meat at all.

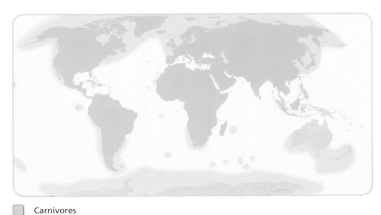

Carnivores

Carnivores can be found worldwide aside from Australia, New Guinea, New Zealand, some islands in the Pacific Ocean, and inland Antarctica.

CARNIVORE FEATURES

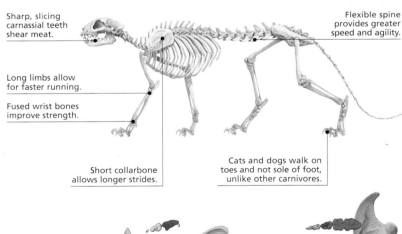

Sharp, slicing carnassial teeth shear meat.

Long limbs allow for faster running.

Fused wrist bones improve strength.

Short collarbone allows longer strides.

Flexible spine provides greater speed and agility.

Cats and dogs walk on toes and not sole of foot, unlike other carnivores.

CARNIVORE TEETH
Carnivores' teeth give clues to their diets. Strict meat-eaters have more developed slicing carnassials (red). Grinding molars (blue) are large and flat in those that eat plants.

Cat: eats only meat.

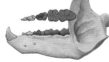
Giant panda: eats no meat.

Dog: eats mostly meat.

Brown bear: eats some meat.

Dogs and foxes

Dogs, foxes, and wolves live on all the world's continents except Antarctica—the dingo was introduced to Australia about 8,000 years ago. All dogs have good eyesight and hearing, as well as a well-developed sense of smell. Dogs eat meat, but some include plant matter, invertebrates, and dead animals in their diets. Members of this family generally live and hunt on open grasslands. Dogs hunt in one of two ways. They either surprise their prey by pouncing on it, or exhaust their prey by pursuing it. Dogs communicate with each other using scent, posture, facial expressions, and a range of barks, yelps, and howls. They live mostly in groups called packs that have well-organized social structures. Packs often work together to care for their young and wounded and to defend their territory.

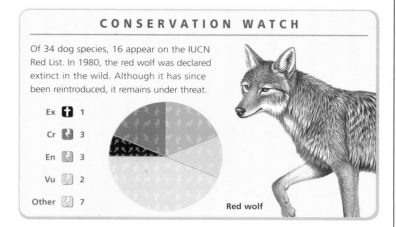

CONSERVATION WATCH

Of 34 dog species, 16 appear on the IUCN Red List. In 1980, the red wolf was declared extinct in the wild. Although it has since been reintroduced, it remains under threat.

Ex ✝ 1
Cr 🗘 3
En 🗘 3
Vu 🗘 2
Other 🗘 7

Red wolf

Black-backed jackal
Canis mesomelas
Male and female pairs share the care of pups.

Coyote
Canis latrans
The coyote's high-pitched howls carry over long distances. It can breed with wolves and domestic dogs.

Red wolf
Canis rufus

Bush dog
Speothos venaticus

Kit fox
Vulpes macrotis

Red fox
North American form
Vulpes vulpes fulva

Gray wolf
Alaskan form
Canis lupus tundrarum

Ethiopian wolf
(Simien jackal)
Canis simensis
The disease rabies has reduced its numbers.

Maned wolf
Chrysocyon brachyurus
When hunting, it taps the ground with its front paw to startle prey, then pounces.

Arctic fox
Alopex lagopus
The Arctic fox burrows into snow to escape cold Arctic winds. It has a dark summer coat and a white winter coat that blends with the snow.

Gray wolf
Scandinavian form
Canis lupus lupus

Cape wild dog
(African wild dog, African hunting dog)
Lycaon pictus
Each dog has a different coat pattern.

Dingo
Canis lupus dingo
Dingos live in Australia and Southeast Asia. In Asia they often live close to villages and are fed by humans.

Bears

Bears have the reputation of being solidly built, powerful, and ferocious predators. Only the polar bear, however, eats meat almost exclusively. Most bears hunt prey but also forage for food such as fruit, nuts, and leaves. Three-quarters of the European brown bear's diet is plant matter, and China's giant panda eats only bamboo shoots and grass. Smell is the best developed sense in bears, which is why they have large snouts. Their eyes and ears are small. Some bears are found in temperate regions of the Northern Hemisphere. When the weather cools, a few species retreat to dens or caves and sleep for as long as six months, living only on stored body fat. This is not true hibernation but is similar to it. Bears live solitary lives, but cubs stay with their protective mothers until her next pregnancy.

Himalayan brown bear
Ursus arctos isabellinus

European brown bear
Ursus arctos arctos
Can stand up on back legs for long periods; ears are so small they can be hidden by long winter coat.

Sun bear
Helarctos malayanus
The sun bear's long tongue laps up honey and insect larvae.

Asiatic black bear
Ursus thibetanus

Sloth bear
Melursus ursinus
Has hair-free lips and a gap in its teeth for sucking up termites; the sound of its slurping can be heard 330 feet (100 m) away.

Giant panda
Ailuropoda melanoleuca
Has a special bone near the thumb of its front paws to grasp bamboo shoots.

FAST FACT

All bear cubs are born tiny, defenseless, blind, and deaf, and most are bald. But they grow fast. Polar bear cubs are just 21 ounces (600 g) at birth but are 20 pounds (9 kg) after a few months.

BEAR FEET

Black bears dig up roots with long claws on their front feet (left). They walk flat on their back feet (right). Giant pandas are the only bears with a "thumb" on their front feet (left), which they use to hold bamboo. They also walk on the toes of their back feet (right).

AMERICAN BLACK BEAR   GIANT PANDA

CONSERVATION WATCH

Of the 9 bear species, 7 appear on the IUCN Red List. Fewer than 1,000 giant pandas survive in the wild. Logging and forest clearing are destroying the panda's high-altitude home. Illegal hunting by poachers is also reducing panda numbers.

Ex	0
Cr	0
En	2
Vu	3
Other	2

Giant panda

TREE CLIMBERS

Many bears scramble up trees to sunbathe and sleep in the branches. Sun bears are the best climbers, reaching as high as 22 feet (7 m) above ground.

American black bear
Ursus americanus
The black bear's coat can be black or brown.

Polar bear
Ursus maritimus
The polar bear has large, paddle-like front paws for swimming.

Red panda
Ailurus fulgens
The smallest bear, and the only one with a long tail

Spectacled bear
Tremarctos ornatus
The only bear that lives in South America

Kodiak bear
Ursus arctos middendorffi
Cubs spend three years with mothers, learning to survive.

BEAR FEATURES

BROWN BEAR
Bears can run as fast as 40 miles per hour (65 km/h) if hunting or threatened.

Long, massive skull

Sturdy frame

Short tail

Powerful limbs

Strong, curved claws that cannot be pulled back

Walks flat-footed on entire sole of foot

Seals and sea lions

Seals, sea lions, and the walrus are called pinnipeds. Their limbs are modified to form flippers—pinniped means "fin foot" in Latin. Their sleek, streamlined bodies help them swim through the oceans with ease, but on land they move with much less grace. Pinnipeds are excellent divers, with some species able to remain submerged for as long as two hours. When they swim underwater the pupils of their eyes open wide to improve their eyesight in the low light. Seals lack external ears and swim using their back flippers, which they cannot bend forward. Sea lions and fur seals have external ears and swim using their front flippers. They can bend their back flippers forward to act as feet on land. The walrus is in a group of its own. It lacks external ears and swims using its back flippers like seals, but can bend them forward like sea lions.

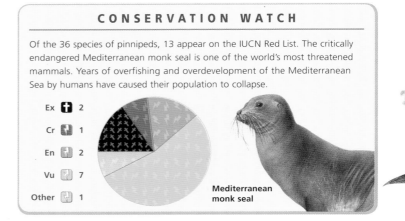

CONSERVATION WATCH

Of the 36 species of pinnipeds, 13 appear on the IUCN Red List. The critically endangered Mediterranean monk seal is one of the world's most threatened mammals. Years of overfishing and overdevelopment of the Mediterranean Sea by humans have caused their population to collapse.

Ex ✝ 2
Cr 🗓 1
En 🗓 2
Vu 🗓 7
Other 🗓 1

Mediterranean monk seal

Hooded seal
Cystophora cristata
Lining of left nostril inflates as part of a mating display.

Ribbon seal
Phoca fasciata

Steller's sea lion
Eumetopias jubatus
The largest sea lion, it hunts and eats fish and otters, as well as the pups of other seals.

Northern fur seal
Callorhinus ursinus
Males lose almost 120 pounds (55 kg) in the breeding season as they fight other males.

Southern elephant seal
Mirounga leonina
This is the largest seal; male elephant seals can weigh more than 2 tons (1.8 t).

Weddell seal
Leptonychotes weddellii

Leopard seal
Hydrurga leptonyx
The leopard seal is a fearsome Antarctic predator of other seals and penguins.

New Zealand fur seal
Arctocephalus forsteri
Hunts mainly at night, for
squid, octopuses, and fish

Walrus
Odobenus rosmarus

Ringed seal
Phoca hispida
The smallest of the pinnipeds

Baikal seal
Phoca sibirica
The only seal that lives
mainly in fresh water

Harp seal
Phoca groenlandica
Pups shed their pure white
coats by three weeks of age.

California sea lion
Zalophus californianus
The sea lion's adaptable and
intelligent nature makes it easy
to train by humans.

Mediterranean monk seal
Monachus monachus
Hunts in shallow coastal waters,
among reefs, caves, and crevices

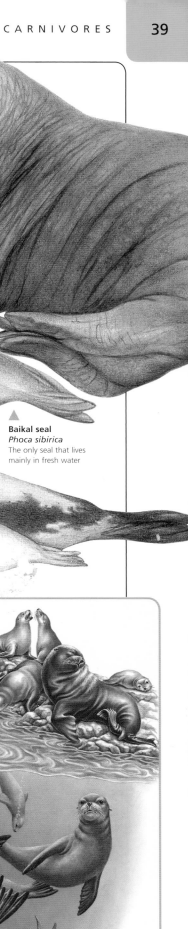

COLONY OF SEA LIONS

Sea lions gather together in large numbers during the
breeding season. Like all pinnipeds, they leave the sea
to breed on land, where they form large, noisy colonies,
called rookeries, on offshore islands. The strongest
males maintain territories containing groups
of females, called harems, with
which they mate.

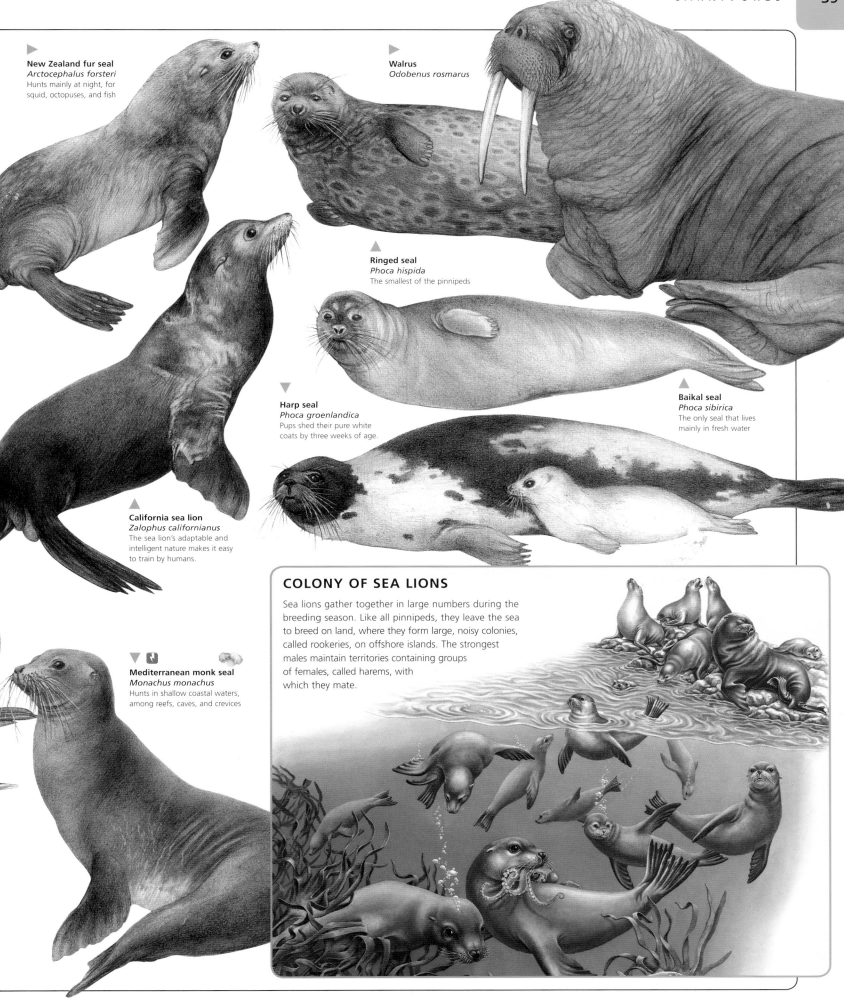

Raccoons and mongooses

Raccoons belong to a family that includes ringtails, coatis, kinkajous, and olingos. This highly social group communicates with each other using noisy barks and squeaks. Feeding on whatever food is available, they thrive in many habitats, even urban areas. Hyenas and the aardwolf look like dogs but have more in common with cats. Hyenas hunt large prey in packs but will also scavenge from the kills of other hunters, such as lions. The solitary, shy aardwolf feeds mainly on termites. Civets, genets, and linsangs are catlike. Most are nocturnal tree dwellers with long tails, claws that pull back into their paws, and pointed, upright ears. Mongooses are relatives of civets. Some are known to kill venomous cobras with their speed and agility. Most live alone but some live in sociable groups.

CONSERVATION WATCH

Of the 98 species of raccoons, hyenas, civets, and mongooses, 39 appear on the IUCN Red List. The ring-tailed mongoose is vulnerable because of the clearing of its forest habitat, as well as increased competition from introduced species.

Ex 1
Cr 1
En 15
Vu 9
Other 13

Ring-tailed mongoose

Ringtail
Bassariscus astutus
Able to clamber
up vertical walls

Kinkajou
Potos flavus
Uses prehensile tail to balance on
and swing between tree branches

Raccoon
Procyon lotor
Raids trash cans in North
America for food scraps

Spotted hyena
Crocuta crocuta
Unlike most mammals,
hyenas can digest
skin and bone.

Suricate (meerkat)
Suricata suricatta
Stands upright to check
for danger

Striped hyena
Hyaena hyaena
Spine slopes from large shoulders
down to the tail. Its powerful jaws
crush the bones of large animals.

White-nosed coati
Nasua narica
Tail is used for balance.

Aardwolf
Proteles cristatus
Mane stands up on back
when stressed to make
aardwolf appear larger.

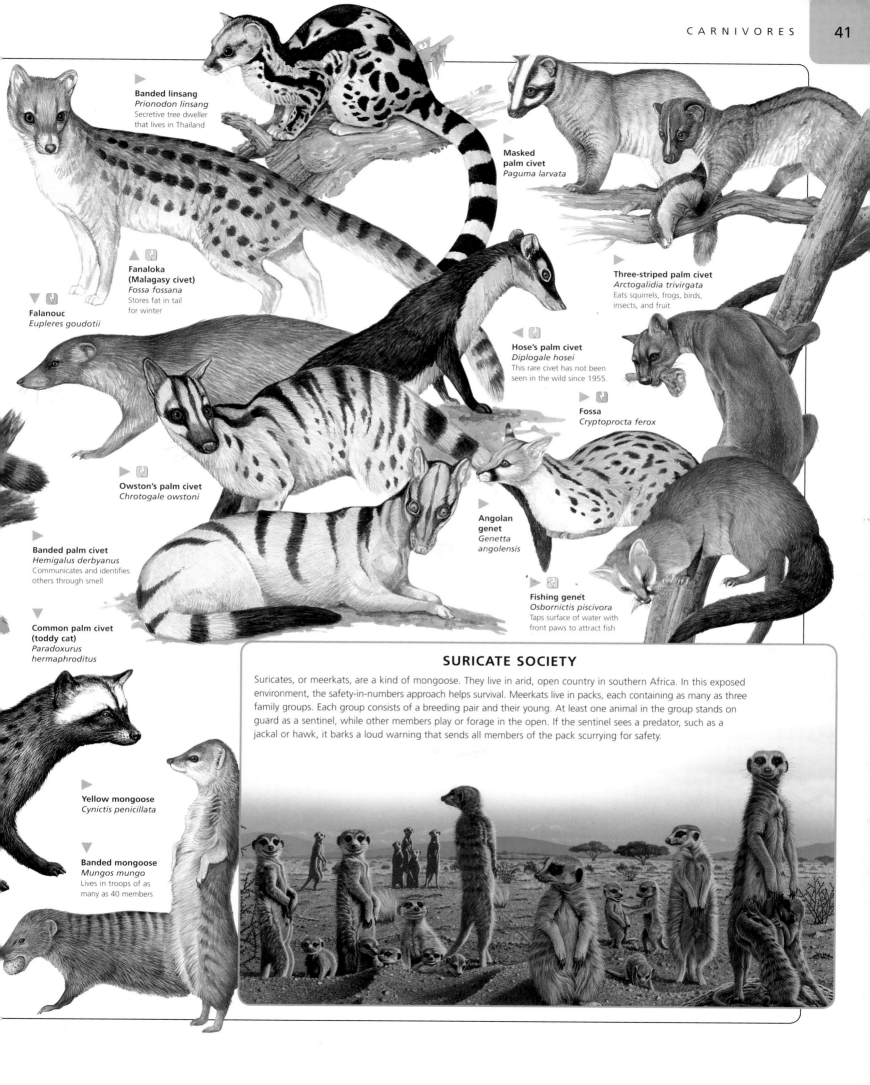

Banded linsang
Prionodon linsang
Secretive tree dweller
that lives in Thailand

**Masked
palm civet**
Paguma larvata

Three-striped palm civet
Arctogalidia trivirgata
Eats squirrels, frogs, birds,
insects, and fruit

**Fanaloka
(Malagasy civet)**
Fossa fossana
Stores fat in tail
for winter

Falanouc
Eupleres goudotii

Hose's palm civet
Diplogale hosei
This rare civet has not been
seen in the wild since 1955.

Fossa
Cryptoprocta ferox

Owston's palm civet
Chrotogale owstoni

**Angolan
genet**
*Genetta
angolensis*

Banded palm civet
Hemigalus derbyanus
Communicates and identifies
others through smell

Fishing genet
Osbornictis piscivora
Taps surface of water with
front paws to attract fish

**Common palm civet
(toddy cat)**
*Paradoxurus
hermaphroditus*

SURICATE SOCIETY

Suricates, or meerkats, are a kind of mongoose. They live in arid, open country in southern Africa. In this exposed
environment, the safety-in-numbers approach helps survival. Meerkats live in packs, each containing as many as three
family groups. Each group consists of a breeding pair and their young. At least one animal in the group stands on
guard as a sentinel, while other members play or forage in the open. If the sentinel sees a predator, such as a
jackal or hawk, it barks a loud warning that sends all members of the pack scurrying for safety.

Yellow mongoose
Cynictis penicillata

Banded mongoose
Mungos mungo
Lives in troops of as
many as 40 members

Otters and weasels

Otters and weasels are mustelids. Mustelids are the largest, most successful family of carnivores. They can be found in almost every habitat on Earth and may dwell above ground, below ground, or in water. They have long bodies with short limbs and curved claws. Their faces are flattened with small eyes and ears but well-developed noses. Otters are well adapted for swimming. Their feet are webbed and their ears and nostrils close when underwater. They have stiff whiskers called vibrissae on their snouts that help detect their prey: frogs, crayfish, and waterbirds. Weasels are highly active animals that are cunning, intelligent, and adaptable. They pursue their small animal prey relentlessly, even following them down burrows and up trees. They can carry as much as half their body weight in meat as they run.

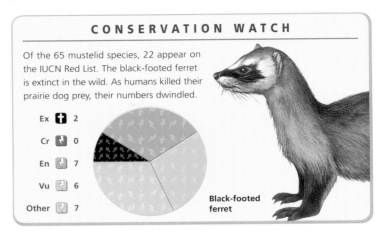

CONSERVATION WATCH

Of the 65 mustelid species, 22 appear on the IUCN Red List. The black-footed ferret is extinct in the wild. As humans killed their prairie dog prey, their numbers dwindled.

Ex   2
Cr   0
En   7
Vu   6
Other   7

Black-footed ferret

Cape clawless otter
Aonyx capensis
Makes a loud, high-pitched scream when attacked

European otter
Lutra lutra
Lives in both freshwater and saltwater habitats

Giant otter
Pteronura brasiliensis
Lives beside streams in family groups of as many as eight

Sea otter
Enhydra lutris
Spends almost its entire life in the water

Fisher
Martes pennanti
Babies are born in dens high in hollow trees.

Yellow-throated marten
Martes flavigula
Also called the honey dog, because it prefers sweet food

Japanese marten
Martes melampus
Eats small mammals, fish, earthworms, insects, and fruit

African weasel
Poecilogale albinucha

Striped polecat (zorilla)
Ictonyx striatus
Introduced into Britain, where it has slaughtered local wildlife.

Siberian weasel
Mustela sibirica

Marbled polecat
Vormela peregusna

Polecat
Mustela putorius
Males can be twice as heavy and a third longer than female polecats.

European mink
Mustela lutreola
Webbed feet help it swim as it hunts underwater.

Tayra
Eira barbara
Size of a medium dog; lives in trees

Grison
Galictis vittata

Stoat (ermine)
Mustela erminea
The stoat's summer coat is brown. Its white winter coat helps it blend in with snow.

Long-tailed weasel
Mustela frenata
Goes on killing sprees when food is available, and stores leftovers for leaner times

Ratel (honey badger)
Mellivora capensis
Tough skin is so loose that ratel can swing around to attack a predator that has bitten down on its neck.

American mink
Mustela vison
Partially webbed toes for swimming

SEA OTTER FEEDING

Like some primates and dolphins, sea otters can use tools. They use rocks like hammers to smash through the shells of abalone, sea urchins, and other prey to reach the soft meat inside. They dive to forage on the seafloor, sometimes as deep as 330 feet (100 m), before they return to the surface to eat, floating on their backs.

Badgers and skunks

Badgers and skunks are closely related to otters and weasels. Badgers live in Europe and Asia, with one species occurring in North America. Skunks are found mainly in the Americas. Almost all mustelids secrete an unpleasant scent from glands around their anus to mark territories and communicate. This is best developed in skunks. When threatened, skunks lift their tails and spray this foul-smelling substance at potential predators. Most skunks are small, about the size of a domestic cat, and can be marked with stripes or spots. Badgers have thick, squat bodies and slowly shuffle along with a rolling gait. They dig small mammals out of the ground using their well-built shoulders and strong claws.

Spotted skunk
Spilogale putorius
This is the only skunk that can climb.

Striped skunk
Mephitis mephitis
Its bold colors are a warning to predators of its nasty smell.

Chinese ferret badger
Melogale moschata
Often sleeps in tree branches

Striped hog-nosed skunk
Conepatus semistriatus

FAST FACT
A skunk gives warning signals before spraying potential attackers with a sulfur compound that smells a little like rotten eggs. It may raise its tail, stamp its feet, pretend to charge, or even do a handstand.

Hog badger
Arctonyx collaris
Uses its piglike snout to search for worms, insects, and roots

Andean hog-nosed skunk
Conepatus chinga
Like all skunks, the Andean hog-nosed skunk has very poor eyesight.

BURROWING BADGERS
Eurasian badgers create elaborate burrows called setts. Setts typically extend about 10 feet (3 m) below ground and include tunnels as long as 30 feet (9 m). They have entrances, nesting chambers, and toilets. Badgers live in these burrows in family groups of about six members, usually a dominant male and female and their offspring. Setts are passed on from one generation to the next and can be hundreds of years old. Badgers leave the sett at night to forage for food.

American badger
Taxidea taxus
Unlike most carnivores, badgers find their prey by digging.

Eurasian badger
Meles meles

Individual badger's nesting chamber

Shared chamber

Entrance

Great cats

Cats are the ultimate hunters, and most species eat nothing but meat. All cats have a strong, muscular body with forward-facing eyes, razor-like teeth, and sharp claws. They have quick reflexes and keen senses that they rely on for stalking or ambushing prey. Many cats live alone, and they are often active at night. Cats are land dwellers. They can all climb trees, and many are good swimmers. There are three groups of cats: the great cats, the small cats, and the cheetah. Lions, tigers, leopards, and jaguars are the great cats. The small cats include lynxes, bobcats, and ocelots. Great cats are grouped together because they roar. They cannot purr like the small cats or the cheetah.

Jaguar
Panthera onca
Excellent climber, fast runner, and good swimmer

Snow leopard
Uncia uncia

Tiger
Panthera tigris
This solitary hunter is the largest cat. Each tiger has its own pattern of stripes.

Lion
Panthera leo
Males are the only cats with manes; they can be twice as large as females.

♂   ♀

Cheetah
Acinonyx jubatus
The fastest animal on land, it can reach a top speed of 60 miles per hour (97 km/h).

Leopard
Panthera pardus
Leopards are covered in spots, or rosettes. Black panthers are leopards with only black pigment in their fur.

LION PRIDE

Usually one but sometimes two related males (often brothers) dominate the family group, or pride.

Lionesses are the pride's main hunters. They hunt together to provide meat for the group.

As many as three generations of females can live in a pride. This may consist of 30 lions.

Cubs suckle for as long as six months before being weaned. They are always the last to feed at kills.

Small cats

The small cats are not only smaller than the great cats, but also have a better developed voice box, or larynx. This lets them purr constantly. Like the great cats, small cats have well-developed shearing teeth, or carnassials, and lack grinding back teeth, or molars. This is because cats feed by tearing flesh, not by grinding plant matter. Small cats have large eyes with pupils that are generally vertical, but can sometimes be rounded. Their coats can be plain, like those of pumas and golden cats; consist of spots or rosettes, like ocelots, bobcats, and servals; contain faint stripes, like wildcats; or be a mixture of all these markings. The main purpose of their coat markings is to blend into their surroundings, or to be camouflaged, which is important for animals that rely on stalking and surprising prey.

CONSERVATION WATCH

Of the 36 species of cats, 25 appear on the IUCN Red List. This includes the Siberian tiger, which is critically endangered. Poachers threaten the largest remaining Siberian tiger population in Russia.

Ex   0
Cr   1
En   4
Vu   12
Other   8

Siberian tiger

Bobcat
Lynx rufus

Wildcat
Felis silvestris
Wildcats rub objects with scent from tail and head glands; they also mark territory with urine.

Caracal
Caracal caracal
Uses old porcupine burrows as dens for young

Puma
(cougar, mountain lion)
Puma concolor

Canada lynx
Lynx canadensis

Marbled cat
Pardofelis marmorata
Lives in rain forests of Southeast Asia

FROM THE WILD

Cats were first tamed by the ancient Egyptians. Even after thousands of years of domestication, pet cats have not lost their hunting instincts, and some go back to the wild. These are known as feral cats. There are more than 100 million domestic or feral cats in North America alone.

Andean cat
Oreailurus jacobita
Long, thick hair protects cat from cold and wind in high mountains.

Margay
Leopardus wiedii

Ocelot
Leopardus pardalis

Kodkod
Oncifelis guigna

African golden cat
Profelis aurata
Night hunter of small antelope,
monkeys, and rodents

Jaguarundi
Herpailurus yaguarondi
Kittens have spots at birth
but lose them as they mature.

Serval
Leptailurus serval
Can leap 10 feet (3 m)
in the air and change
direction mid-leap

Asiatic golden cat
Catopuma temminckii
Known as the "fire tiger"
by local Thai tribes

Leopard cat
*Prionailurus
bengalensis*

Iberian lynx
Lynx pardinus

Eurasian lynx
Lynx lynx
Furry feet act like
snowshoes to help the
lynx travel over soft snow.

Jungle cat
Felis chaus

Fishing cat
*Prionailurus
viverrinus*
Webbed toes
on front paws

DEFENSE SIGNALS

BACK OFF
Cats use facial expressions when threatened. The
margay, of Central and South America, signals it
can defend itself by staring with wide eyes.

READY TO ATTACK
The margay tucks its ears out of the way, opens
its mouth wide, and bares its sharp teeth to give
a final warning signal before attacking.

7 ORDERS • 28 FAMILIES • 139 GENERA • 329 SPECIES

Hoofed Mammals

Zebras and wildebeest surge through the Mara River together as they complete their annual migration across the Serengeti. Their large herds offer protection from predators.

Hard hooves evolved to help plant-eating mammals survive on grasslands. They make it easier to run fast and escape predators. Only two groups of hoofed mammals, or ungulates, have true hooves: odd-toed ungulates—tapirs, rhinoceroses, and horses—and even-toed ungulates—pigs, hippopotamuses, camels, deer, cattle, and giraffes. The other ungulates have their own specializations.

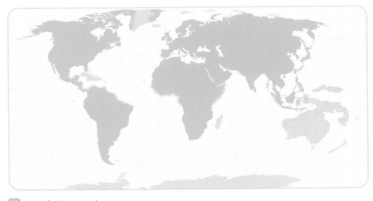

Hoofed mammals

Hoofed mammals occur on all landmasses except Australia, Antarctica, and some islands. Sirenians live in shallow waters off the coasts of the Americas, Africa, Asia, and Australia.

HORNS

Antelope horns have a bony core encased in keratin.

Deer antlers are made of bone that is shed each year.

Rhinoceros horns are made of modified hair.

Horns and antlers are used by males as weapons; they fight each other for the right to mate with females.

HOOVES

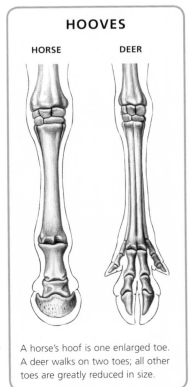

HORSE   DEER

A horse's hoof is one enlarged toe. A deer walks on two toes; all other toes are greatly reduced in size.

Elephants

Elephants are the world's biggest land animals. There are just two living species: the Asiatic elephant and the African elephant. Both species live in hot, tropical climates. An elephant's trunk is a combination of the upper lip and nose. It is made up of more than 150,000 muscle bands. The trunk is strong enough to carry heavy objects but agile enough to pick up a delicate twig. They have limbs like pillars and broad feet to support their huge bulk. Heat from their bodies is dispersed through their large, thin ears, which have many blood vessels running through them. Elephants are mostly social animals. Adult males gather in small bachelor herds, or they may live alone. Related adult females and their young live in strong family groups led by the oldest animals.

CONSERVATION WATCH

Both species of elephants appear on the IUCN Red List. African elephants have been hunted for their ivory tusks for centuries. An increase in hunting in recent years is the main cause of huge losses.

Ex   0
Cr   0
En   1
Vu   1
Other   0

African elephant

Asiatic elephant
Elephas maximus
It has smaller ears than African elephant; one "finger" at tip of trunk; and four nails on back foot. Only males have large tusks: modified teeth that never stop growing.

Adult

African elephant
Loxodonta africana
Heavier and taller than Asiatic elephant, it has larger ears; three nails on its back foot; and its trunk has two "fingers" at tip. Both males and females can have large tusks.

Juvenile

ELEPHANT GROWTH

Newborn elephants are a fraction of their adult size. A male African elephant weighs 250 pounds (110 kg) at birth but will add almost 14,000 more pounds (6,400 kg) during its life. Elephants nurse for as long as 3 years. They are dependent on their mothers for 8 to 10 years. Like humans, they are adolescents at 12 to 14 years. Females can produce young at 16 years. Elephants grow rapidly when they are young. They achieve most of their growth by about 20 but will continue to grow throughout their lives. They live for 65 to 70 years.

40 years
15 years
10 years
6 years
3 years
1 year
Less than 1 year

Dugong and manatees

There are only four living sirenians, the dugong and three species of manatees. These marine mammals spend their entire lives in water. They live in tropical and subtropical regions, grazing on the seagrasses and plants that grow in shallow seas. Their ancestors would have been land dwellers; the closest living relatives of sirenians are probably elephants and hyraxes. Today, their front legs have become flippers and their back legs have almost disappeared. The dugong's tail is fluked like a whale's. Manatees have a tail like a large, flat paddle. The vegetarian diet of sirenians produces a lot of gas. To stop them from floating too high in the water, their heavy bones weigh them down. Fleeting glimpses of sirenians by confused sailors inspired the myth of the mermaid, or siren, for which they are named.

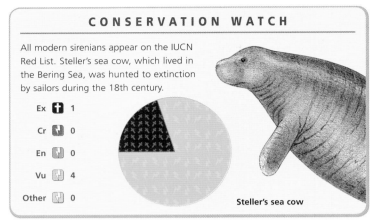

CONSERVATION WATCH

All modern sirenians appear on the IUCN Red List. Steller's sea cow, which lived in the Bering Sea, was hunted to extinction by sailors during the 18th century.

Ex   1
Cr   0
En   0
Vu   4
Other   0

Steller's sea cow

GRIZZLED GRAZERS

Sirenians graze on algae and seagrasses growing in shallow, warm waters. Their poor eyesight means they locate food by touch, with sensitive, bristle-like hairs on their pig-like snouts. Their mobile, muscular lips grasp plant material and pull it from the sediment. Sirenians may use their flippers to pass food to the mouth. The disturbed sediment can form a murky feeding trail behind them.

Dugong
Dugong dugon
Dugongs have no nails on their flippers; these have calluses on them from crawling across the seabed.

Caribbean manatee
Trichechus manatus
Has nails on its flippers; algae and barnacles grow on its skin; it lives in both salt and fresh water.

Amazonian manatee
Trichechus inunguis
This species lives in lagoons and lakes among dense vegetation, where it feeds on floating grasses.

African manatee
Trichechus senegalensis
This manatee lives in rivers and coastal waters off the west coast of Africa.

Hyraxes, tapirs, and aardvark

Hyraxes are rabbit-size mammals that look like guinea pigs. These distant relatives of elephants and sirenians live in Africa and the Middle East. They have flattened, hooflike nails on their feet. Their upper incisor teeth grow constantly and look like small tusks. Hyraxes keep warm by huddling together in groups and basking in the sun. Tapirs have a trunklike nose similar to elephants, but they are more closely related to rhinoceroses. There are four living species. Three inhabit the tropical rain forests of Central and South America; one lives in Southeast Asia. All are shy plant-eaters with poor vision but excellent senses of hearing and smell. Unlike most hoofed mammals, the aardvark is not herbivorous. It eats ants and termites instead, and can gulp as many as 50,000 of them in one nighttime feeding session.

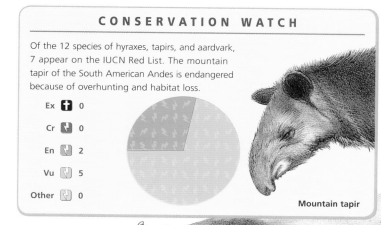

CONSERVATION WATCH

Of the 12 species of hyraxes, tapirs, and aardvark, 7 appear on the IUCN Red List. The mountain tapir of the South American Andes is endangered because of overhunting and habitat loss.

Ex	✝	0
Cr		0
En		2
Vu		5
Other		0

Mountain tapir

Rock hyrax
Procavia capensis
Medicine made from rock hyrax dung is used to treat epilepsy.

Malayan tapir
Tapirus indicus
Coat markings camouflage it in its shady rain forest home.

Yellow-spotted hyrax
Heterohyrax brucei

Southern tree hyrax
Dendrohyrax arboreus
Scent glands on back are covered by tuft of hair.

Juvenile

Adult

Brazilian tapir
Tapirus terrestris
This tapir has regular baths to remove parasites. Young are mottled and striped.

Aardvark
Orycteropus afer

AARDVARK ANATOMY

Tops of ears fold back to keep out dirt during digging.

Poor eyesight; it is known to run into objects when startled.

Excellent sense of smell sniffs out termites in the dark.

Horses, asses, and zebras

Horses, asses, and zebras are known as equids. Equids occur in the grasslands, savannas, and deserts of Africa and Asia, but feral herds live on most continents. Their ancestors evolved in North America, but equids vanished from there by the end of the last ice age. Equids commonly live in large female herds led by a harem male. All equids run on a single toe. Their teeth are highly specialized for eating plants: They have incisor teeth to snip at leaves and ridged cheek teeth to grind them. Eyes on the sides of their heads and sharp hearing help them keep alert for danger. Equids communicate with each other by moving their tails, ears, and mouths. Many also use sounds such as whinnies, brays, nickers, and squeals. Most species groom each other to reinforce herd relationships.

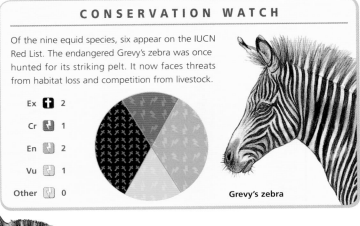

CONSERVATION WATCH

Of the nine equid species, six appear on the IUCN Red List. The endangered Grevy's zebra was once hunted for its striking pelt. It now faces threats from habitat loss and competition from livestock.

Ex ✝ 2
Cr 🗲 1
En 🗲 2
Vu 🗲 1
Other 🗲 0

Grevy's zebra

Horse
wild form
Equus ferus
The horse is extinct in the wild but lives on in domestic breeds.

Kiang
Equus kiang
Forms family groups of as many as 400 members, led by a mature female

Onager
Equus onager
This equid can reach speeds of 40 miles per hour (65 km/h) in short bursts.

Ass wild form
Equus africanus
Domestic donkey was bred from this species.

Zebra
northern form
Equus burchelli
Every zebra has its own pattern of stripes, which probably helps herd members identify each other.

Mountain zebra
Equus zebra
Responds to alarm calls from wildebeest, as well as zebras

Adult

Juvenile

Mongolian wild ass
Equus hemionus
Grazes on grass but will eat shrubs and trees when grass is scarce

Rhinoceroses

Rhinoceroses might look similar to elephants, but they are more closely related to tapirs and horses. There are just five living rhinoceros species. Three live in Asia; two are found in Africa. Africa's white rhinoceros is the third largest living land animal after the elephants. All rhinoceroses have one or two large horns protruding from their snouts. Males use these to fight each other for females. Females use them to guide their young with gentle nudges. Both sexes use their horns to defend against predators or to push dung into scented signposts. Their bodies are large and stumpy; their three-toed feet leave tracks like the "ace of clubs" playing card. Rhinoceroses are generally solitary herbivores that come together for a few months to breed. Females or young males may form temporary herds.

CONSERVATION WATCH

All five rhinoceros species appear on the IUCN Red List. The black rhinoceros is critically endangered: Just over 3,000 individuals remain in the wild. Its biggest threat is being hunted for its horn.

Ex 0
Cr 3
En 1
Vu 0
Other 1

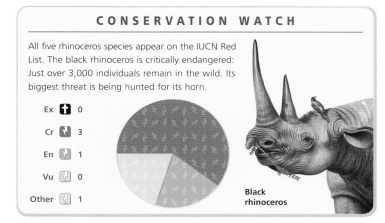

Black rhinoceros

Indian rhinoceros
Rhinoceros unicornis

Adult

Javan rhinoceros
Rhinoceros sondaicus
Browses on leaves using prehensile upper lip

Sumatran rhinoceros
Dicerorhinus sumatrensis

Juvenile

Black rhinoceros
Diceros bicornis
Calf may stay with its mother for almost four years.

White rhinoceros
Ceratotherium simum

FAST FACT

The largest land animal ever was a rhinoceros that lived about 40 million years ago, called *Indricotherium*. It stood 18 feet (5.5 m) tall at the shoulder and may have weighed more than 22 tons (20 t).

CHARGING RHINO

Black rhinoceroses can be aggressive and charge when threatened or startled. They are capable of surprising bursts of speed over short distances. Loud snorts add to the terrifying display. Adults can weigh almost 3,000 pounds (1,400 kg). With this weight charging at speed, horns cause serious damage when they connect with attackers.

Black rhinoceroses will gore and toss attackers with their horns.

Horns are made of keratin, the same substance as human fingernails.

Spotted hyena

Cattle

Cattle, goats, and sheep, along with buffalo, antelope, and gazelles, are bovids. All males, and many females, have horns made of bone and covered in keratin. These are never shed. Bovids bear their weight on the two middle toes of each foot. These toes form a split, or cloven, hoof. Bovids are plant-eaters. Their stomachs have four chambers. After they swallow, food passes through the first two stomachs. The partially digested meal, called cud, is returned to the mouth to be chewed and swallowed again. It then enters the final two stomachs. This process helps to break down the tough walls of plant cells in the grasses bovids eat. The pronghorn looks like an antelope but is in a group of its own. Its horns are made of bone and keratin like bovids' horns, but the keratin is shed every year like deer's horns.

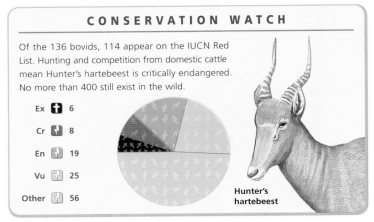

CONSERVATION WATCH

Of the 136 bovids, 114 appear on the IUCN Red List. Hunting and competition from domestic cattle mean Hunter's hartebeest is critically endangered. No more than 400 still exist in the wild.

Ex	✝	6
Cr		8
En		19
Vu		25
Other		56

Hunter's hartebeest

◀ Arabian tahr
Hemitragus jayakari

◀ Spanish ibex
Capra pyrenaica

▲ Chamois
Rupicapra rupicapra
Flexible hoof pads grip
the ground.

▼ Mountain anoa
Bubalus quarlesi
A kind of water buffalo
that looks more like
a deer

▶ Thomson's gazelle
Gazella thomsonii
Usually lives in small groups,
but thousands may migrate
together to grasslands in
the rainy season.

▼ Yak
Bos grunniens

◀ Serow
*Capricornis
sumatraensis*

▲ Wildebeest
*Connochaetes
taurinus*

▼ Bison
Bison bison

▶ Saola (Vu Quang ox)
Pseudoryx nghetinhensis

▲ Gemsbok
Oryx gazella

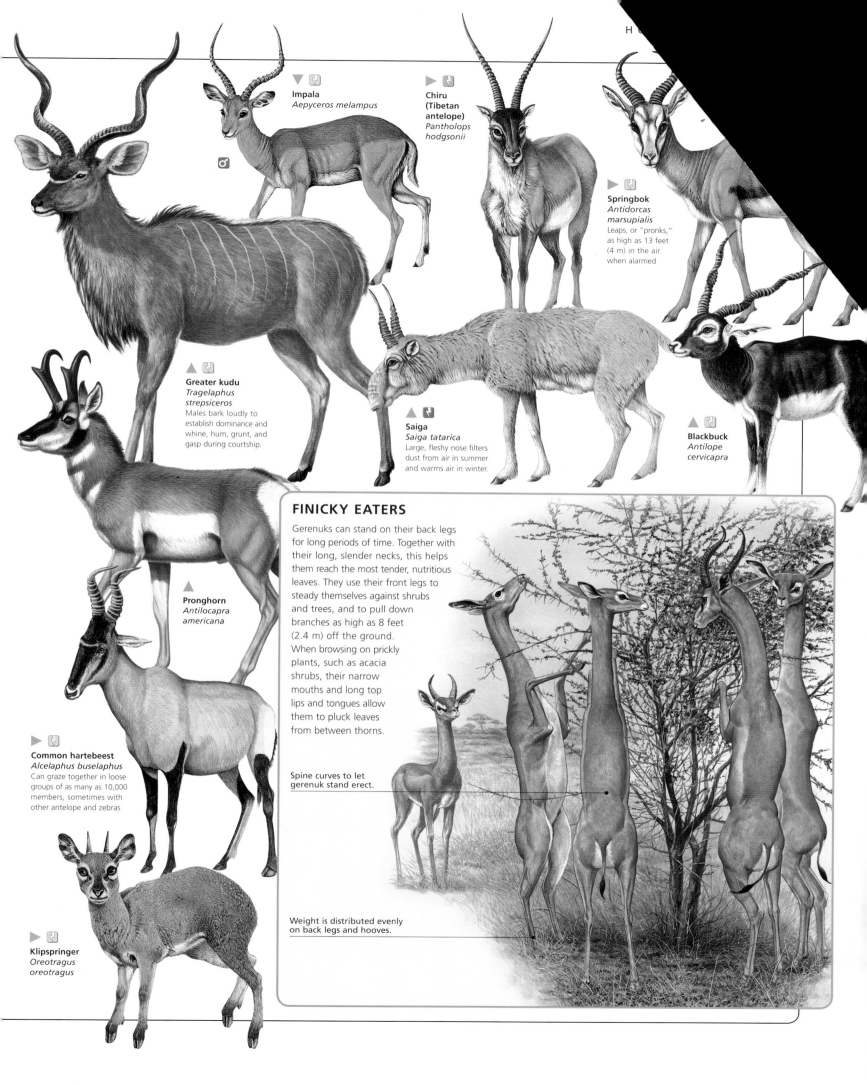

Impala
Aepyceros melampus

**Chiru
(Tibetan
antelope)**
*Pantholops
hodgsonii*

Springbok
*Antidorcas
marsupialis*
Leaps, or "pronks,"
as high as 13 feet
(4 m) in the air
when alarmed

Greater kudu
*Tragelaphus
strepsiceros*
Males bark loudly to
establish dominance and
whine, hum, grunt, and
gasp during courtship.

Saiga
Saiga tatarica
Large, fleshy nose filters
dust from air in summer
and warms air in winter.

Blackbuck
*Antilope
cervicapra*

Pronghorn
*Antilocapra
americana*

Common hartebeest
Alcelaphus buselaphus
Can graze together in loose
groups of as many as 10,000
members, sometimes with
other antelope and zebras

FINICKY EATERS

Gerenuks can stand on their back legs
for long periods of time. Together with
their long, slender necks, this helps
them reach the most tender, nutritious
leaves. They use their front legs to
steady themselves against shrubs
and trees, and to pull down
branches as high as 8 feet
(2.4 m) off the ground.
When browsing on prickly
plants, such as acacia
shrubs, their narrow
mouths and long top
lips and tongues allow
them to pluck leaves
from between thorns.

Spine curves to let
gerenuk stand erect.

Weight is distributed evenly
on back legs and hooves.

Klipspringer
*Oreotragus
oreotragus*

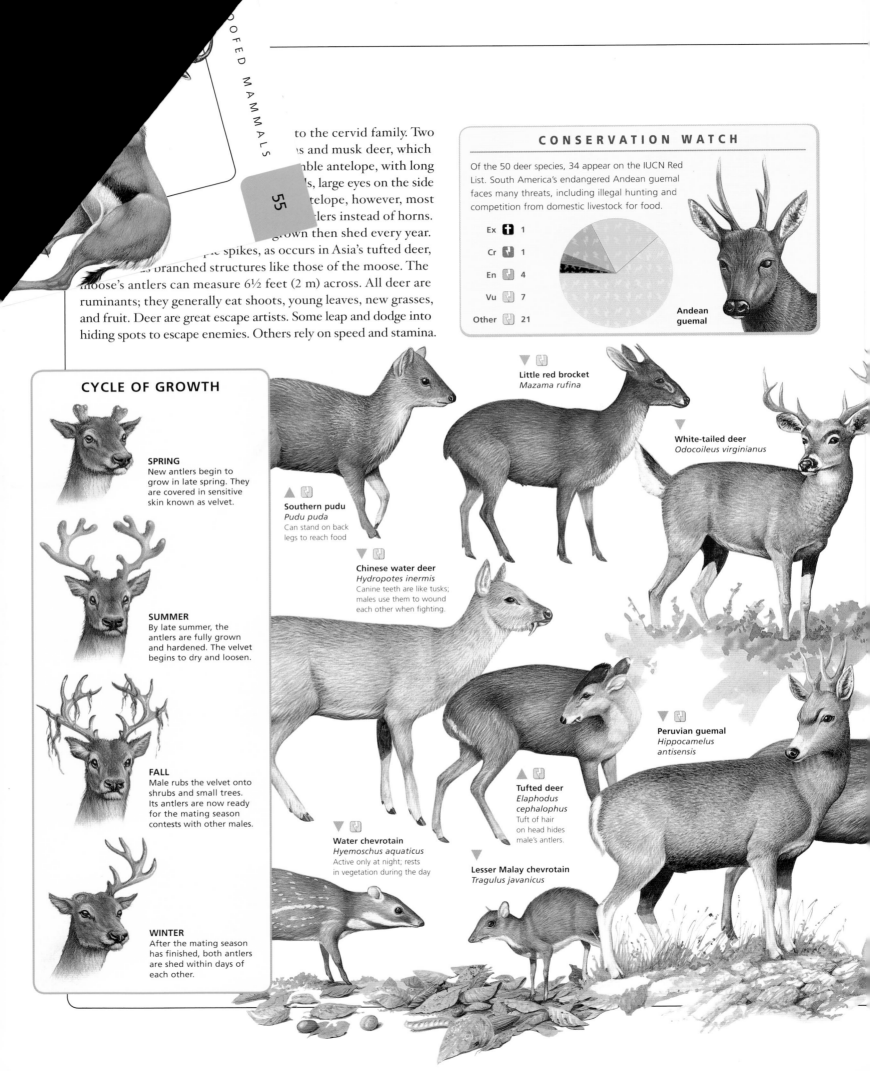

... to the cervid family. Two
... s and musk deer, which
... ble antelope, with long
... s, large eyes on the side
... telope, however, most
... lers instead of horns.
... grown then shed every year.
... e spikes, as occurs in Asia's tufted deer,
... branched structures like those of the moose. The
moose's antlers can measure 6½ feet (2 m) across. All deer are
ruminants; they generally eat shoots, young leaves, new grasses,
and fruit. Deer are great escape artists. Some leap and dodge into
hiding spots to escape enemies. Others rely on speed and stamina.

CONSERVATION WATCH

Of the 50 deer species, 34 appear on the IUCN Red List. South America's endangered Andean guemal faces many threats, including illegal hunting and competition from domestic livestock for food.

Ex 1
Cr 1
En 4
Vu 7
Other 21

Andean guemal

CYCLE OF GROWTH

SPRING
New antlers begin to grow in late spring. They are covered in sensitive skin known as velvet.

SUMMER
By late summer, the antlers are fully grown and hardened. The velvet begins to dry and loosen.

FALL
Male rubs the velvet onto shrubs and small trees. Its antlers are now ready for the mating season contests with other males.

WINTER
After the mating season has finished, both antlers are shed within days of each other.

Little red brocket
Mazama rufina

White-tailed deer
Odocoileus virginianus

Southern pudu
Pudu puda
Can stand on back legs to reach food

Chinese water deer
Hydropotes inermis
Canine teeth are like tusks; males use them to wound each other when fighting.

Peruvian guemal
Hippocamelus antisensis

Tufted deer
Elaphodus cephalophus
Tuft of hair on head hides male's antlers.

Water chevrotain
Hyemoschus aquaticus
Active only at night; rests in vegetation during the day

Lesser Malay chevrotain
Tragulus javanicus

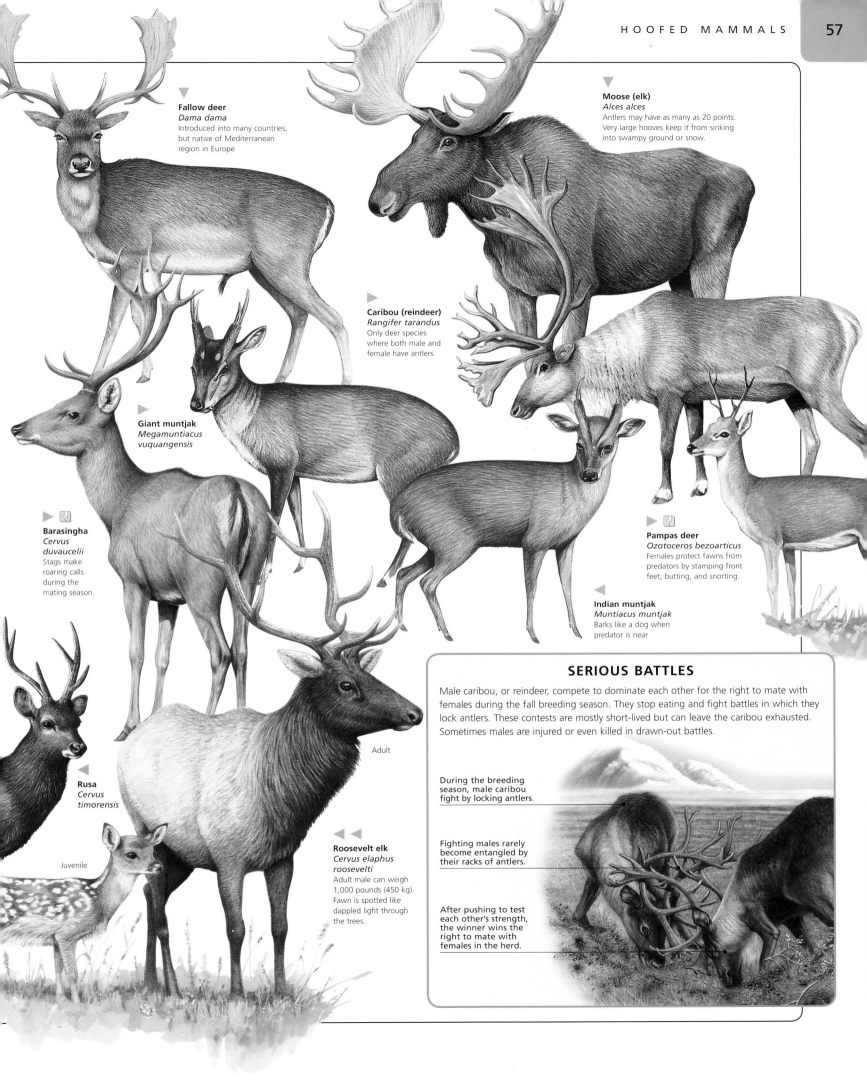

Fallow deer
Dama dama
Introduced into many countries, but native of Mediterranean region in Europe

Moose (elk)
Alces alces
Antlers may have as many as 20 points. Very large hooves keep it from sinking into swampy ground or snow.

Caribou (reindeer)
Rangifer tarandus
Only deer species where both male and female have antlers

Giant muntjak
Megamuntiacus vuquangensis

Barasingha
Cervus duvaucelii
Stags make roaring calls during the mating season.

Pampas deer
Ozotoceros bezoarticus
Females protect fawns from predators by stamping front feet, butting, and snorting.

Indian muntjak
Muntiacus muntjak
Barks like a dog when predator is near

Rusa
Cervus timorensis

Juvenile

Adult

Roosevelt elk
Cervus elaphus roosevelti
Adult male can weigh 1,000 pounds (450 kg). Fawn is spotted like dappled light through the trees.

SERIOUS BATTLES

Male caribou, or reindeer, compete to dominate each other for the right to mate with females during the fall breeding season. They stop eating and fight battles in which they lock antlers. These contests are mostly short-lived but can leave the caribou exhausted. Sometimes males are injured or even killed in drawn-out battles.

During the breeding season, male caribou fight by locking antlers.

Fighting males rarely become entangled by their racks of antlers.

After pushing to test each other's strength, the winner wins the right to mate with females in the herd.

Giraffes and okapi

Giraffes and the okapi are the only living members of the giraffe family. They are distantly related to cattle, sheep, and antelope. Both have long necks, tails, and limbs. Their front legs are longer than their back legs. This causes their backs to slope down toward the tail. A fully grown giraffe's neck is so long that it can reach as high as 18 feet (5.5 m) above the ground. This makes it the tallest animal in the world. Giraffes and the okapi have small bony horns covered by furred skin; thin, movable lips; and large eyes and ears. Giraffes live in small herds in wooded areas of Africa's savannas. Their striking coats mimic the dappled light of these regions. The okapi prefers to live alone in the dark rain forests of central Africa. The distinctive stripes on its rear break up its outline in the dense undergrowth.

Reticulated giraffe
Giraffa camelopardalis reticulata
Has seven neck bones, like humans, only longer; young males have contests with their necks, much like arm wrestling.

Southern giraffe
Giraffa camelopardalis giraffa
A giraffe's coat pattern provides for excellent camouflage on open savannas. These markings fade along lower limbs.

Okapi
Okapia johnstoni
Has poor vision, but sharp hearing and good sense of smell

Kenyan giraffe
Giraffa camelopardalis tippelskirschi
Kicks with front legs to defend itself

Nubian giraffe
Giraffa camelopardalis camelopardalis
Spreads its front legs wide and bends down to reach the water, making it easy prey for predators

PICKING AT ACACIAS

Acacia leaves contain poisons and the branches have sharp thorns. Giraffes have special adaptations that allow them to eat these leaves in large quantities.

Giraffes select the most tender, and least poisonous, new leaves from acacia trees.

Mobile, grasping tongue can be 21 inches (53 cm) long in adults.

Acacia thorns

Camels

Two kinds of camels, together with the guanaco, vicuña, and the domesticated llama and alpaca, are known as camelids. Camelids are social animals. In the wild, they live in female groups, or harems, that have one dominant male. Young males sometimes form small bachelor herds. All camelids are well adapted to life in desert or semidesert conditions. Their three-chambered stomachs extract nutrients from the leaves and stems that they eat. The two camels also have a fatty hump that stores food. Only the front of a camelid's hoof touches the ground. Its weight rests instead on a fleshy pad on the foot's sole. When they walk, camelids move the front and back legs of one side together, creating a rolling gait. This has led some domestic camels to be called "ships of the desert."

CONSERVATION WATCH

Of the six camelids, three appear on the IUCN Red List. The critically endangered Bactrian camel is under threat from hunting. However, many survive in domestic herds.

Ex ✝ 1
Cr 🗲 1
En 🗲 0
Vu 🗲 0
Other 🗲 1

Bactrian camel

Dromedary
Camelus dromedarius
Can drink 30 gallons (110 L) of water in 10 minutes, but can go for days without drinking

Bactrian camel
Camelus bactrianus
Long winter coat sheds in summer. Its humps are mainly stored fat, and shrink during food shortages.

Alpaca
Lama pacos
Probably a cross between wild vicuña and tame llama; its silky wool is used to make clothing.

Llama
Lama glama

Vicuña
Vicugna vicugna

Guanaco
Lama guanicoe
Spits when threatened

INSIDE A CAMEL'S HUMP

Shaggy fur

Fatty tissue, connective tissue, and blood vessels

Skin

Woolly fur

Pigs and hippopotamuses

Pigs, hogs, boars, and the babirusa are all hoofed mammals but are not strict herbivores. While they eat plant matter, they also eat grubs, earthworms, eggs, and small animals. They forage for food in leaf litter and dirt with their long snouts. A pig's snout is surrounded by tough cartilage, which is similar to flexible bone. The upper and lower canines form sharp tusks that are used as weapons and for displaying status. Social peccaries look like pigs but have long, slender limbs; a scent gland on the rump; and a complex stomach to digest the plant matter they eat. Hippopotamuses also look like pigs, but their closest relatives are probably whales. These barrel-shaped herbivores are strong swimmers and spend most of the day resting in water before emerging at night to feed.

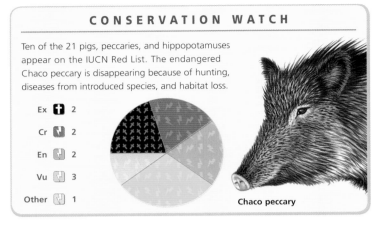

CONSERVATION WATCH

Ten of the 21 pigs, peccaries, and hippopotamuses appear on the IUCN Red List. The endangered Chaco peccary is disappearing because of hunting, diseases from introduced species, and habitat loss.

Ex 🕆 2
Cr 🗷 2
En 🗷 2
Vu 🗷 3
Other 🗷 1

Chaco peccary

Babirusa
Babyrousa babyrussa
Skin is mostly hairless, with large folds and wrinkles.

Giant hog
Hylocherus meinertzhageni
Males have puffy cheek pads that contain scent glands.

Red river hog
Potamochoerus porcus
Butt heads and whip each other with tails during fights

Pygmy hog
Sus salvanius
Smallest pig: Males reach maximum weight of only 20 pounds (9 kg).

Adults

Hippopotamus
Hippopotamus amphibius
Although this mammal does not have sweat glands, its skin is protected by mucus glands that stain the skin red.

Wild boar
Sus scrofa
Wild boars wallow in mud or water for protection from sun and insects. Piglets' camouflaging stripes fade with age.

Juveniles

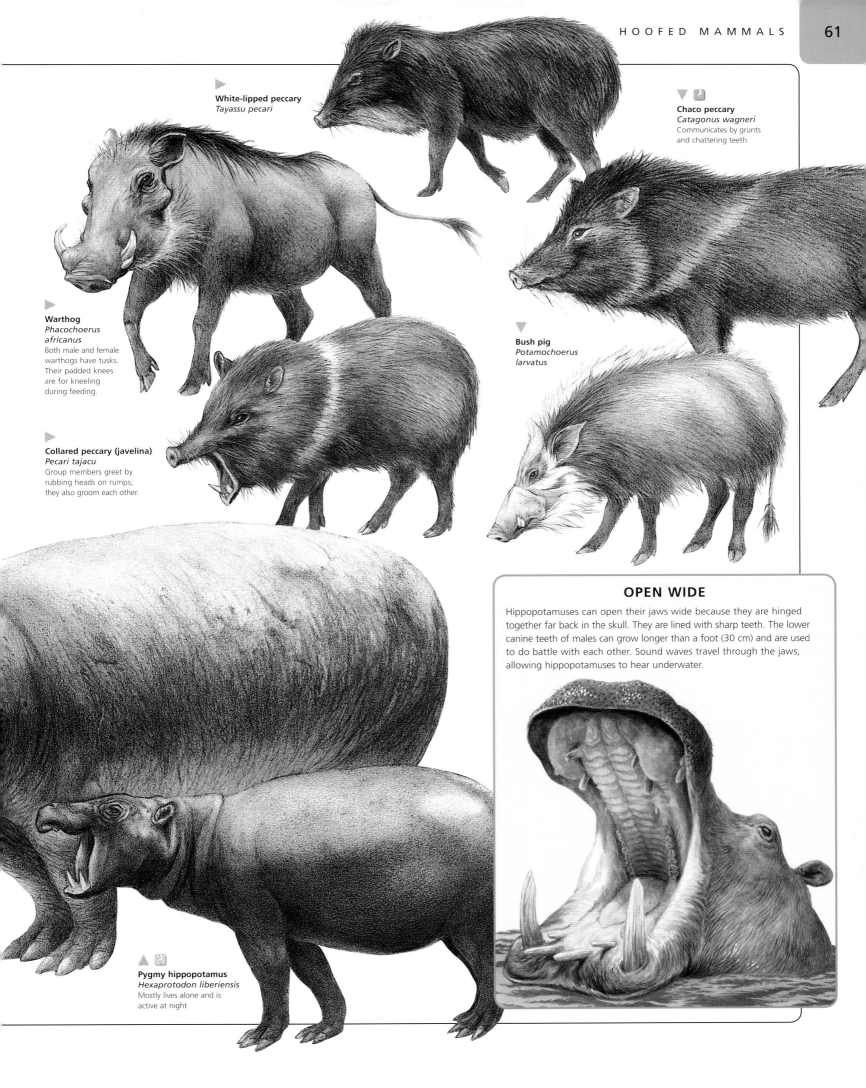

White-lipped peccary
Tayassu pecari

Chaco peccary
Catagonus wagneri
Communicates by grunts
and chattering teeth

Warthog
*Phacochoerus
africanus*
Both male and female
warthogs have tusks.
Their padded knees
are for kneeling
during feeding.

Bush pig
*Potamochoerus
larvatus*

Collared peccary (javelina)
Pecari tajacu
Group members greet by
rubbing heads on rumps;
they also groom each other.

OPEN WIDE

Hippopotamuses can open their jaws wide because they are hinged
together far back in the skull. They are lined with sharp teeth. The lower
canine teeth of males can grow longer than a foot (30 cm) and are used
to do battle with each other. Sound waves travel through the jaws,
allowing hippopotamuses to hear underwater.

Pygmy hippopotamus
Hexaprotodon liberiensis
Mostly lives alone and is
active at night

Baleen whales

Whales, dolphins, and porpoises are called cetaceans. Whale ancestors lived entirely on land, and were probably also those of hippopotamuses. Over time, whales became as streamlined as fish, modifying their front legs into flippers, losing their back legs entirely, and developing a powerful tail with two flattened flukes. All cetaceans now feed, rest, mate, give birth, and raise young entirely in the water. There are two groups of cetaceans: baleen whales and toothed whales. Baleen whales, the giants of the ocean, feed on tiny prey. They have thin, meshlike plates of a bony substance called baleen that hang down from their top jaw. This strains the water for tiny animals that are then swallowed. Many baleen whales communicate with moaning sounds. Some species form long and complicated songs.

Humpback whale
Megaptera novaeangliae

Bowhead whale
Balaena mysticetus
Kept warm by a 24-inch (60-cm) layer of blubber just under skin

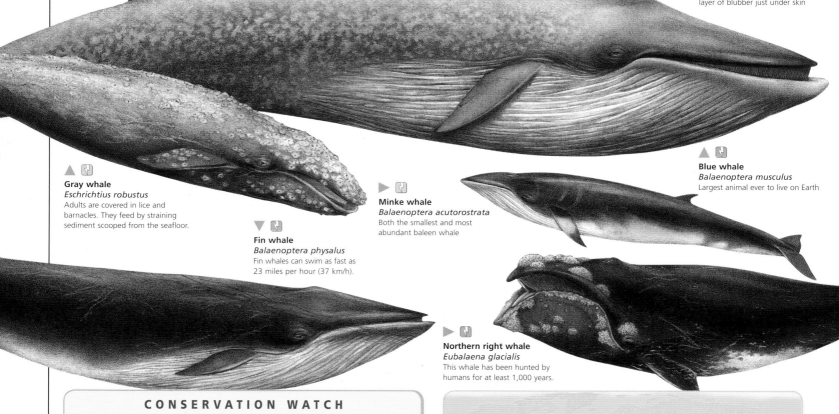

Gray whale
Eschrichtius robustus
Adults are covered in lice and barnacles. They feed by straining sediment scooped from the seafloor.

Minke whale
Balaenoptera acutorostrata
Both the smallest and most abundant baleen whale

Blue whale
Balaenoptera musculus
Largest animal ever to live on Earth

Fin whale
Balaenoptera physalus
Fin whales can swim as fast as 23 miles per hour (37 km/h).

Northern right whale
Eubalaena glacialis
This whale has been hunted by humans for at least 1,000 years.

CONSERVATION WATCH

Of 13 baleen whale species, 12 appear on the IUCN Red List. The endangered fin whale was overhunted in the 20th century by commercial whalers. Thanks to whaling bans, the species is recovering.

Ex 🕆 0
Cr 0
En 5
Vu 1
Other 6

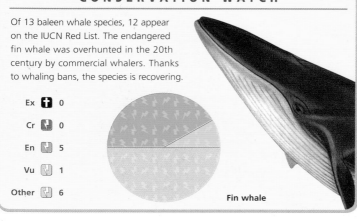

Fin whale

☐ Whales, dolphins, and porpoises

Whales, dolphins, and porpoises live in all the world's oceans and seas, except under the ice caps and in the Caspian Sea. River dolphins live in some of the world's major rivers.

CATCH OF THE DAY

HUNTING TACTICS

Whales use strategies and tricks when hunting. Baleen whales have enormous mouths to engulf huge quantities of tiny animals. Toothed whales pursue single prey, using sonar to find it. Many whales hunt together, calling out their next move as they swim. Humpback whales use bubbles as a group hunting tactic. One humpback swims around a school of fish to herd them together. While circling upward, it breathes out to produce a "net" of bubbles, which the prey cannot swim through. The whales then take turns swimming through the trapped school with their mouths open, eating the fish.

Orcas regularly patrol sites where their favorite prey dwell. Here an orca lunges right up onto the beach to snatch a sea lion pup.

The school of fish trapped by a "net" of bubbles move closer together.

One member of the humpback hunting team swims up through the trapped fish with its mouth open, scooping in both prey and water.

Another member of the team swims in a spiral around the school of fish, breathing out to create the "bubblenet."

Humpback whales live and migrate together in small groups called pods. This enables close bonds to develop. These bonds are necessary so that the whales cooperate well enough for behaviors like bubblenetting to work.

Toothed whales

Most cetaceans are toothed whales. The group includes sperm whales, narwhals and belugas, beaked whales, dolphins, porpoises, and river dolphins. Compared to the massive baleen whales, most toothed whales are medium-size. They also tend to live in larger groups and have more complex relationships. Toothed whales are among the most intelligent mammals. They are vocal when they communicate and can be very playful. Toothed whales use echolocation to "see" underwater with sound. They emit high-pitched clicks, then use the echoes that bounce back from objects in the water around them to determine their location. Fish and squid are their preferred prey. Toothed whales' jaws are lined with sharp, cone-shaped teeth that allow them to grasp prey firmly, but not to chew it.

CONSERVATION WATCH

Of the 69 species of toothed whales, 35 appear on the IUCN Red List. China's baiji is critically endangered. Fishermen often catch and kill baijis by accident. Its habitat is being destroyed by pollution and other causes.

Ex	0
Cr	2
En	2
Vu	1
Other	30

Baiji

Common porpoise (harbor porpoise)
Phocoena phocoena

Spectacled porpoise
Australophocaena dioptrica
Lives with one or two others, or alone

Finless porpoise
Neophocaena phocaenoides
Has no dorsal fin

Common dolphin
Delphinus delphis
Lives in herds of several hundred, or even a thousand, members

Risso's dolphin
Grampus griseus
Crisscross scars from battles with squid prey

False killer whale
Pseudorca crassidens
Mothers nurse calves for two years.

Pygmy sperm whale
Kogia breviceps

Sperm whale
Physeter catodon
Large "melon" on head is filled with oil.

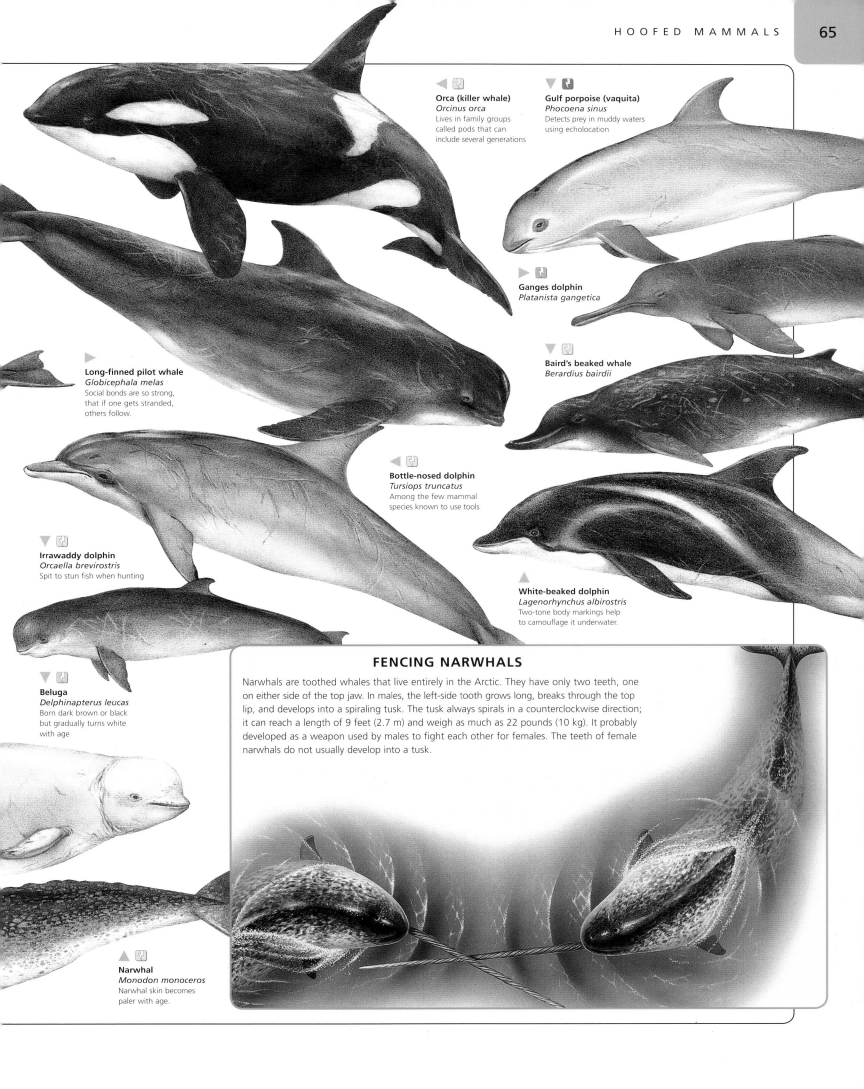

Orca (killer whale)
Orcinus orca
Lives in family groups
called pods that can
include several generations

Gulf porpoise (vaquita)
Phocoena sinus
Detects prey in muddy waters
using echolocation

Ganges dolphin
Platanista gangetica

Long-finned pilot whale
Globicephala melas
Social bonds are so strong,
that if one gets stranded,
others follow.

Baird's beaked whale
Berardius bairdii

Bottle-nosed dolphin
Tursiops truncatus
Among the few mammal
species known to use tools

Irrawaddy dolphin
Orcaella brevirostris
Spit to stun fish when hunting

White-beaked dolphin
Lagenorhynchus albirostris
Two-tone body markings help
to camouflage it underwater.

Beluga
Delphinapterus leucas
Born dark brown or black
but gradually turns white
with age

FENCING NARWHALS

Narwhals are toothed whales that live entirely in the Arctic. They have only two teeth, one
on either side of the top jaw. In males, the left-side tooth grows long, breaks through the top
lip, and develops into a spiraling tusk. The tusk always spirals in a counterclockwise direction;
it can reach a length of 9 feet (2.7 m) and weigh as much as 22 pounds (10 kg). It probably
developed as a weapon used by males to fight each other for females. The teeth of female
narwhals do not usually develop into a tusk.

Narwhal
Monodon monoceros
Narwhal skin becomes
paler with age.

1 ORDER • 29 FAMILIES • 442 GENERA • 2,010 SPECIES

Rodents

Almost half of all mammal species are rodents. Rodents tend to be small animals with stocky bodies and short limbs and tails. They have a pair of chisel-like incisor teeth in each jaw. There are three main groups of rodents: the squirrel-like, mouse-like, and cavy-like rodents. All squirrel-like rodents have jaw muscles arranged to give them a strong bite. Many squirrels live in trees, feeding on fruit, nuts, leaves, and insects. Mouse-like rodents mainly have pointed faces with long whiskers. They all have chewing muscles that let them gnaw readily. Most are seed-eaters that live on the ground, but some spend time in trees, underground, or in water. Most cavy-like rodents have large heads, plump bodies, short limbs, and small tails. Cavy-like rodents, such as guinea pigs and porcupines, have chewing muscles that give them a strong bite.

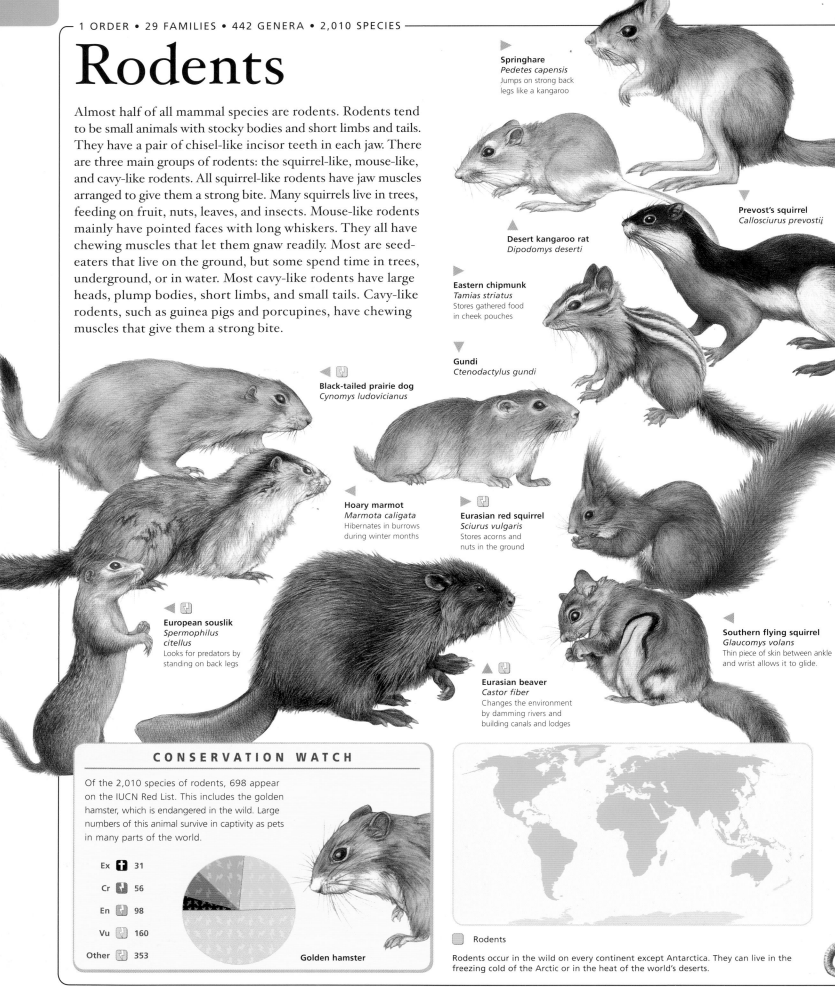

Springhare
Pedetes capensis
Jumps on strong back legs like a kangaroo

Desert kangaroo rat
Dipodomys deserti

Prevost's squirrel
Callosciurus prevostii

Eastern chipmunk
Tamias striatus
Stores gathered food in cheek pouches

Gundi
Ctenodactylus gundi

Black-tailed prairie dog
Cynomys ludovicianus

Hoary marmot
Marmota caligata
Hibernates in burrows during winter months

Eurasian red squirrel
Sciurus vulgaris
Stores acorns and nuts in the ground

European souslik
Spermophilus citellus
Looks for predators by standing on back legs

Eurasian beaver
Castor fiber
Changes the environment by damming rivers and building canals and lodges

Southern flying squirrel
Glaucomys volans
Thin piece of skin between ankle and wrist allows it to glide.

CONSERVATION WATCH

Of the 2,010 species of rodents, 698 appear on the IUCN Red List. This includes the golden hamster, which is endangered in the wild. Large numbers of this animal survive in captivity as pets in many parts of the world.

Ex	✝	31
Cr		56
En		98
Vu		160
Other		353

Golden hamster

☐ Rodents

Rodents occur in the wild on every continent except Antarctica. They can live in the freezing cold of the Arctic or in the heat of the world's deserts.

Harvest mouse
Micromys minutus
Climbs using tail like
a fifth limb

**Siberian collared lemming
(Arctic lemming)**
Dicrostonyx torquatus
Brown summer coat changes
to white in the winter months.

Demarest's hutia
Capromys pilorides
Waddles on short limbs

Paca
Agouti paca

Garden dormouse
Eliomys quercinus
Can hibernate for more
than half the year

Dassie rat
Petromus typicus

Pacarana
Dinomys branickii

**Large
bamboo rat**
*Rhizomys
sumatrensis*

Brazilian porcupine
Coendou prehensilis

Gray agouti
*Dasyprocta
fuliginosa*

Chinchilla
Chinchilla lanigera

**Fawn
hopping
mouse**
*Notomys
cervinus*

**European hamster
(common hamster)**
Cricetus cricetus

Muskrat
Ondatra zibethicus

Malayan porcupine
Hystrix brachyura

Plains viscacha
Lagostomus maximus

**Greater
bandicoot rat**
Bandicota indica

Coypu (nutria)
Myocastor coypus

Greater stick-nest rat
Leporillus conditor

Great gerbil
*Rhombomys
opimus*

**Black rat
(roof rat, ship rat)**
Rattus rattus

**Northern three-
toed jerboa**
Dipus sagitta

Capybara
Hydrochaeris hydrochaeris
The largest rodent, it weighs
as much as 150 pounds (70 kg).

2 ORDERS • 3 FAMILIES • 19 GENERA • 97 SPECIES

Rabbits and Elephant Shrews

Rabbits, hares, and pikas look similar to large rodents, but they belong to an order called the lagomorphs. Like rodents, they have large, constantly growing incisors and produce many offspring quickly. Unlike rodents, a second pair of incisors, known as peg teeth, sit behind the first. Plant-eaters, lagomorphs all have eyes on the sides of their heads to keep on the lookout for predators. Rabbits and hares have large ears for sharp hearing; pikas have shorter, rounded ears. With their powerful back legs, many species can outrun predators. Elephant shrews are named for their long, mobile snouts. They live on the ground, eat insects, and have excellent sight and hearing. They scamper or leap away from predators on their slender limbs. Most elephant shrews share a territory with a lifelong mate.

Arctic hare
Lepus timidus
Brown summer coat blends in with the tundra vegetation. This coat turns white in winter, for camouflage in the snow.

Central African hare
Poelagus marjorita

Pygmy rabbit
Brachylagus idahoensis

Hispid hare
Caprolagus hispidus

Brown hare
Lepus europaeus
Can run at speeds of 35 miles per hour (56 km/h)

Sumatran rabbit
Nesolagus netscheri

Eastern cottontail
Sylvilagus floridanus

Forest rabbit
Sylvilagus brasiliensis

European rabbit
Oryctolagus cuniculus

CONSERVATION WATCH

Of the 97 species of lagomorphs and elephant shrews, 34 appear on the IUCN Red List. South Africa's riverine rabbit is critically endangered because of the clearing of its habitat. Feral cats and dogs, as well as illegal trapping by hunters, are other threats.

Ex	🕆	1
Cr		4
En		10
Vu		7
Other		12

Riverine rabbit

Lagomorphs   Lagomorphs and elephant shrews

Lagomorphs occur naturally worldwide except Australia, Antarctica, southern South America, and parts of Southeast Asia. Elephant shrews live throughout much of Africa.

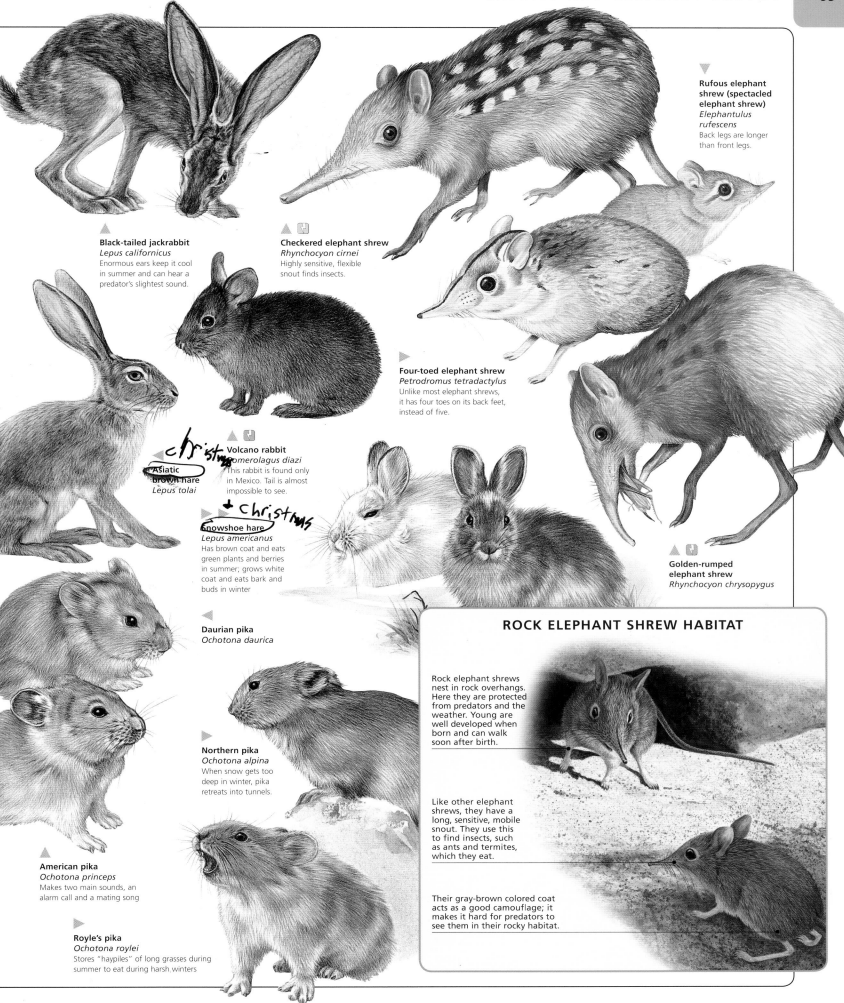

Black-tailed jackrabbit
Lepus californicus
Enormous ears keep it cool in summer and can hear a predator's slightest sound.

Checkered elephant shrew
Rhynchocyon cirnei
Highly sensitive, flexible snout finds insects.

Rufous elephant shrew (spectacled elephant shrew)
Elephantulus rufescens
Back legs are longer than front legs.

Four-toed elephant shrew
Petrodromus tetradactylus
Unlike most elephant shrews, it has four toes on its back feet, instead of five.

christmas
Asiatic brown hare
Lepus tolai

Volcano rabbit
Romerolagus diazi
This rabbit is found only in Mexico. Tail is almost impossible to see.

+ christmas
Snowshoe hare
Lepus americanus
Has brown coat and eats green plants and berries in summer; grows white coat and eats bark and buds in winter

Golden-rumped elephant shrew
Rhynchocyon chrysopygus

Daurian pika
Ochotona daurica

Northern pika
Ochotona alpina
When snow gets too deep in winter, pika retreats into tunnels.

American pika
Ochotona princeps
Makes two main sounds, an alarm call and a mating song

Royle's pika
Ochotona roylei
Stores "haypiles" of long grasses during summer to eat during harsh winters

ROCK ELEPHANT SHREW HABITAT

Rock elephant shrews nest in rock overhangs. Here they are protected from predators and the weather. Young are well developed when born and can walk soon after birth.

Like other elephant shrews, they have a long, sensitive, mobile snout. They use this to find insects, such as ants and termites, which they eat.

Their gray-brown colored coat acts as a good camouflage; it makes it hard for predators to see them in their rocky habitat.

Flamingos take flight to avoid danger. They need to run a few steps to gain enough speed to take off. In flight, they stretch out their long necks and trail their legs behind them.

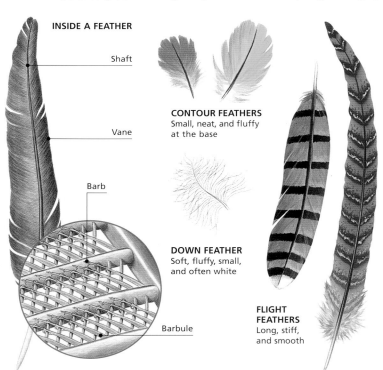

INSIDE A FEATHER

Shaft

Vane

Barb

Barbule

CONTOUR FEATHERS
Small, neat, and fluffy at the base

DOWN FEATHER
Soft, fluffy, small, and often white

FLIGHT FEATHERS
Long, stiff, and smooth

KINDS OF FEATHERS

Feathers are made of keratin. Each feather consists of a central shaft with vanes branching off it. In some feathers, the vane is made of barbs, lined with hooked barbules that interlock to hold the vane stiff. There are three main kinds of feathers: down feathers protect the bird from the cold; contour feathers keep it streamlined so it moves smoothly through the air; and flight feathers on the wing and tail allow the bird to take off, fly, and land.

Light yet strong, flight feathers allow the Galápagos hawk to soar high in the air while hunting.

Birds live in almost every habitat on Earth, from the freezing cold of the Antarctic to arid deserts and even urban areas. The ostrich, which can grow taller than 9 feet (2.7 m) and weigh more than 300 pounds (136 kg), is the largest bird. The smallest is the bee hummingbird, which weighs just ⅟₁₀ ounce (2.8 g). The first birds developed from dinosaurs more than 150 million years ago. These early species had feathers and could fly. Today, all birds still have feathers and most can fly, but some have lost this ability. Like their reptile ancestors, birds have scales on their legs and lay eggs. Unlike reptiles, they are endothermic, or warm-blooded. The bodies of flying birds are rather bullet-like in shape, which reduces the effort of flight. Birds have fewer bones than mammals, so their bodies are light as well as strong. They spend much of their waking lives searching for food. Many species feed on seeds and fruit; others eat insects; some hunt small mammals and even other birds. The ability to fly has made many birds great travelers, migrating long distances every year to escape cold winters and find food. The need to react quickly and maneuver on the wing means that sight is the best developed sense in birds. Hearing is the next most important sense, even though birds do not have external ears. Birds mainly communicate by sight and sound. Some birds form lifelong pair bonds with their mate; many live and breed in large flocks; others are solitary. Most birds build nests for their eggs and young.

FROM EGG TO CHICK

Male birds fertilize eggs inside females' bodies. The albumen layers, yolk, membranes, and shell develop before the egg is laid. The egg, which has a hard, protective shell, is usually laid in a nest. The parents often take turns sitting on the nest to keep the eggs warm. Inside, the developing embryo is nourished by yolk and albumen. Body waste is stored in a sac. When it is ready to hatch, the chick has to crack the shell so it can break out.

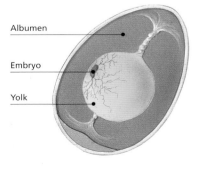

Albumen

Embryo

Yolk

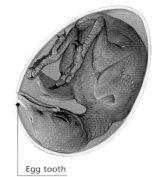

Egg tooth

NEWLY LAID EGG
Yolk provides the growing embryo with food; albumen provides it with water.

READY TO HATCH
The chick uses its egg tooth to crack through the shell.

The great gray owl hunts to feed its chicks until they can fend for themselves.

— 3 ORDERS • 5 FAMILIES • 15 GENERA • 60 SPECIES —

Ratites and Tinamous

Most flightless birds—ostriches, rheas, emus, cassowaries, and kiwis—are known as ratites. Their breastbones lack the keel of flying birds because they do not have large flight muscles. Most have stubby wings and soft flight feathers. Ratites probably lost the ability to fly because they either lacked predators or could evade them more easily by other means. They are powerful runners that can use their strong, long legs for kicking. The ostrich is so fast it can outrun a racehorse. Rheas have large, cloaklike wings, which they sometimes spread to act like a sail as they run. Tinamous are small, plump flying birds, closely related to ratites. They have a keeled breastbone and many can fly, although not very well. They usually avoid predators either by standing still or by creeping through undergrowth.

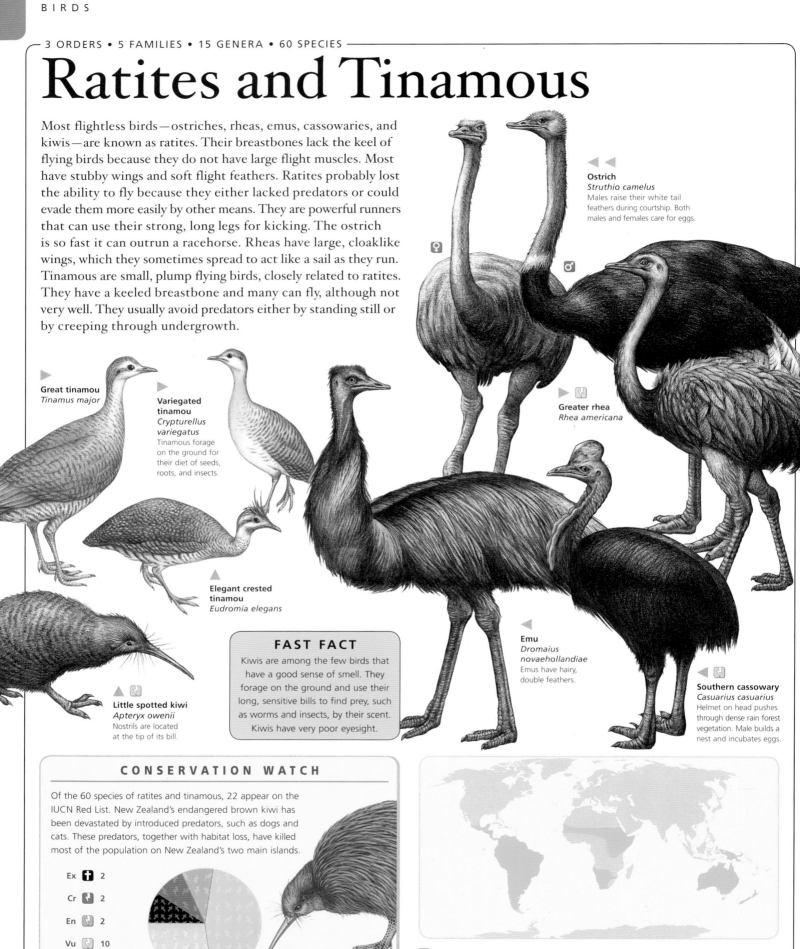

Ostrich
Struthio camelus
Males raise their white tail feathers during courtship. Both males and females care for eggs.

Great tinamou
Tinamus major

Variegated tinamou
Crypturellus variegatus
Tinamous forage on the ground for their diet of seeds, roots, and insects.

Greater rhea
Rhea americana

Elegant crested tinamou
Eudromia elegans

Emu
Dromaius novaehollandiae
Emus have hairy, double feathers.

Southern cassowary
Casuarius casuarius
Helmet on head pushes through dense rain forest vegetation. Male builds a nest and incubates eggs.

Little spotted kiwi
Apteryx owenii
Nostrils are located at the tip of its bill.

FAST FACT

Kiwis are among the few birds that have a good sense of smell. They forage on the ground and use their long, sensitive bills to find prey, such as worms and insects, by their scent. Kiwis have very poor eyesight.

CONSERVATION WATCH

Of the 60 species of ratites and tinamous, 22 appear on the IUCN Red List. New Zealand's endangered brown kiwi has been devastated by introduced predators, such as dogs and cats. These predators, together with habitat loss, have killed most of the population on New Zealand's two main islands.

Ex	🕆	2
Cr		2
En		2
Vu		10
Other		6

Brown kiwi

☐ Ratites and tinamous

Ostriches are found in Africa. Emus and cassowaries are strictly Australasian. Kiwis occur in New Zealand. Rheas and tinamous live in Central and South America.

1 ORDER • 5 FAMILIES • 80 GENERA • 290 SPECIES

Gamebirds

Pheasants, partridges, grouse, quail, and their relatives are called gamebirds because many of them are hunted by humans. They have stocky bodies, relatively small heads, and short, broad wings. While most can fly fast and low over short distances, many live mainly on the ground. Gamebirds usually have strong legs and can run well. The chicks of ground-dwelling species run quickly soon after hatching. Because they are the favored food of many predators, most gamebirds have dull-colored plumage that acts as camouflage. Others, like male pheasants and peafowl, are brilliantly colored. Males use their bright plumage, or elaborate feathery outgrowths, to make themselves stand out to females. They may court females with calls or complex dances.

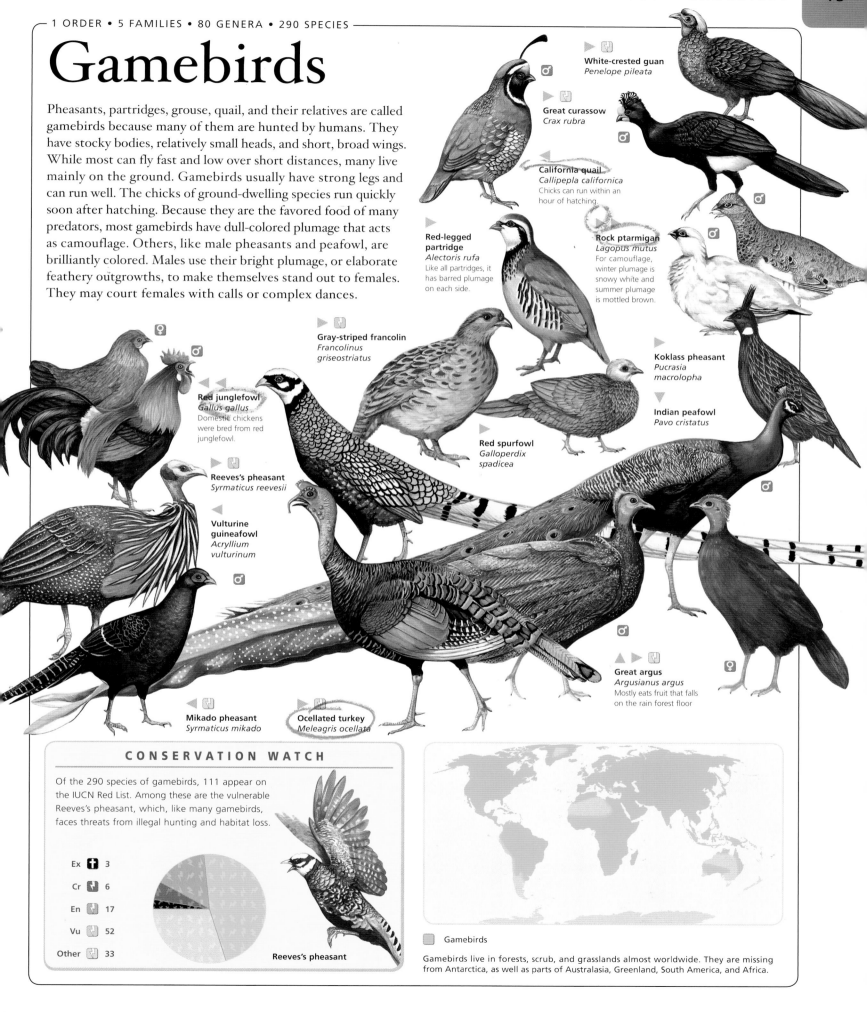

White-crested guan
Penelope pileata

Great curassow
Crax rubra

California quail
Callipepla californica
Chicks can run within an hour of hatching.

Red-legged partridge
Alectoris rufa
Like all partridges, it has barred plumage on each side.

Rock ptarmigan
Lagopus mutus
For camouflage, winter plumage is snowy white and summer plumage is mottled brown.

Gray-striped francolin
Francolinus griseostriatus

Koklass pheasant
Pucrasia macrolopha

Red junglefowl
Gallus gallus
Domestic chickens were bred from red junglefowl.

Red spurfowl
Galloperdix spadicea

Indian peafowl
Pavo cristatus

Reeves's pheasant
Syrmaticus reevesii

Vulturine guineafowl
Acryllium vulturinum

Great argus
Argusianus argus
Mostly eats fruit that falls on the rain forest floor

Mikado pheasant
Syrmaticus mikado

Ocellated turkey
Meleagris ocellata

CONSERVATION WATCH

Of the 290 species of gamebirds, 111 appear on the IUCN Red List. Among these are the vulnerable Reeves's pheasant, which, like many gamebirds, faces threats from illegal hunting and habitat loss.

Ex	✝	3
Cr		6
En		17
Vu		52
Other		33

Reeves's pheasant

Gamebirds

Gamebirds live in forests, scrub, and grasslands almost worldwide. They are missing from Antarctica, as well as parts of Australasia, Greenland, South America, and Africa.

1 ORDER • 3 FAMILIES • 52 GENERA • 162 SPECIES

Waterfowl

Ducks, geese, and swans are known as waterfowl and often live on or near water. Waterfowl are excellent swimmers with short legs and webbed feet. Those that live on land have less webbing. Waterfowl have broad, flat bills and necks that are long compared to their bodies. Their bodies are covered in dense, waterproof feathers and a thick layer of down to protect them from cold water. These feathers can be brightly colored and patterned. Some waterfowl species do not fly, but most are strong fliers and many migrate between their summer and winter homes. They migrate in search of food, such as plant matter or fish and shellfish. Screamers are related to waterfowl. They live in South America on riverbanks and uproot aquatic vegetation with their hooked bills.

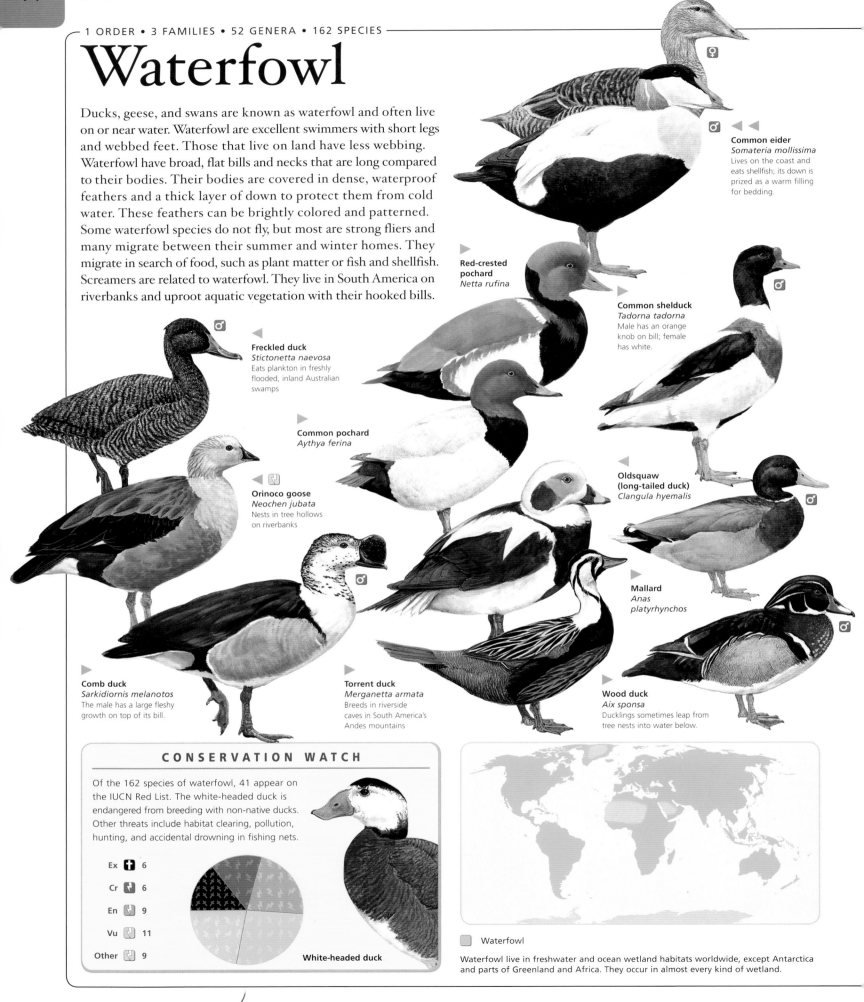

Common eider
Somateria mollissima
Lives on the coast and eats shellfish; its down is prized as a warm filling for bedding.

Red-crested pochard
Netta rufina

Common shelduck
Tadorna tadorna
Male has an orange knob on bill; female has white.

Freckled duck
Stictonetta naevosa
Eats plankton in freshly flooded, inland Australian swamps

Common pochard
Aythya ferina

Orinoco goose
Neochen jubata
Nests in tree hollows on riverbanks

Oldsquaw (long-tailed duck)
Clangula hyemalis

Mallard
Anas platyrhynchos

Comb duck
Sarkidiornis melanotos
The male has a large fleshy growth on top of its bill.

Torrent duck
Merganetta armata
Breeds in riverside caves in South America's Andes mountains

Wood duck
Aix sponsa
Ducklings sometimes leap from tree nests into water below.

CONSERVATION WATCH

Of the 162 species of waterfowl, 41 appear on the IUCN Red List. The white-headed duck is endangered from breeding with non-native ducks. Other threats include habitat clearing, pollution, hunting, and accidental drowning in fishing nets.

Ex 🕆 6
Cr 🕆 6
En 🕆 9
Vu 🕆 11
Other 🕆 9

White-headed duck

Waterfowl

Waterfowl live in freshwater and ocean wetland habitats worldwide, except Antarctica and parts of Greenland and Africa. They occur in almost every kind of wetland.

Muscovy duck
Cairina moschata
Isolated groups live in
South America and Africa.

**White-faced
whistling-duck**
*Dendrocygna
viduata*

Southern screamer
Chauna torquata
Alarm calls can be heard
more than 2 miles
(3.2 km) away.

Northern shoveler
Anas clypeata
Northern shovelers live in
small groups of up to 20
birds, but larger numbers
may migrate together.

Snow goose
Anser caerulescens
Breeds in North American
tundra; migrates in winter
to southern North America

Canada goose
Branta canadensis
Lives in flocks, aside from
nesting time

Red-breasted goose
Branta ruficollis

Mute swan
Cygnus olor
Mute swans mate
for life. Females
incubate the eggs,
but both parents
care for young.

Whooper swan
Cygnus cygnus

Black-necked swan
*Cygnus
melanocoryphus*

Bean goose
Anser fabalis
Breeds in Arctic during
summer; flies south to
the Mediterranean and
China for winter

Magpie goose
Anseranas semipalmata
Lives in northern Australian
swamps; it is a good
swimmer although its feet
are only partially webbed.

Coscoroba swan
Coscoroba coscoroba

MIGRATING GEESE

Barnacle geese breed in Greenland
during summer, before flying south
to Europe for the cold winter months.
Like many waterfowl, flocks fly in
a V-shaped formation when migrating.
This is an efficient way to travel long
distances. The lead goose breaks
up the air, creating small updrafts
that make flight easier for the
birds behind it. The geese can
also see clearly what is ahead of
them. Each bird takes a turn at
being in the lead.

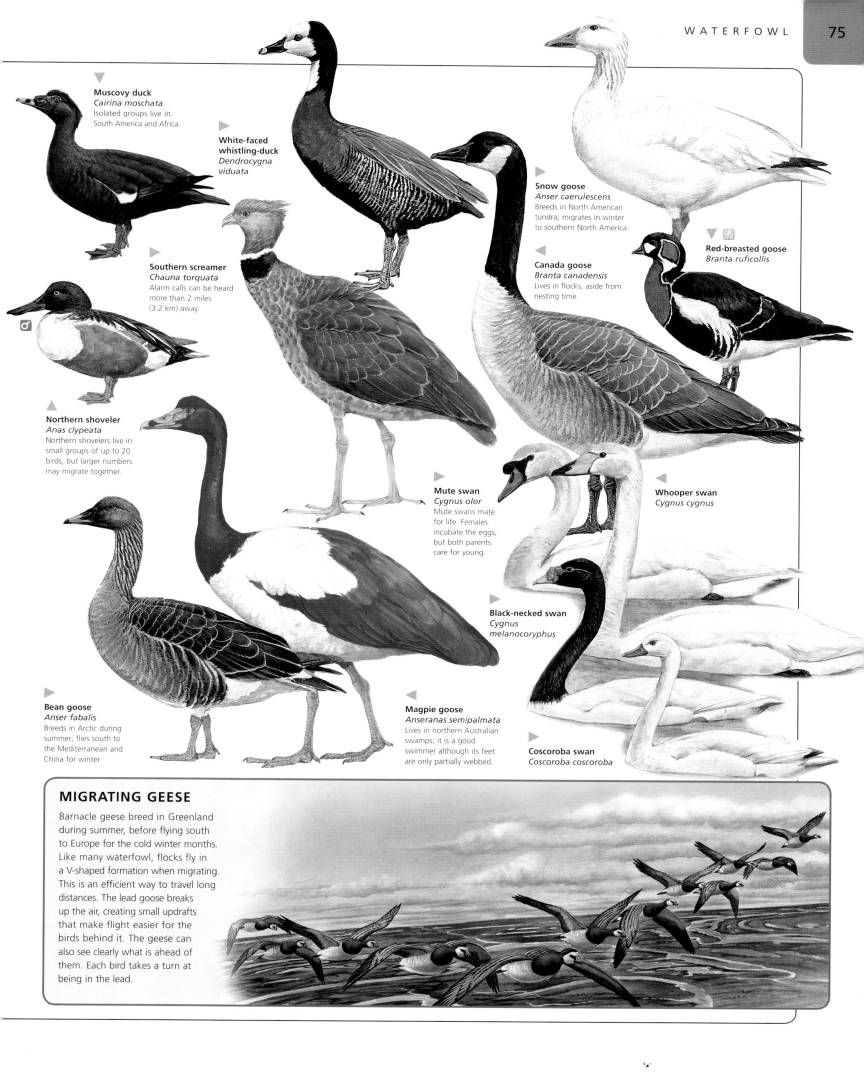

3 ORDERS • 6 FAMILIES • 33 GENERA • 139 SPECIES

Albatrosses and Grebes

Albatrosses and petrels, or tubenoses, are well adapted to life at sea. They are called tubenoses because of their long, external, tubelike nostrils. They use their sense of smell to locate food, breeding sites, and each other. Tubenoses are excellent fliers, often flying hundreds of miles in search of squid, fish, and other marine animals. They may travel for days across open water without seeing or stopping on dry land. Grebes, too, spend their lives around water. They even nest on floating platform nests made of plant material. Larger grebes are slim and elegant; smaller species look like ducklings. Grebes have lobed toes that propel them rapidly in water. Distantly related to grebes, loons have webbed feet. Loons and grebes are both poor fliers, and prefer to dive underwater to avoid danger.

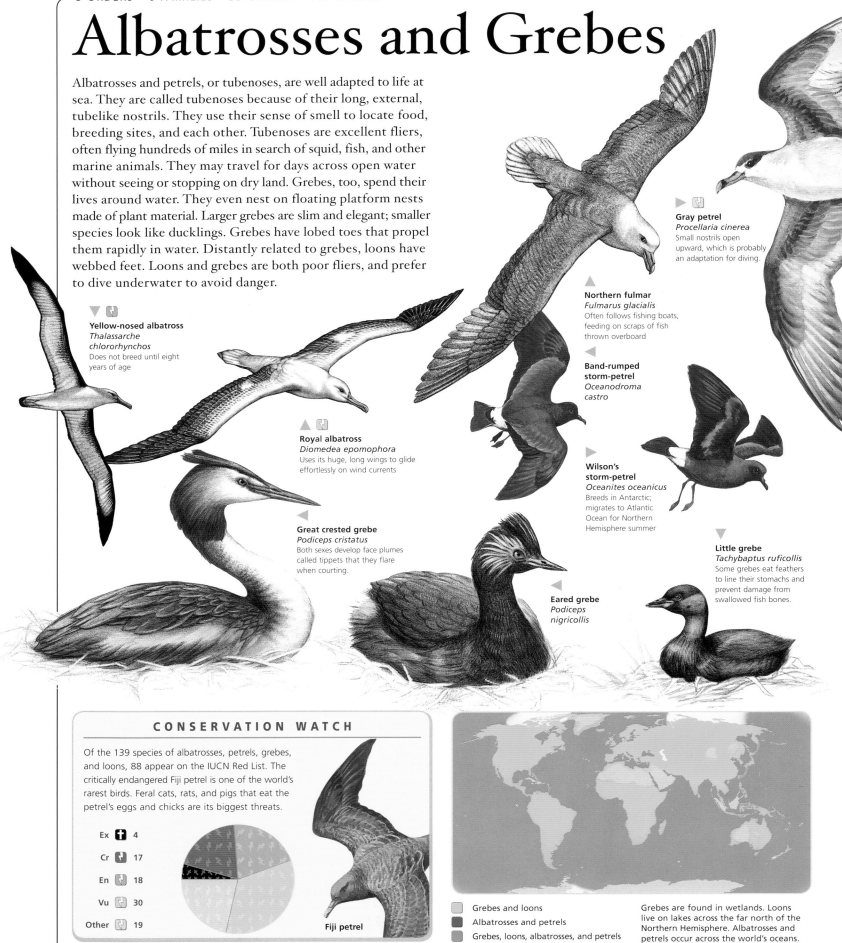

Gray petrel
Procellaria cinerea
Small nostrils open upward, which is probably an adaptation for diving.

Northern fulmar
Fulmarus glacialis
Often follows fishing boats, feeding on scraps of fish thrown overboard

Band-rumped storm-petrel
Oceanodroma castro

Wilson's storm-petrel
Oceanites oceanicus
Breeds in Antarctic; migrates to Atlantic Ocean for Northern Hemisphere summer

Yellow-nosed albatross
Thalassarche chlororhynchos
Does not breed until eight years of age

Royal albatross
Diomedea epomophora
Uses its huge, long wings to glide effortlessly on wind currents

Great crested grebe
Podiceps cristatus
Both sexes develop face plumes called tippets that they flare when courting.

Eared grebe
Podiceps nigricollis

Little grebe
Tachybaptus ruficollis
Some grebes eat feathers to line their stomachs and prevent damage from swallowed fish bones.

CONSERVATION WATCH

Of the 139 species of albatrosses, petrels, grebes, and loons, 88 appear on the IUCN Red List. The critically endangered Fiji petrel is one of the world's rarest birds. Feral cats, rats, and pigs that eat the petrel's eggs and chicks are its biggest threats.

Ex 🕆 4
Cr ⬇ 17
En ⬇ 18
Vu ⬇ 30
Other ⬇ 19

Fiji petrel

Grebes and loons
Albatrosses and petrels
Grebes, loons, albatrosses, and petrels

Grebes are found in wetlands. Loons live on lakes across the far north of the Northern Hemisphere. Albatrosses and petrels occur across the world's oceans.

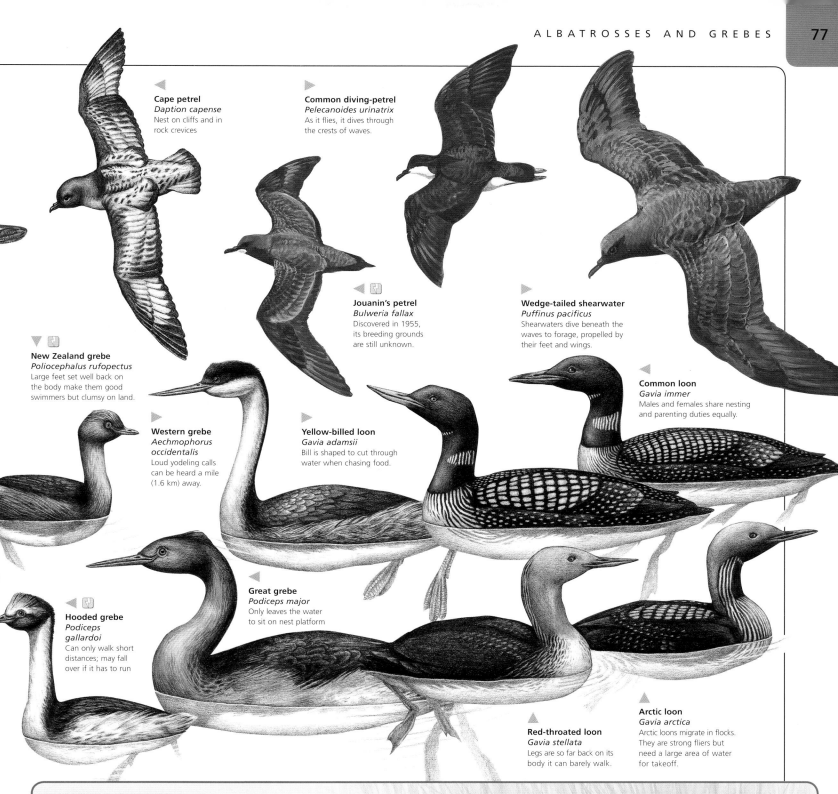

Cape petrel
Daption capense
Nest on cliffs and in rock crevices

Common diving-petrel
Pelecanoides urinatrix
As it flies, it dives through the crests of waves.

Jouanin's petrel
Bulweria fallax
Discovered in 1955, its breeding grounds are still unknown.

Wedge-tailed shearwater
Puffinus pacificus
Shearwaters dive beneath the waves to forage, propelled by their feet and wings.

New Zealand grebe
Poliocephalus rufopectus
Large feet set well back on the body make them good swimmers but clumsy on land.

Western grebe
Aechmophorus occidentalis
Loud yodeling calls can be heard a mile (1.6 km) away.

Yellow-billed loon
Gavia adamsii
Bill is shaped to cut through water when chasing food.

Common loon
Gavia immer
Males and females share nesting and parenting duties equally.

Hooded grebe
Podiceps gallardoi
Can only walk short distances; may fall over if it has to run

Great grebe
Podiceps major
Only leaves the water to sit on nest platform

Red-throated loon
Gavia stellata
Legs are so far back on its body it can barely walk.

Arctic loon
Gavia arctica
Arctic loons migrate in flocks. They are strong fliers but need a large area of water for takeoff.

DANCING GREBES

Grebes choose and bond with their mates, and courtship can be complex and last for hours. Both sexes take part in spectacular courtship dances, which involve pairs dancing together and performing matching moves. Each species has its own dance that courting pairs follow precisely. Western grebes begin courting with a "weed dance," which involves holding strands of vegetation in their bills. Then they rise up and race across the water's surface, moving in time like dance partners. This part of their performance, shown here, is called rushing.

2 ORDERS • 4 FAMILIES • 44 GENERA • 123 SPECIES

Herons and Flamingos

Herons and their relatives—storks, ibises, spoonbills, egrets, bitterns, and the hamerkop—wade in shallow water or swampy areas to hunt for fish, insects, and frogs. Their long legs let them stride through water without getting their feathers wet. All herons have long beaks and necks; they fold these back on their shoulders when they fly. Herons have patches of special feathers, called powder-down, that do not molt, but the tips fray into a fine powder, which the bird collects in its bill and uses to clean its feathers. Flamingos are also wading birds. Their distinctive reddish feathers come from pigments in the tiny plants and animals that they eat. These birds have a specially designed bill that strains this food from the surface of lakes, where they gather in huge numbers.

Greater flamingo
Phoenicopterus ruber

Great blue heron
Ardea herodias
Often seen stalking along the edges of lakes or marshes

Whistling heron
Syrigma sibilatrix

Boat-billed heron
Cochlearius cochlearius

White-crested bittern
Tigriornis leucolophus

Hamerkop
Scopus umbretta

Andean flamingo
Phoenicoparrus andinus

Cattle egret
Bubulcus ibis
Often perches on cattle, eating insects that the cattle's hooves stir up

Sacred ibis
Threskiornis aethiopicus
An important bird in ancient Egyptian mythology, sacred ibises were often mummified.

Wood stork
Mycteria americana
Sensitive bill finds prey by touch in muddy water.

CONSERVATION WATCH

Of the 123 species of herons, their relatives, and flamingos, 37 appear on the IUCN Red List. The crested ibis is endangered because of the destruction and pollution of its habitat. These birds are now found only in central China.

Ex		5
Cr		4
En		12
Vu		7
Other		9

Crested ibis

Herons

Herons and flamingos

Herons and their relatives can be found in freshwater habitats worldwide, except near the Poles. Flamingos live on most continents, around shallow lakes and coastal regions.

1 ORDER • 6 FAMILIES • 8 GENERA • 63 SPECIES

Pelicans

Pelicans are related to five other families of waterbirds: gannets and boobies; tropicbirds; cormorants; anhingas and darters; and frigatebirds. All of these birds have four toes on each foot that are connected by webbing. Pelicans and their relatives are true waterbirds. They are all excellent swimmers, and some can barely walk on land. Most, except cormorants and darters, have waterproof feathers. Many species have a large throat sac that has no feathers. This sac is used to catch fish, as well as to impress mates during courtship displays. This group nests in colonies, often with other seabirds. They are long-lived birds, and may return to the same nesting sites and breed with the same partners every year for 20 years. The males and females of all species share nesting and parenting duties.

Great white pelican
Pelecanus onocrotalus

Red-tailed tropicbird
Phaethon rubricauda

Northern gannet
Morus bassanus

Lesser frigatebird
Fregata ariel

Dalmatian pelican
Pelecanus crispus
Chick puts entire head into parent's mouth for a meal of partly digested fish.

Double-crested cormorant
Phalacrocorax auritus
Perches with its wings spread out to dry them after diving

European shag
Phalacrocorax aristotelis
Communicates using grunts and clicks

Pelagic cormorant
Phalacrocorax pelagicus
Dives as deep as 100 feet (30 m) in coastal waters to feed on the sea bottom

Darter
Anhinga melanogaster

Great cormorant
Phalacrocorax carbo
White patches develop on the birds' legs at breeding time.

Peruvian booby
Sula variegata
Can dive from 50 feet (15 m) high to catch fish

Anhinga
Anhinga anhinga

Blue-footed booby
Sula nebouxii
The blue-footed booby incubates its eggs with its webbed feet.

CONSERVATION WATCH

Of the 63 species of pelicans and their relatives, 23 appear on the IUCN Red List. The vulnerable rough-faced shag is found only around four tiny New Zealand islands. In the past, it was hunted by indigenous people; now it is sometimes caught accidentally by commercial fishing operations.

Ex 🕆 1
Cr 🐦 2
En 🐦 3
Vu 🐦 11
Other 🐦 6

Rough-faced shag

☐ Pelicans

Pelicans and their relatives live in watery environments throughout much of the world. Most species tend to be found in tropical or temperate areas.

1 ORDER • 3 FAMILIES • 83 GENERA • 304 SPECIES

Birds of Prey

Birds of prey are known as raptors, a Latin word meaning "one who seizes and carries away." Many of these birds hunt by swooping down from the sky to snatch up prey. Raptors are one of the largest bird orders. All raptors are carnivorous, and most are well adapted to hunting live prey. Strong feet armed with sharp claws called talons seize onto struggling animals. Sharp, hooked bills tear through their prey's flesh. Most raptors have long, broad wings on which they soar high above open habitats as they look for food far below. They watch for the slightest movements of prey with their exceptional eyesight. Those that dwell in forests have shorter, rounded wings to change direction quickly. The secretary bird is the only raptor that actively hunts on the ground, stalking and flushing out prey with its long, graceful legs.

Crowned eagle
Harpyhaliaetus coronatus
This eagle lives in isolated pockets of open country in South America.

Javan hawk-eagle
Spizaetus bartelsi
Lives in rain forests and eats birds and small mammals

Collared falconet
Microhierax caerulescens

Harris's hawk
Parabuteo unicinctus
Often two males and one female look after a nest.

African cuckoo-hawk
Aviceda cuculoides
Eats large insects and small reptiles

Juvenile

Yellow-headed caracara
Milvago chimachima
This bird often feeds by plucking ticks off the backs of cattle.

Adult

Common kestrel
Falco tinnunculus
It hovers in the air, facing into the wind, on the lookout for prey below.

Osprey
Pandion haliaetus
The osprey lives worldwide near rivers, lakes, and seashores where it hunts for fish. When it dives for fish, nasal valves stop water from entering its nostrils.

Black baza
Aviceda leuphotes

Andean condor
Vultur gryphus
With a wingspan of more than 10 feet (3 m), this is the largest flying raptor.

CONSERVATION WATCH

Of the 304 raptor species, 81 appear on the IUCN Red List. The critically endangered California condor came close to extinction in the wild during the 1980s. It is threatened by hunters and egg collectors, the trapping of its prey, and lead poisoning from eating animals killed by lead shot.

Ex	2
Cr	9
En	8
Vu	26
Other	36

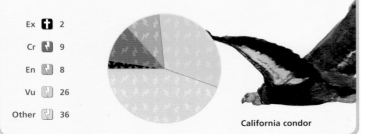

California condor

Birds of prey

Birds of prey are found throughout most of the world. They range from sparse, bitterly cold Arctic tundra to hot, lush tropical rain forests and dry, desolate deserts.

▶ Cinereous vulture
Aegypius monachus
This large raptor nests in tall trees. Similarly to other vultures, it eats dead animals but it also hunts live prey.

◀ Black harrier
Circus maurus
A small raptor found in southern Africa

▶ Bald eagle
Haliaeetus leucocephalus
Its huge stick nest is added to each year and can end up weighing 2 tons (1.8 t).

▼ European honey-buzzard
Pernis apivorus
The honey-buzzard does not eat honey. It feeds mainly on bees and wasps, digging them out of their hives to eat.

▶ Eurasian griffon
Gyps fulvus
This Old World vulture nests in mountainous areas but flies to open plains to feed.

▲ Black kite
Milvus migrans
The black kite is widespread through much of Europe.

◀ Secretary bird
Sagittarius serpentarius
The secretary bird is the only surviving member of its family and has no close relatives. It uses its long legs to kick its prey and subdue it.

▶ Crested serpent-eagle
Spilornis cheela
Eats tree snakes but also hunts lizards

SCAVENGING VULTURES

Ruppell's griffons are vultures. They do not usually hunt live prey but feed on the leftovers of other carnivores' kills. Their strong bills tear easily through hide and bone. To find meals, they cruise as high as 20,000 feet (6,100 m) across arid African plains, relying on their excellent eyesight to spot dead animals or feeding carnivores. Hundreds of them may descend on a single kill. Ruppell's griffons often eat so much they are too heavy to fly and must wait for a short period before they are able to take off.

1 ORDER • 1 FAMILY • 6 GENERA • 17 SPECIES

Penguins

Penguins are flightless birds. They spend three-quarters of their lives in the sea, where they hunt fish and other small marine animals. Their wings act like flat, stiff paddles that propel them through water. Beneath the skin, a layer of fat called blubber provides insulation from frigid waters. Their dense, waterproof feathers protect them from cold by trapping warm air. On land, they molt old feathers and grow new ones, which may take more than a month. They mate and lay eggs in large, noisy colonies. Chicks have down feathers for warmth. They cannot enter the water until they grow their first waterproof feathers. Before then they are dependent on their parents for food. Skuas and gulls prey on eggs and chicks, but adults have few predators on land. In the ocean, they are hunted by sharks and leopard seals.

Jackass penguin
Spheniscus demersus

Adelie penguin
Pygoscelis adeliae
This quite aggressive penguin nests on mainland Antarctica.

Yellow-eyed penguin
Megadyptes antipodes
Nests in coastal forest and scrub on New Zealand's South Island

Snares penguin
Eudyptes robustus
Nests only on the Snares Islands, New Zealand, in colonies of as many as 200 birds

Emperor penguin
Aptenodytes forsteri
The largest penguin; female lays one egg in winter and leaves it with male, returning only in spring.

King penguin
Aptenodytes patagonicus
Parent can travel as far as 250 miles (400 km) in search of food for chick.

Little penguin
Eudyptula minor
Also known as the fairy penguin, this is the smallest of the penguins.

Royal penguin
Eudyptes schlegeli
Breeds off Macquarie Island, in Antarctic waters; of two eggs laid, only one is reared.

CONSERVATION WATCH

Of the 17 penguin species, 12 appear on the IUCN Red List. New Zealand's yellow-eyed penguin is one of the most endangered penguins. Their eggs and chicks are snatched from their nesting sites by introduced animals, or they are trampled by domestic livestock.

Ex 🕆 0
Cr 🕆 0
En 🕆 3
Vu 🕆 7
Other 🕆 2

Yellow-eyed penguin

Penguins

Penguins live in the cooler waters of the world's southern oceans. They breed along mainland and island coasts. Only the Galápagos penguin strays across the Equator.

2 ORDERS • 12 FAMILIES • 62 GENERA • 213 SPECIES

Cranes

Cranes belong to a diverse order that includes limpkins and trumpeters, rails and crakes, bustards, and buttonquails. Many do not appear to have a lot in common: Cranes tend to be large, long-legged birds; buttonquails have small, plump bodies and short legs. But they are all descended from an ancient ground-dwelling shorebird. Cranes and their relatives spend much of their lives on the ground. Many prefer to walk rather than fly or swim. Some have even lost the ability to fly. Cranes usually make their nests on the ground or on platforms in shallow water. Their young can walk almost as soon as they hatch. Most cranes use sound to communicate. Males and females of many species sing together. They may also perform elaborate dances to form new mating pairs or renew old bonds.

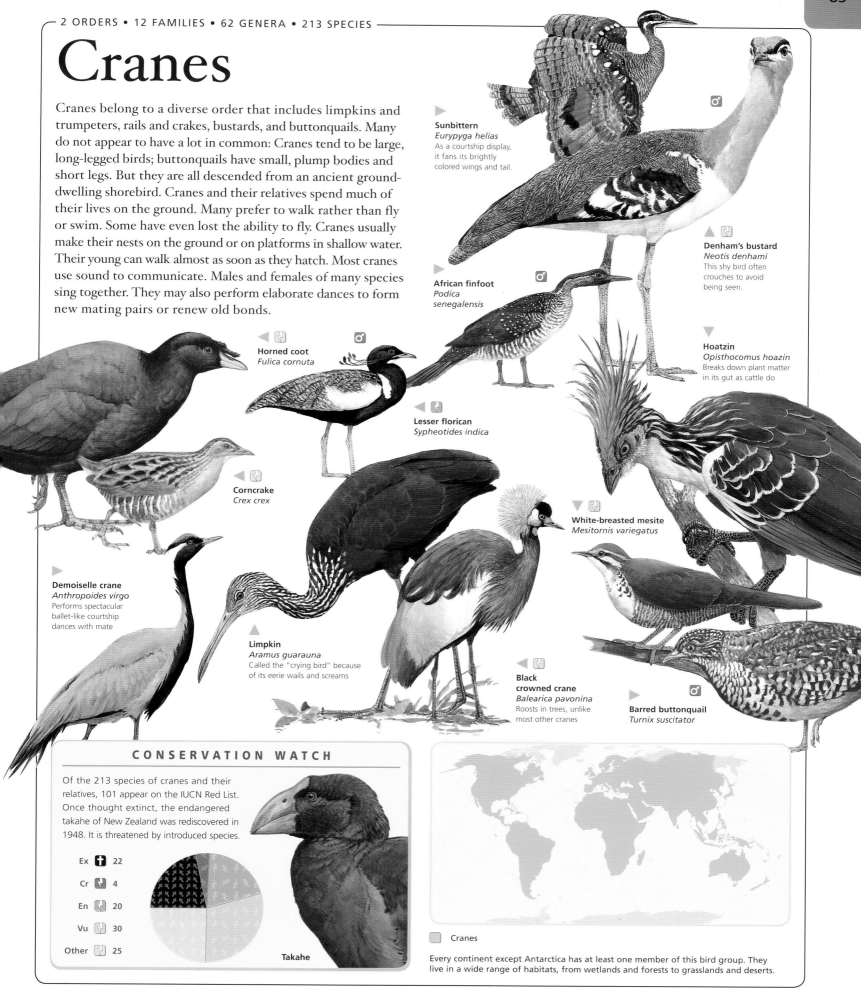

Sunbittern
Eurypyga helias
As a courtship display, it fans its brightly colored wings and tail.

Denham's bustard
Neotis denhami
This shy bird often crouches to avoid being seen.

African finfoot
Podica senegalensis

Hoatzin
Opisthocomus hoazin
Breaks down plant matter in its gut as cattle do

Horned coot
Fulica cornuta

Lesser florican
Sypheotides indica

Corncrake
Crex crex

White-breasted mesite
Mesitornis variegatus

Demoiselle crane
Anthropoides virgo
Performs spectacular ballet-like courtship dances with mate

Limpkin
Aramus guarauna
Called the "crying bird" because of its eerie wails and screams

Black crowned crane
Balearica pavonina
Roosts in trees, unlike most other cranes

Barred buttonquail
Turnix suscitator

CONSERVATION WATCH

Of the 213 species of cranes and their relatives, 101 appear on the IUCN Red List. Once thought extinct, the endangered takahe of New Zealand was rediscovered in 1948. It is threatened by introduced species.

Ex	✝	22
Cr		4
En		20
Vu		30
Other		25

Takahe

☐ Cranes

Every continent except Antarctica has at least one member of this bird group. They live in a wide range of habitats, from wetlands and forests to grasslands and deserts.

1 ORDER • 16 FAMILIES • 86 GENERA • 351 SPECIES

Waders and Shorebirds

Waders and shorebirds live near the sea or around lakes, pools, and puddles. They feed mainly on small animals and are all strong fliers. They belong to three main subgroups: waders, gulls and terns, and auks. Many of these birds look different from each other because of the distinct roles they fill in the environment. Waders, such as oystercatchers, curlews, and stilts, tend to have long bodies, narrow wings, and long, thin legs. They stride through shallow waters and along shorelines, foraging in sediment. Gulls are mostly seabirds. They scavenge along shorelines but also may swim out to hunt prey in deeper water. Terns are plunge-divers that hover when they spot a fish, then plunge headfirst to catch their meal. Auks find food by swimming underwater, like penguins. Unlike penguins, they can also fly.

Ruff
Philomachus pugnax
Ruff of long, loose feathers around male's neck and head is used in courtship displays.

Curlew sandpiper
Calidris ferruginea
Forages for worms on tidal mudflats, washing them before eating

Collared pratincole
Glareola pratincola
Feeds on insects while flying in flocks at dawn and dusk

Red-necked phalarope
Phalaropus lobatus
Swims gracefully, holding its head high and nodding

Common redshank
Tringa totanus
Feeds day and night on coastal mudflats when the tide is out

Southern lapwing
Vanellus chilensis
Hunts by running then freezing like a statue as it looks around for prey

Common snipe
Gallinago gallinago
A special tip at the end of its bill allows it to eat prey in mud.

Black-tailed godwit
Limosa limosa
This sociable bird often forms large feeding flocks. Breeding pairs migrate separately but find each other at the breeding ground every year.

CONSERVATION WATCH

Of the 351 species of waders and shorebirds, 71 appear on the IUCN Red List. The flightless great auk was hunted into extinction for its feathers and meat. The last known living pair was found in Iceland in 1844.

Ex 4
Cr 8
En 8
Vu 21
Other 30

Great auk

Waders and shorebirds

These birds are found near bodies of water, such as lakes, rivers, and oceans. Some species can live far inland, even in semidesert regions.

Fairy tern (white tern)
Sterna nereis
Although they have webbed
feet, terns rarely swim.

Atlantic puffin
Fratercula arctica
Nests in colonies, sometimes
in burrows dug by rabbits

Crested auklet
*Aethia
cristatella*

Common tern
Sterna hirundo
These birds nest in noisy
colonies; intruders are
attacked from the air
by angry terns.

Tufted puffin
Fratercula cirrhata
Nests in burrows as
deep as 6 feet (1.8 m)
on coastal shores

Ibisbill
Ibidorhyncha struthersii
This central Asian bird forages
along streams and ponds, using
its downward-curved bill to
search for insects under rocks.

Black-winged stilt
Himantopus himantopus
Because of its long legs, this
stilt can feed in deeper water
than many other waders.

Black skimmer
Rynchops niger
Flies low along surface of
water with its bill open,
scooping up any prey it finds

Black-faced sheathbill
Chionis minor
Uses small spur on wing as a
weapon; a fatty layer keeps it
warm in its Antarctic habitat.

Great black-backed gull
Larus marinus
Eats almost anything,
including smaller birds

Pied avocet
Recurvirostra avosetta
Avocets use their upward-curved
bills to sift tiny animals from
the mud.

Beach stone curlew
Esacus magnirostris
Hunts on beaches, reefs,
mangroves, and tidal flats in
Australia and Southeast Asia

Herring gull
Larus argentatus
Often seen with
groups of great
black-backed gulls

2 ORDERS • 3 FAMILIES • 46 GENERA • 327 SPECIES

Pigeons and Sandgrouse

Pigeons and sandgrouse forage in flocks and travel large distances between feeding and nesting areas every day. Pigeons and doves are tree-dwelling birds that eat seeds and fruit. The term "dove" is used for smaller birds; "pigeon" describes larger species. Pigeons and doves have bills that let them suck up water rather than sip it. They are able to produce "crop milk." The crop is a pouch at the beginning of the digestive system. Glands in the crops of both males and females produce a thick, milky substance that is fed to chicks. Desert-dwelling sandgrouse do not produce crop milk. These strong, fast fliers need to drink regularly and may fly more than 40 miles (65 km) between waterholes and feeding areas. They nest on the ground. Sandgrouse chicks leave the nest a few hours after hatching.

Victoria crowned pigeon
Goura victoria
Males repeatedly bow their elaborate crests to impress females during courtship.

Seychelles blue pigeon
Alectroenas pulcherrima
These striking birds became rare because they were once shot for food, but their numbers have since recovered.

Zebra dove
Geopelia striata
Scurry around like rodents, feeding on grass seeds

Pied imperial pigeon
Ducula bicolor

Chestnut-bellied sandgrouse
Pterocles exustus
Adults soak up water in their feathers; chicks drink from the wet feathers.

Emerald dove
Chalcophaps indica
Feeds on fallen rain forest fruit and sometimes termites

Pallas's sandgrouse
Syrrhaptes paradoxus

Rock dove
Columba livia
Known as the common pigeon, huge flocks are seen in cities worldwide.

Banded fruit dove
Ptilinopus cinctus
Fruit doves have a specialized digestive system to cope with a diet of fruit.

CONSERVATION WATCH

Of the 327 species of pigeons and sandgrouse, 112 appear on the IUCN Red List. The extinct flightless dodo lived only on the Indian Ocean island of Mauritius. Explorers in the late 1600s slaughtered it for food and sport.

Ex ✝ 14
Cr 🕭 12
En 🕭 15
Vu 🕭 34
Other 🕭 37

Dodo

☐ Pigeons and sandgrouse

Pigeons and doves occur worldwide, but most species live in the tropics and subtropics. Sandgrouse are found only in regions of Africa and Eurasia that have low rainfall.

2 ORDERS • 2 FAMILIES • 41 GENERA • 161 SPECIES

Cuckoos and Turacos

Even though cuckoos and turacos are related, they look and behave differently. Cuckoos are infamous for laying their eggs in other birds' nests for those birds to raise. While about 50 species behave like this, most do not. These include the social anis and guiras, which live in distinct territories; the roadrunners and ground cuckoos, which rarely fly and prefer to run; and the couas and coucals. Most members of the cuckoo family have drab-colored feathers that provide them with good camouflage. In contrast, turacos are brightly colored birds with long tails and short wings. They are more agile running along branches than flapping among them. All except one species have crests on their heads. These noisy birds live in groups of as many as 10 and communicate with loud, barking calls.

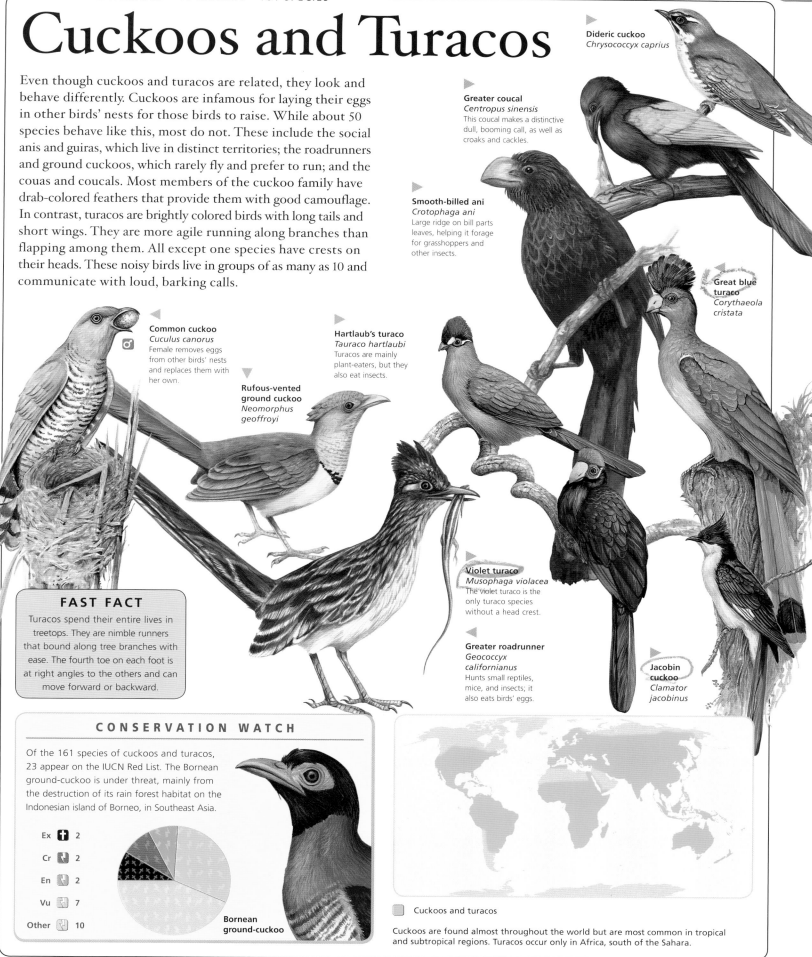

Dideric cuckoo
Chrysococcyx caprius

Greater coucal
Centropus sinensis
This coucal makes a distinctive dull, booming call, as well as croaks and cackles.

Smooth-billed ani
Crotophaga ani
Large ridge on bill parts leaves, helping it forage for grasshoppers and other insects.

Great blue turaco
Corythaeola cristata

Common cuckoo
Cuculus canorus
Female removes eggs from other birds' nests and replaces them with her own.

Hartlaub's turaco
Tauraco hartlaubi
Turacos are mainly plant-eaters, but they also eat insects.

Rufous-vented ground cuckoo
Neomorphus geoffroyi

Violet turaco
Musophaga violacea
The violet turaco is the only turaco species without a head crest.

Greater roadrunner
Geococcyx californianus
Hunts small reptiles, mice, and insects; it also eats birds' eggs.

Jacobin cuckoo
Clamator jacobinus

FAST FACT

Turacos spend their entire lives in treetops. They are nimble runners that bound along tree branches with ease. The fourth toe on each foot is at right angles to the others and can move forward or backward.

CONSERVATION WATCH

Of the 161 species of cuckoos and turacos, 23 appear on the IUCN Red List. The Bornean ground-cuckoo is under threat, mainly from the destruction of its rain forest habitat on the Indonesian island of Borneo, in Southeast Asia.

Ex	2
Cr	2
En	2
Vu	7
Other	10

Bornean ground-cuckoo

Cuckoos and turacos

Cuckoos are found almost throughout the world but are most common in tropical and subtropical regions. Turacos occur only in Africa, south of the Sahara.

1 ORDER • 3 FAMILIES • 85 GENERA • 364 SPECIES

Parrots

Parrots are some of the easiest birds in the world to recognize. Their unique bill is short and strong, with the top section curving downward. This design is perfect for crushing the seeds and nuts that make up most of their diet. Parrot feet are distinctive: two toes point forward and two toes point backward. This arrangement allows them to grasp objects with their feet and move with great agility in trees. Most parrots have brilliantly colored feathers, usually in shades of green with splashes of red, yellow, and blue. A few species are drab for camouflage. Their bright colors, along with their sociable natures, have made them popular as pets. As a result, many wild birds are poached for the caged bird market. This is one reason why parrots are among the most common birds on endangered species lists.

Eclectus parrot
Eclectus roratus
Males and females look so different they were once thought to belong to different species.

Buff-faced pygmy parrot
Micropsitta pusio

Rainbow lorikeet
Trichoglossus haematodus

Galah
Eolophus roseicapilla

Blue-fronted parrot
Amazona aestiva

White-crowned parrot
Pionus senilis

Kakapo
Strigops habroptilus
Male produces deep booming sounds from a special throat sac and digs "arenas" where he dances for females.

Kea
Nestor notabilis
Eats seeds, flowers, and insects, but will also eat dead animals and sometimes even attacks live sheep

CONSERVATION WATCH

Of the 364 parrot species, 146 appear on the IUCN Red List. Mexico's thick-billed parrot is endangered, mainly because of the logging of its pine forest home. Its striking red and green plumage has also made it popular with the illegal pet trade.

Thick-billed parrot

Ex	🕆	19
Cr	🕆	15
En	🕆	30
Vu	🕆	45
Other	🕆	37

☐ Parrots

Parrots live mainly in the tropical regions of the Southern Hemisphere; they occur as far north as eastern Afghanistan. Australasia and South America boast the most species.

Hyacinth macaw
Anodorhynchus hyacinthinus
Eats the nut of South America's acuri palm; the nut is so tough it needs to pass through a cow's digestive system before the macaw can crack it.

Yellow-collared lovebird
Agapornis personatus
Mates form close, usually lifelong, bonds.

Fischer's lovebird
Agapornis fischeri

Swift parrot
Lathamus discolor

Senegal parrot
Poicephalus senegalus
Lives alone or in pairs, sometimes in groups of as many as 10 members

Plum-headed parakeet
Psittacula cyanocephala

Maroon-faced parakeet
Pyrrhura leucotis

Scarlet macaw
Ara macao
Young can stay with parents for as long as two years after hatching.

Ground parrot
Pezoporus wallicus

Military macaw
Ara militaris
Macaws are long-lived birds: some have survived to age 65 in captivity.

Burrowing parakeet
Cyanoliseus patagonus
Digs tunnels into sandstone or limestone cliffs, where it breeds in colonies

DESIGNED FOR CRUSHING

Position of upper bill when jaw is open

Well-muscled base of bill has a cutting edge for cracking tough foods, such as hard-shelled nuts.

Hooked for grabbing and holding food

Well-developed upper hinge opens like a lever; aids bird when climbing.

Lower hinge

Position of lower bill when jaw is open

2 ORDERS • 7 FAMILIES • 51 GENERA • 314 SPECIES

Nightjars and Owls

Nightjars, their relatives, and owls are predators that hunt almost exclusively at night or twilight. Most have drab, mottled plumage that provides camouflage when they are at rest. Nightjars and their relatives are expert at striking poses that make them look like broken-off tree limbs. Owls have sharp, hooked bills to tear flesh; strong legs; and feet with talons to grasp and hold struggling prey. They have large, round eyes that face forward. This gives owls binocular vision, which helps them to judge distances. Their eyes are designed to work best at low light levels, with many light-sensitive cells known as rods. Similarly to owls, nightjars and their relatives have eyes adapted for seeing at low light levels. Unlike owls, these are not forward facing. They also do not have talons. Their hearing is excellent.

Tawny frogmouth
Podargus strigoides
Perches completely still, then pounces when it spots prey

Spotted nightjar
Eurostopodus argus

Common pauraque
Nyctidromus albicollis

Oilbird
Steatornis caripensis
Lives in dark caves and finds its way around using echolocation, like bats

Common potoo
Nyctibius griseus
Mottled feathers and habit of posing like a branch give excellent camouflage.

European nightjar (Eurasian nightjar)
Caprimulgus europaeus

Common poorwill
Phalaenoptilus nuttallii

CONSERVATION WATCH

Of the 314 species of nightjars and owls, 81 appear on the IUCN Red List. The spotted owl, found in Central and North America, is near threatened. In many areas its forest habitat is being disrupted or destroyed by logging and clear-felling of trees.

Ex 🕆 4
Cr 🗗 8
En 🗗 12
Vu 🗗 16
Other 🗗 41

Spotted owl

Owls   Owls and nightjars

Owls live in forested areas throughout most of the world. Frogmouths are found in and around forests in Australasia. Nightjars occur in warm climates across the world.

FLIGHT OF THE HUMMINGBIRD

BUSY LIKE BEES

Most birds only fly forward, but hummingbirds can fly backward, forward, up and down, and hover, much like helicopters. Hummingbird wings beat as fast as 90 times a second, which can create a humming noise. The special structure of their wings lets them maneuver in this way. A bird's wing is like a human arm, with shoulder, elbow, wrist, and hand joints. While the hummingbird's shoulder joint moves, the permanently bent elbow and wrist joints do not. The hand is enlarged compared to the rest of the arm. This transfers enormous power to the flight feathers, which take up almost the entire wing. The breastbone is strong enough to support the muscles needed for high-energy flight. Hummingbirds need to produce a lot of energy to fuel the way they fly. They feed almost constantly throughout the day. At night, they reduce their needs by allowing their body temperatures to drop; this is called torpor.

INSIDE THE WING

The arrangement of the wing bones gives great power to the flight feathers. To fly forward, hummingbirds flap their wings up and down. To hover, they move their wings rapidly in a figure-eight shape.

Flight feathers, attached to finger and forearm bones

Elongated fourth finger bone

Elongated middle finger bone

Shortened forearm bones

Shoulder joint

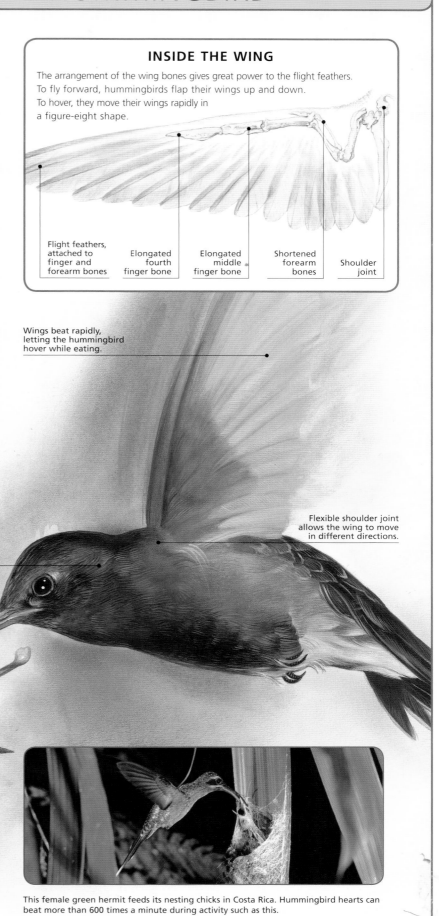

The scintillant hummingbird has such fine control over its flight that it can position itself at just the right angle to reach the nectar deep inside a flower.

To produce the energy they need to fly, hummingbirds must eat almost their body weight in nectar each day.

Bill is long and slender so it can reach deep inside flowers. Tongue is tipped with a brush to capture nectar.

Wings beat rapidly, letting the hummingbird hover while eating.

Flexible shoulder joint allows the wing to move in different directions.

Nectar-rich flower

This female green hermit feeds its nesting chicks in Costa Rica. Hummingbird hearts can beat more than 600 times a minute during activity such as this.

3 ORDERS • 13 FAMILIES • 59 GENERA • 254 SPECIES

Kingfishers

The kingfisher order includes many related birds—hornbills, todies, motmots, rollers, bee-eaters, wood-hoopoes, and the hoopoe. Trogons and mousebirds form two separate orders. All kingfishers have small feet with four toes. The three toes that point forward are fused together. They all use their large, strong, straight bills to dig nests in soil or rotten trees. Kingfishers usually sit on a perch, waiting and watching for small land or water animals, before swooping suddenly. The plumage of most kingfishers is brightly colored. Trogons, such as the resplendent quetzal, can be even more spectacular. These birds live in tropical forests and eat insects and small lizards. Some species also eat fruit. Mousebirds are far more drab. They creep among bushes like mice or hang upside down with their tails high in the air.

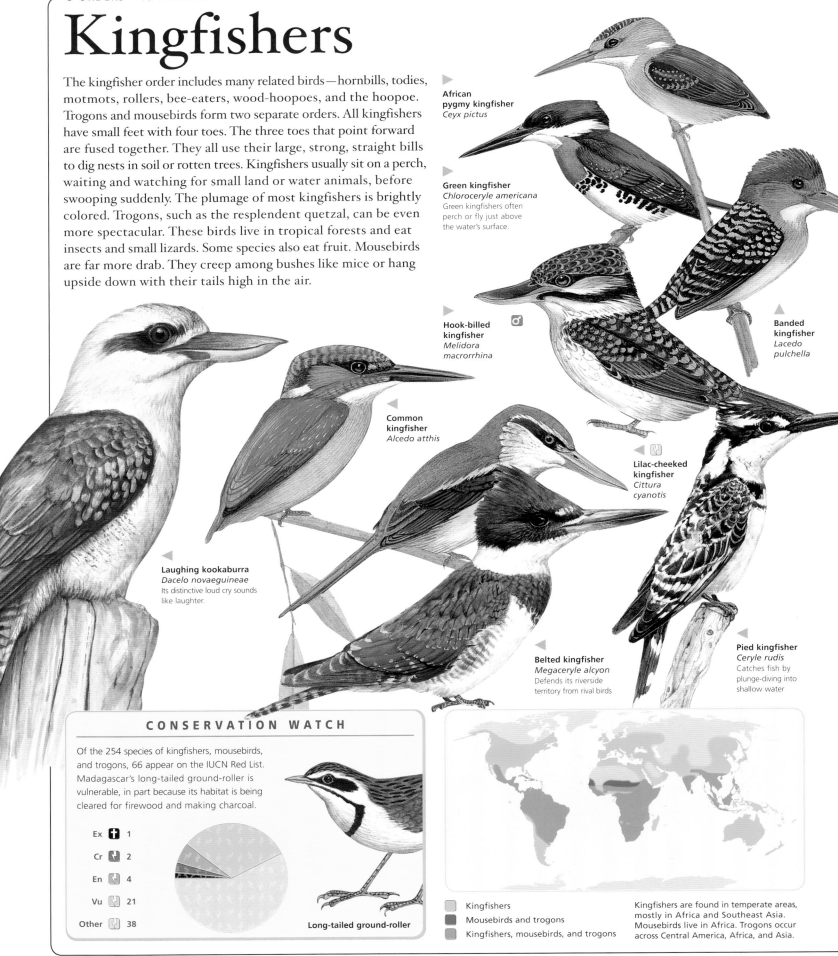

African pygmy kingfisher
Ceyx pictus

Green kingfisher
Chloroceryle americana
Green kingfishers often perch or fly just above the water's surface.

Banded kingfisher
Lacedo pulchella

Hook-billed kingfisher
Melidora macrorrhina ♂

Common kingfisher
Alcedo atthis

Lilac-cheeked kingfisher
Cittura cyanotis

Laughing kookaburra
Dacelo novaeguineae
Its distinctive loud cry sounds like laughter.

Belted kingfisher
Megaceryle alcyon
Defends its riverside territory from rival birds

Pied kingfisher
Ceryle rudis
Catches fish by plunge-diving into shallow water

CONSERVATION WATCH

Of the 254 species of kingfishers, mousebirds, and trogons, 66 appear on the IUCN Red List. Madagascar's long-tailed ground-roller is vulnerable, in part because its habitat is being cleared for firewood and making charcoal.

Ex 🕀 1
Cr 📋 2
En 📋 4
Vu 📋 21
Other 📋 38

Long-tailed ground-roller

Kingfishers
Mousebirds and trogons
Kingfishers, mousebirds, and trogons

Kingfishers are found in temperate areas, mostly in Africa and Southeast Asia. Mousebirds live in Africa. Trogons occur across Central America, Africa, and Asia.

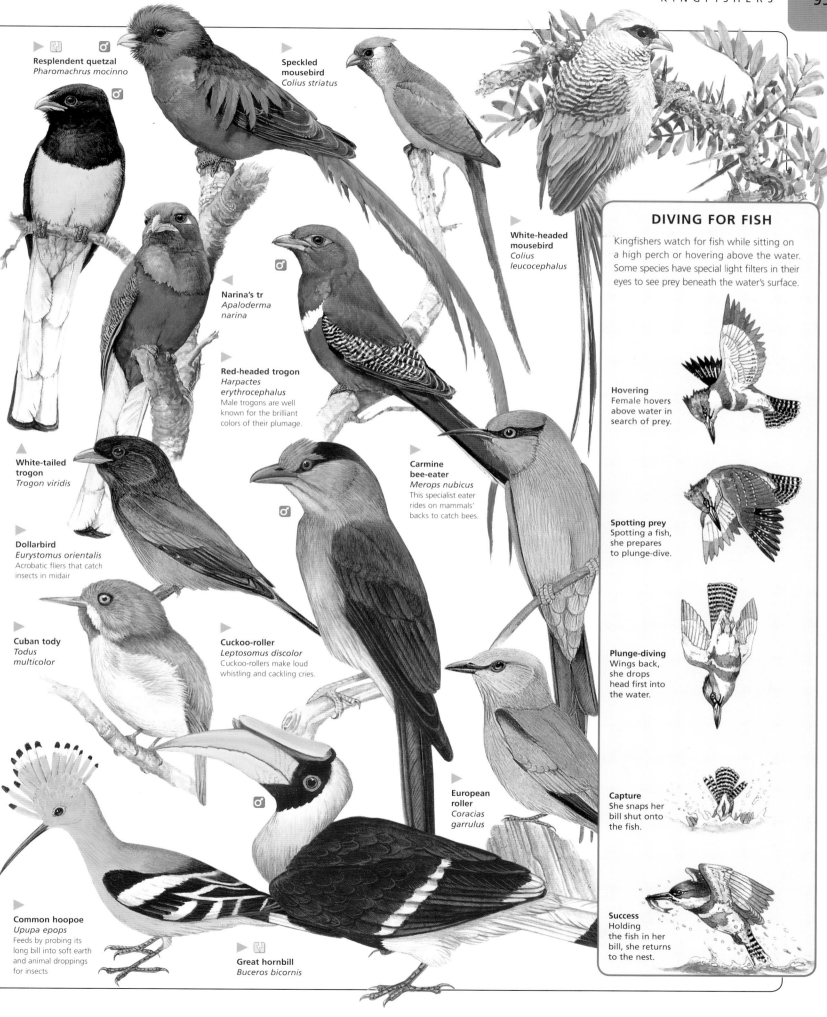

Resplendent quetzal
Pharomachrus mocinno

Speckled mousebird
Colius striatus

White-headed mousebird
Colius leucocephalus

Narina's tr
Apaloderma narina

Red-headed trogon
Harpactes erythrocephalus
Male trogons are well known for the brilliant colors of their plumage.

White-tailed trogon
Trogon viridis

Dollarbird
Eurystomus orientalis
Acrobatic fliers that catch insects in midair

Cuban tody
Todus multicolor

Cuckoo-roller
Leptosomus discolor
Cuckoo-rollers make loud whistling and cackling cries.

Carmine bee-eater
Merops nubicus
This specialist eater rides on mammals' backs to catch bees.

European roller
Coracias garrulus

Common hoopoe
Upupa epops
Feeds by probing its long bill into soft earth and animal droppings for insects

Great hornbill
Buceros bicornis

DIVING FOR FISH

Kingfishers watch for fish while sitting on a high perch or hovering above the water. Some species have special light filters in their eyes to see prey beneath the water's surface.

Hovering
Female hovers above water in search of prey.

Spotting prey
Spotting a fish, she prepares to plunge-dive.

Plunge-diving
Wings back, she drops head first into the water.

Capture
She snaps her bill shut onto the fish.

Success
Holding the fish in her bill, she returns to the nest.

2 ORDERS • 5 FAMILIES • 68 GENERA • 398 SPECIES

Woodpeckers

Woodpeckers are related to honeyguides, jacamars, puffbirds, barbets, and toucans. All have two toes pointing forward and two pointing backward, which helps them grasp tree branches. Most are colorful birds that live in the tropics. They lay their eggs in trees, termite mounds, or the ground. Woodpeckers hang onto tree bark with strong toes and long claws. They use their chisel-like bills to break through tough bark to find insects. Honeyguides eat insects and beeswax. Females trick other birds to raise young honeyguides as their own. Jacamars and puffbirds are both insect-eaters: Jacamars have long, pointed bills; puffbirds have short, solid bills and big heads. Brightly colored barbets and toucans are fruit-eaters. Toucans are well camouflaged in rain forest trees despite their enormous bills.

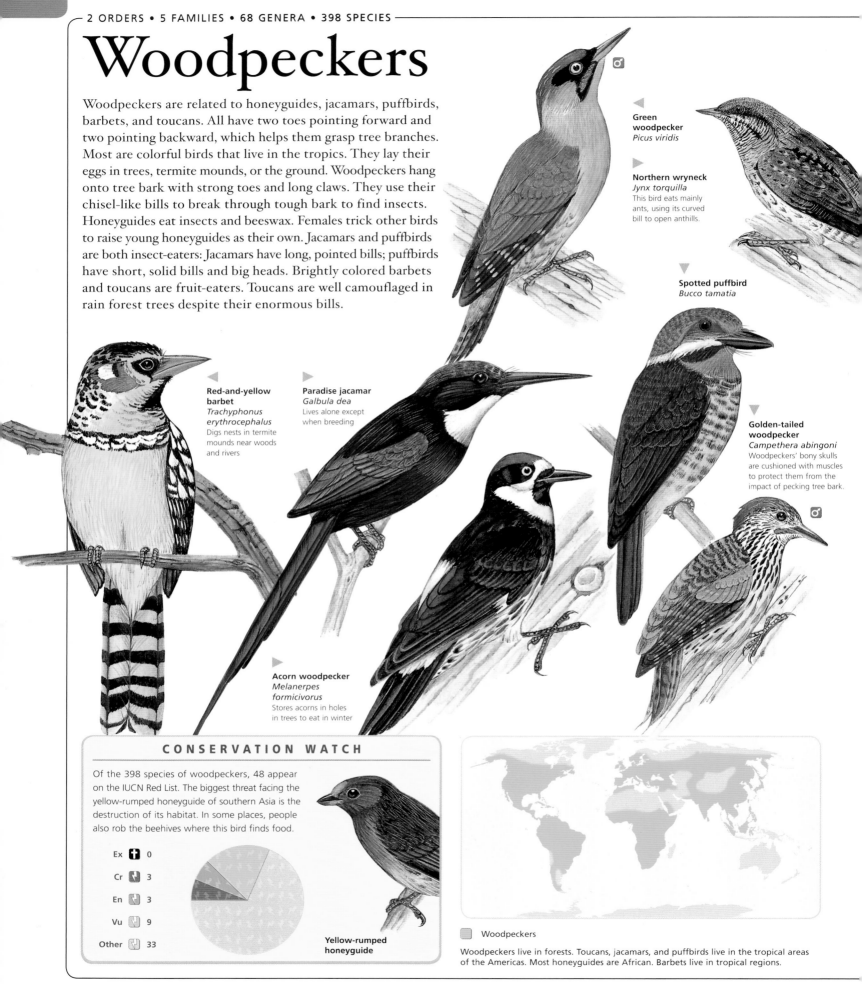

Green woodpecker
Picus viridis

Northern wryneck
Jynx torquilla
This bird eats mainly ants, using its curved bill to open anthills.

Spotted puffbird
Bucco tamatia

Red-and-yellow barbet
Trachyphonus erythrocephalus
Digs nests in termite mounds near woods and rivers

Paradise jacamar
Galbula dea
Lives alone except when breeding

Golden-tailed woodpecker
Campethera abingoni
Woodpeckers' bony skulls are cushioned with muscles to protect them from the impact of pecking tree bark.

Acorn woodpecker
Melanerpes formicivorus
Stores acorns in holes in trees to eat in winter

CONSERVATION WATCH

Of the 398 species of woodpeckers, 48 appear on the IUCN Red List. The biggest threat facing the yellow-rumped honeyguide of southern Asia is the destruction of its habitat. In some places, people also rob the beehives where this bird finds food.

Ex	✝	0
Cr		3
En		3
Vu		9
Other		33

Yellow-rumped honeyguide

Woodpeckers

Woodpeckers live in forests. Toucans, jacamars, and puffbirds live in the tropical areas of the Americas. Most honeyguides are African. Barbets live in tropical regions.

Pileated woodpecker
Dryocopus pileatus
♀

Black-rumped woodpecker
Dinopium benghalense
Forages in trees for ants and other insects
♀

Gray woodpecker
Dendropicos goertae
♂

Yellow-bellied sapsucker
Sphyrapicus varius

TOCO TOUCAN

Large bill is light and mostly hollow but has a honeycomb structure that makes it strong.

Bill is used to pick off fruit, which is then tossed back in the mouth to be swallowed.

Two toes in the front and two at the back help to grasp tree branches firmly.

It sleeps by folding tail over its head and resting long bill over its back.

Greater honeyguide
Indicator indicator

Emerald toucanet
Aulacorhynchus prasinus

Blue-throated barbet
Megalaima asiatica

Rufous woodpecker
Celeus brachyurus

Gray-breasted mountain toucan
Andigena hypoglauca

Ground woodpecker
Geocolaptes olivaceus
Digs its bill into ant nests and sticks out its tongue to catch and eat the ants inside

Curl-crested aracari
Pteroglossus beauharnaesii

Channel-billed toucan
Ramphastos vitellinus
This bird drinks water from tropical plants or by holding its bill open in the rain.

1 ORDER • 96 FAMILIES • 1,218 GENERA • 5,754 SPECIES

Perching Birds

The canary is a finch from the Canary Islands in the Atlantic Ocean. Its beautiful songs have made it a prized pet for 400 years; it is now one of the most popular caged birds.

The largest order of birds is the perching birds, or passerines. This order contains more than half of all birds. Their flexible toes are well adapted for gripping perches, such as twigs and branches. The muscles and tendons of their legs are arranged so their toes grip tightly. Three toes face forward and one faces backward. The smallest perching birds can perch on blades of grass. A perching bird's syrinx, or voice box, is a structure at the base of its windpipe. It is well developed, allowing the birds to sing complex, musical songs. These songs can be used to mark out territory or to find mates. Most perching birds raise young with the same partner, usually working together to raise chicks. They eat insects and plants. During the breeding season, they tend to eat more insects for their protein.

CONSERVATION WATCH

Of 5,754 species of perching birds, 1,066 appear on the IUCN Red List. Southeast Asia's white-eyed river martin was discovered in 1968 and has not been seen since 1978. Hunting of this bird at its winter roosting sites has probably reduced its numbers.

Ex		42
Cr		71
En		166
Vu		339
Other		448

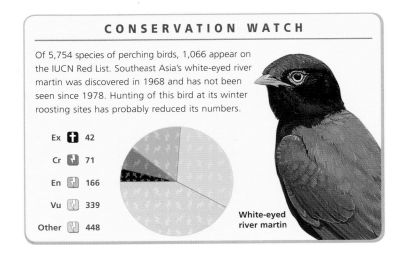

White-eyed river martin

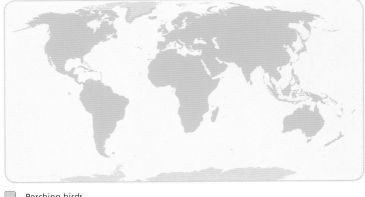

Perching birds

Perching birds are found throughout the world except Antarctica. They are adapted to live in a wide range of environments, from deserts to rain forests.

Perching birds

Woodcreepers, ovenbirds, antbirds, and tapaculos occur in the forests of South and Central America. Many prefer to live in dense foliage and hop between leaves, eating insects and spiders. A few species eat small frogs and snakes, eggs, and the chicks of other birds. Woodcreepers use their tails to brace themselves against tree trunks, similarly to woodpeckers. Antbirds feed on swarms of army ants. They avoid stings by darting in and out to pick off single ants. Manakins, cotingas, and tyrant flycatchers live in South and Central America, but many extend into North America. Manakins and cotingas are small fruit-eaters. Males can be brightly colored; most females are drab. Tyrant flycatchers eat insects or fruit. Many distinct species can live in one area because each species uses different resources.

Tufted flycatcher
Mitrephanes phaeocercus
Both parents help raise their chicks.

Black phoebe
Sayornis nigricans

Three-wattled bellbird
Procnias tricarunculata
This bellbird has three wattles on its beak that grow as long as 5 inches (12.5 cm).

Red-billed scythebill
Campylorhamphus trochilirostris
Thin, semicircular bill probes for insects in small, deep holes.

Blue-crowned manakin
Pipra coronata
Male manakins perform complex dances to attract mates.

Turquoise cotinga
Cotinga ridgwayi

Golden-headed manakin
Pipra erythrocephala

Ruddy treerunner
Margarornis rubiginosus

Barred antshrike
Thamnophilus doliatus
Noisy bird that raises its crest while singing

Streak-chested antpitta
Hylopezus perspicillatus

Black-bellied gnateater
Conopophaga melanogaster
The largest and most brightly colored gnateater

Black-throated huet-huet
Pteroptochos tarnii
This bird has covered nostrils, which may help it forage through dense undergrowth.

HORNERO NEST

South America's rufous hornero and many of its relatives build nests that look like clay ovens. Some use mud for their nests; others use twigs or moss. Not surprisingly, they are known as oven birds. These nests protect chicks from sun, cold, and predators.

Perching birds

Colorful pittas are insect-eaters that live in tropical forests. Honeyeaters and white-eyes are woodland birds. Honeyeaters have tongues with fringed tips to collect nectar. Insect-eating tits and flycatchers use their tails in special ways: Fantails spread their tails like fans and monarch flycatchers flick theirs. Many crows—such as choughs, nutcrackers, magpies, ravens, and jays—hide food and can find it after a long time. Swallows are some of the most widespread perching birds. Like their relatives the martins, they feed on insects caught in midair. Dippers feed on the larvae of water insects and sometimes on small fish. Most dippers catch prey by diving into a stream and walking along the bottom.

Cape sugarbird
Promerops cafer
Sugarbirds are nectar-eaters with long, curved bills and even longer tails.

Asian paradise-flycatcher
Terpsiphone paradisi

Brown-throated sunbird
Anthreptes malacensis

Oriental white-eye
Zosterops palpebrosus

Yellow-bellied fantail
Rhipidura hypoxantha

Penduline tit
Remiz pendulinus
Male builds a nest of feathers and plants that hangs like a paper bag from a tree branch.

Crimson chat
Epthianura tricolor

Red-headed honeyeater
Myzomela erythrocephala

Red-billed blue magpie
Urocissa erythrorhyncha
Tail feathers are as long as 17 inches (43 cm).

Red-browed treecreeper
Climacteris erythrops

Fairy gerygone
Gerygone palpebrosa

Superb lyrebird
Menura novaehollandiae
These expert mimics can copy the sounds of birds, animals—even chainsaws.

Variegated fairy-wren
Malurus lamberti
This fairy-wren lives in family groups of as many as seven birds.

Red-bellied pitta
Pitta erythrogaster

Western parotia
Parotia sefilata

Red-whiskered bulbul
Pycnonotus jocosus
Chicks are fed caterpillars,
whereas adults eat fruit.

Orange-bellied leafbird
Chloropsis hardwickei

Golden bowerbird
Prionodura newtoniana

Scarlet minivet
Pericrocotus flammeus

Greater short-toed lark
Calandrella brachydactyla

Red-throated pipit
Anthus cervinus
Pipits nest mostly on the
ground and feed on insects.

Madagascan wagtail
Motacilla flaviventris
Wagtails almost constantly
wag their long tails up
and down.

Marsh wren
Cistothorus palustris

White-browed woodswallow
Artamus superciliosus

White-banded swallow
Atticora fasciata

Red-backed shrike
Lanius collurio

Eurasian golden oriole
Oriolus oriolus

White-necked raven
Corvus albicollis
Drops tortoises to crack
their hard shells and eat
the meat inside

White-capped dipper
Cinclus leucocephalus

Perching birds

Just as there are tyrant flycatchers in the Americas, the Old World flycatchers fill the same insect-eating roles in the rest of the world. Many sit on perches and dart out to snap up passing prey. Others hop through forests picking insects and caterpillars from leaves. Sparrows and finches rely on insects to feed their chicks. Adults eat mostly seeds with their short, cone-shaped bills. Thrushes eat fruit and small animals, usually found on the ground. Some of the best known perching birds are the thrushes, such as the European blackbird and the American robin. Starlings are common garden birds and are easily recognized. Less easy to identify by sight are the members of the warbler family, because of their dull plumage. However, each warbler species tends to have its own lovely, rich, loud song.

Shining starling
Aplonis metallica
Feathers are dark with a metallic sheen that glistens purple and green in the sun.

Southern red bishop
Euplectes orix

Tropical gnatcatcher
Polioptila plumbea
Flocks with other insect-eating birds

Goldcrest
Regulus regulus

Black-throated accentor
Prunella atrogularis
Eats mainly insects in summer and berries and seeds in winter

Black-thighed grosbeak
Pheucticus tibialis
Has a cone-shaped bill for eating seeds

Snow bunting
Plectrophenax nivalis

Icterine warbler
Hippolais icterina

White-browed shortwing
Brachypteryx montana

Eastern paradise whydah
Vidua paradisaea
Whydahs lay their eggs in waxbills' nests to be cared for by waxbills.

American goldfinch
Carduelis tristis

White-necked picathartes
Picathartes gymnocephalus

Northern scrub robin
Drymodes superciliaris
This bird looks like a robin but is more closely related to crows.

Bluethroat
Luscinia svecica

Collared redstart
Myioborus torquatus
Like most American wood warblers, this is a small woodland bird.

Eastern whipbird
Psophodes olivaceus

American robin
Turdus migratorius
The robin hops across the ground, feeding on fruit and berries, as well as worms and insects.

Bananaquit
Coereba flaveola
Bananaquits are very small birds with slender, curved bills for taking nectar.

Black-throated thrush
Turdus atrogularis

Red-winged blackbird
Agelaius phoeniceus

Scarlet tanager
Piranga olivacea

Fluffy-backed tit-babbler
Macronous ptilosus

Chestnut-crowned babbler
Pomatostomus ruficeps

Red-billed buffalo weaver
Bubalornis niger

Gouldian finch
Erythrura gouldiae

Blue-faced parrotfinch
Erythrura trichroa

Black-capped vireo
Vireo atricapilla
Vireos build their nests in trees or low shrubs. They suspend the woven nests from forked branches.

DIVERSE BILLS

1. CRESTED HONEYCREEPER

Rapid spread
Some honeycreepers eat insects (1 and 3) or seeds (2). They developed from one species of seed-eating finch that arrived in Hawaii long ago.

2. LAYSAN FINCH

3. ANIANIAU

Different appetites
Many honeycreepers are seed-eaters that have strong, stout bills to crack hard shells (4). Others have developed long, curved bills that let them probe flowers for nectar (5).

4. MAUI PARROTBILL

5. IIWI

Limitations
Despite bills that allowed them to eat well on the Hawaiian islands, many honeyeaters became extinct (6). They could not adapt fast enough to cope with introduced predators and other threats.

6. BLACK MAMO (EXTINCT)

The shape and size of a bird's bill relates to its diet and the way that it gathers food. Sometimes many bird species share the same habitat. This happens because each has a bill suited to eating a different food. There are more than 30 species of honeycreepers on the islands of Hawaii (although some are now extinct). They have the same ancestor, a finch species that settled in Hawaii millions of years ago. Some species kept the short, strong bills of their seed-eating ancestor, but many have developed bills designed to eat nectar from different-shaped flowers.

Chameleons are a kind of lizard. They change their skin color for camouflage or to communicate. Some color changes warn enemies to stay away, and others attract potential mates.

SKIN AND SCALES

Reptile skin is covered with scales. This allows reptiles to live out of water without drying out. Like mammal hair, scales are made of keratin. Each species has a different shape and arrangement of scales to help them move, protect them from danger, or even direct water into their mouths. Scales may overlap for greater protection; in some species they form defensive spines. Some reptiles also have bony plates under their scales called osteoderms.

Snakes and lizards periodically shed their entire outer layer of skin cells.

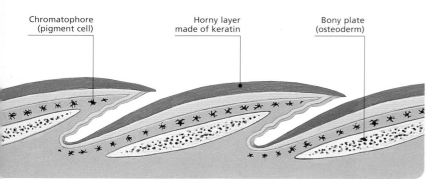

Chromatophore (pigment cell)

Horny layer made of keratin

Bony plate (osteoderm)

GRANULAR SCALES

KEELED SCALES

SMOOTH SCALES

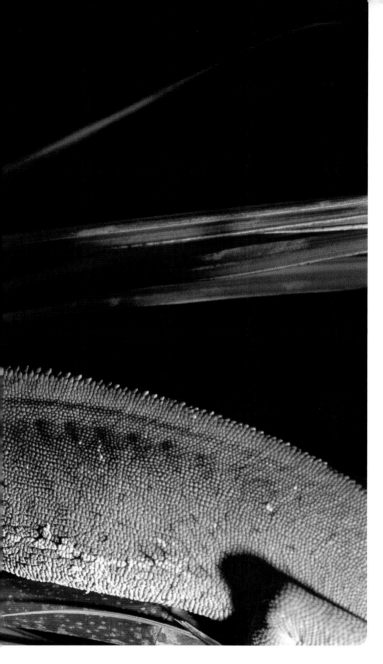

Reptiles have lived on Earth for more than 300 million years. There are several groups of reptiles: ruling reptiles, such as alligators and crocodiles; scaly reptiles, which include lizards and snakes; tuatara; and turtles. Reptiles can be found in salt water, fresh water, on land, underground, and in trees. They are most common in tropical or temperate regions because they are cold-blooded, or ectothermic. This means that most of their body heat is drawn from their surroundings, not produced by themselves. Despite this, at least two species live in the Arctic, and some are found in the cold environment of high mountains. They survive by sitting in the sun to warm themselves. Those that live in hot environments are either nocturnal or remain underground or in the shade during the heat of the day. Most reptiles do not have to eat as often as mammals or birds, because they do not need to burn as much energy to warm their bodies. Some can go for days or even weeks without eating. Like mammals and birds, reptiles have internal fertilization: Males deposit sperm inside females to fertilize eggs. Because of this, reptiles have developed many different ways of finding each other, courting, and choosing mates. Reptiles differ from mammals and birds in the amount of care they give their young. While some species are devoted parents, many leave their young to develop on their own. Reptiles rarely feed their young. As a result, many die, and only a few survive to reach adulthood.

REPTILE REPRODUCTION

Reptiles develop inside eggs that are usually laid outside the mother's body. Some snakes and lizards keep eggs in their bodies and give birth to live young. The shell is waterproof to keep the embryo moist. Oxygen enters through the chorion. The embryo is nourished by yolk and cushioned by fluid-filled sacs.

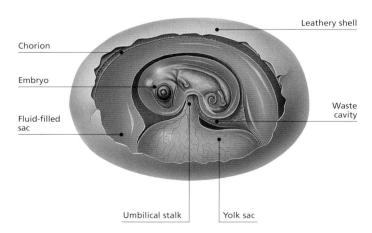

Crocodile eggs have soft shells; they need to be buried to limit water loss.

Leathery shell

Chorion

Embryo

Waste cavity

Fluid-filled sac

Umbilical stalk   Yolk sac

2 ORDERS • 4 FAMILIES • 9 GENERA • 25 SPECIES

Crocodilians and Tuatara

Crocodiles, alligators, caimans, and gharials are known as crocodilians. They belong to a reptile group that included the dinosaurs and have lived on Earth for more than 220 million years. Crocodilians have long bodies with short, muscular limbs and tails flattened at the sides for swimming. Their massive skulls hold powerful jaws with sharp teeth. They spend much of their lives in water and are often seen basking on the shorelines of estuaries, rivers, or swamps. They lay eggs in nests near the water. Mothers are protective of eggs and hatchlings. The two species of tuatara are known as "living fossils": They are the only survivors of a group that existed more than 225 million years ago. Tuatara are nocturnal and spend their days in burrows. They eat insects and other small animals.

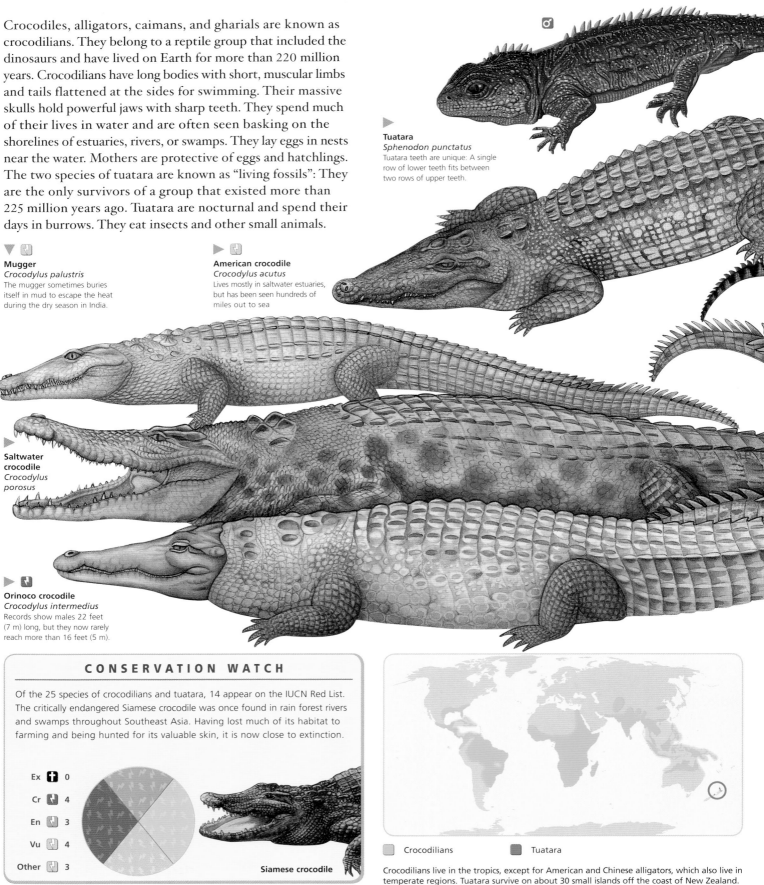

Tuatara
Sphenodon punctatus
Tuatara teeth are unique: A single row of lower teeth fits between two rows of upper teeth.

Mugger
Crocodylus palustris
The mugger sometimes buries itself in mud to escape the heat during the dry season in India.

American crocodile
Crocodylus acutus
Lives mostly in saltwater estuaries, but has been seen hundreds of miles out to sea

Saltwater crocodile
Crocodylus porosus

Orinoco crocodile
Crocodylus intermedius
Records show males 22 feet (7 m) long, but they now rarely reach more than 16 feet (5 m).

CONSERVATION WATCH

Of the 25 species of crocodilians and tuatara, 14 appear on the IUCN Red List. The critically endangered Siamese crocodile was once found in rain forest rivers and swamps throughout Southeast Asia. Having lost much of its habitat to farming and being hunted for its valuable skin, it is now close to extinction.

Ex ☦ 0
Cr 🐊 4
En 🐊 3
Vu 🐊 4
Other 🐊 3

Siamese crocodile

▢ Crocodilians   ▢ Tuatara

Crocodilians live in the tropics, except for American and Chinese alligators, which also live in temperate regions. Tuatara survive on about 30 small islands off the coast of New Zealand.

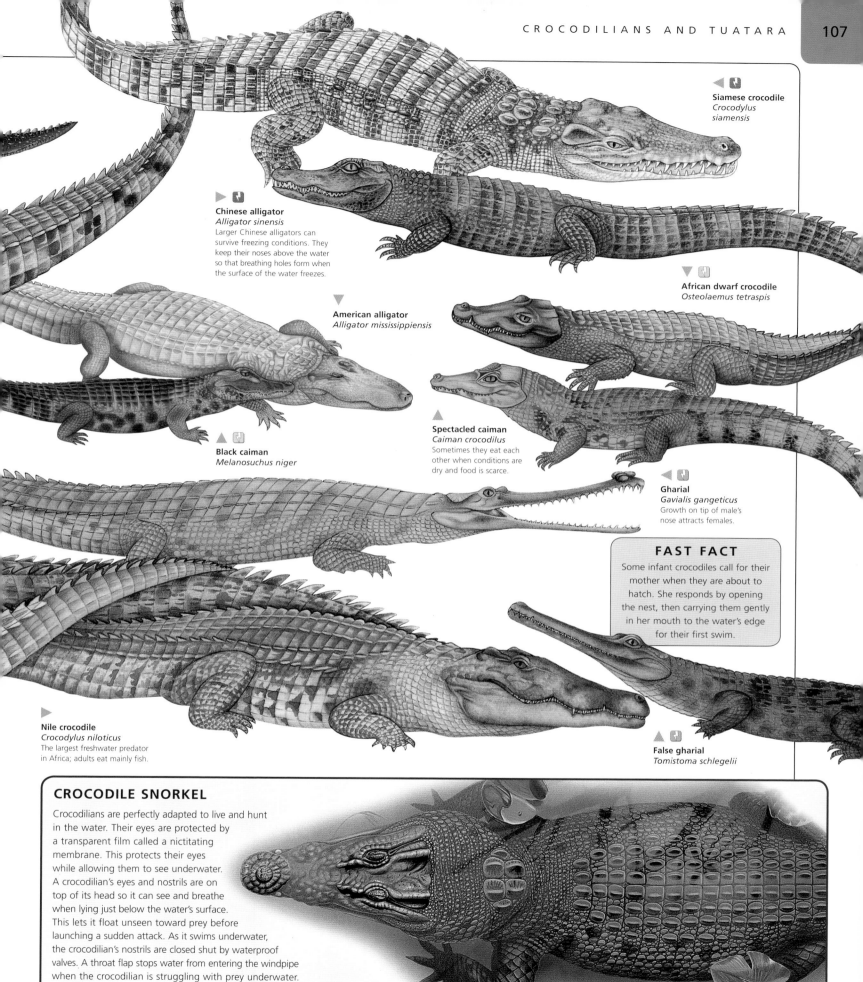

Siamese crocodile
Crocodylus siamensis

Chinese alligator
Alligator sinensis
Larger Chinese alligators can survive freezing conditions. They keep their noses above the water so that breathing holes form when the surface of the water freezes.

American alligator
Alligator mississippiensis

African dwarf crocodile
Osteolaemus tetraspis

Black caiman
Melanosuchus niger

Spectacled caiman
Caiman crocodilus
Sometimes they eat each other when conditions are dry and food is scarce.

Gharial
Gavialis gangeticus
Growth on tip of male's nose attracts females.

FAST FACT
Some infant crocodiles call for their mother when they are about to hatch. She responds by opening the nest, then carrying them gently in her mouth to the water's edge for their first swim.

Nile crocodile
Crocodylus niloticus
The largest freshwater predator in Africa; adults eat mainly fish.

False gharial
Tomistoma schlegelii

CROCODILE SNORKEL

Crocodilians are perfectly adapted to live and hunt in the water. Their eyes are protected by a transparent film called a nictitating membrane. This protects their eyes while allowing them to see underwater. A crocodilian's eyes and nostrils are on top of its head so it can see and breathe when lying just below the water's surface. This lets it float unseen toward prey before launching a sudden attack. As it swims underwater, the crocodilian's nostrils are closed shut by waterproof valves. A throat flap stops water from entering the windpipe when the crocodilian is struggling with prey underwater.

1 ORDER • 14 FAMILIES • 99 GENERA • 293 SPECIES

Turtles and Tortoises

Turtles and tortoises are found mainly in tropical and temperate regions. Many divide their lives between water and land habitats. Some live almost their entire lives in water. The limbs of sea turtles have developed into paddles, making them fast and agile swimmers but slow and awkward walkers. Others have adapted to life in dry environments, such as deserts and savanna grasslands. There are species of land tortoises that have probably never encountered any open bodies of water in their lifetimes. The shells of turtles and tortoises are built into the skeleton, with the backbone running along the inside. They are made up of an inner layer of bones and an outer layer of horny plates. The shell's structure varies among species. Softshell turtles have soft, leathery, and flexible plates on their shells.

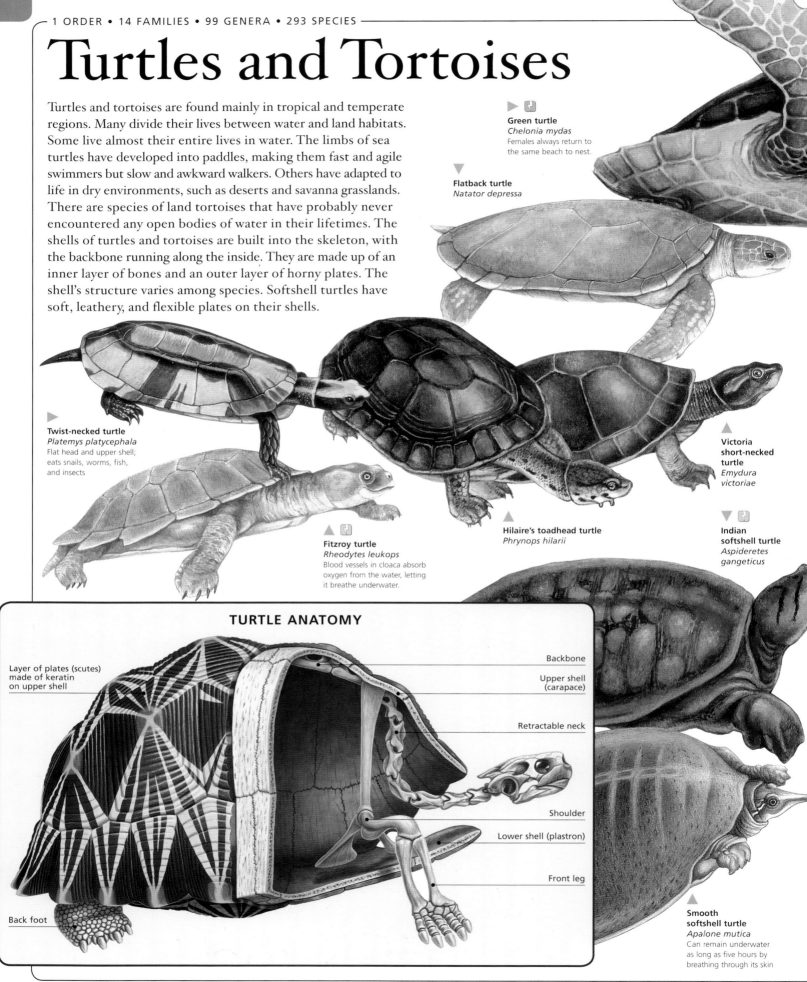

Green turtle
Chelonia mydas
Females always return to the same beach to nest.

Flatback turtle
Natator depressa

Twist-necked turtle
Platemys platycephala
Flat head and upper shell; eats snails, worms, fish, and insects

Fitzroy turtle
Rheodytes leukops
Blood vessels in cloaca absorb oxygen from the water, letting it breathe underwater.

Hilaire's toadhead turtle
Phrynops hilarii

Victoria short-necked turtle
Emydura victoriae

Indian softshell turtle
Aspideretes gangeticus

Smooth softshell turtle
Apalone mutica
Can remain underwater as long as five hours by breathing through its skin

TURTLE ANATOMY

Layer of plates (scutes) made of keratin on upper shell

Back foot

Backbone

Upper shell (carapace)

Retractable neck

Shoulder

Lower shell (plastron)

Front leg

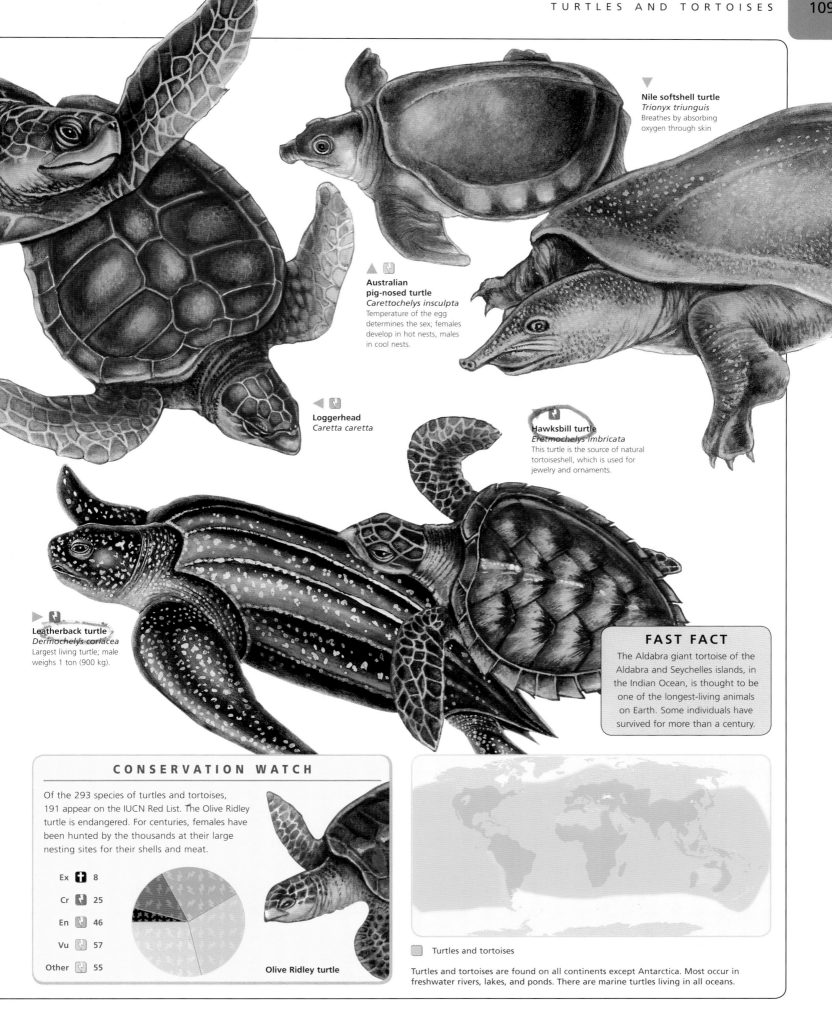

Nile softshell turtle
Trionyx triunguis
Breathes by absorbing
oxygen through skin

**Australian
pig-nosed turtle**
Carettochelys insculpta
Temperature of the egg
determines the sex; females
develop in hot nests, males
in cool nests.

Loggerhead
Caretta caretta

Hawksbill turtle
Eretmochelys imbricata
This turtle is the source of natural
tortoiseshell, which is used for
jewelry and ornaments.

Leatherback turtle
Dermochelys coriacea
Largest living turtle; male
weighs 1 ton (900 kg).

FAST FACT

The Aldabra giant tortoise of the
Aldabra and Seychelles islands, in
the Indian Ocean, is thought to be
one of the longest-living animals
on Earth. Some individuals have
survived for more than a century.

CONSERVATION WATCH

Of the 293 species of turtles and tortoises,
191 appear on the IUCN Red List. The Olive Ridley
turtle is endangered. For centuries, females have
been hunted by the thousands at their large
nesting sites for their shells and meat.

Ex	8
Cr	25
En	46
Vu	57
Other	55

Olive Ridley turtle

Turtles and tortoises

Turtles and tortoises are found on all continents except Antarctica. Most occur in
freshwater rivers, lakes, and ponds. There are marine turtles living in all oceans.

Turtles and tortoises

There are two main groups of turtles and tortoises: side-necked turtles and hidden-necked turtles. Side-necked turtles use a sideways movement to fold their necks and bring their heads under the front edge of the upper shell. Hidden-necked turtles draw their necks directly back into the shell. Some cannot do this completely, so their heads always stick out a little. Tortoises are land-dwelling species of hidden-necked turtles. Turtles and tortoises do not have teeth. Instead, they all have hard ridges covering the top and bottom jaws. They eat a variety of foods: the soft parts of plants; small invertebrates like worms and insects; crayfish; and sometimes fish or birds. Meat-eating species have sharp ridges that work like shears. The ridges of plant-eaters have sawlike outer edges.

Gopher tortoise
Gopherus polyphemus
Lives in burrows as deep as 10 feet (3 m)

Painted turtle
Chrysemys picta

European pond turtle
Emys orbicularis

Alligator snapping turtle
Macrochelys temminckii

Ringed sawback
Graptemys oculifera

Painted terrapin
Callagur borneoensis
Male's head turns white with a red stripe in breeding season.

Central American river turtle
Dermatemys mawii

Bell's hinge-back tortoise
Kinixys belliana

Black-breasted leaf turtle
Geoemyda spengleri

Malayan snail-eating turtle
Malayemys subtrijuga

River terrapin
Batagur basca

1 SUBORDER • 27 FAMILIES • 442 GENERA • 4,560 SPECIES

Lizards

Most lizards prey on insects and other small animals, but the green iguana is strictly a plant-eater. It is almost perfectly camouflaged in the lush vegetation of its tropical home.

izards have existed for more than 100 million years. While dinosaurs and most other large reptiles died out about 65 million years ago, lizards survived. They now form the largest group of living reptiles. One reason that there are so many lizards is that they are small in size: Most are no bigger than a foot (30 cm) long. This means many species can exist in the same habitat. Their small size also makes them the popular prey of mammals and birds. Many have developed ways of avoiding or escaping predators. Most are well camouflaged. The sharp spines of some can injure a predator's mouth. The slippery scales of others make them hard to grip. Iguanas and monitors use their tails like weapons to beat off attackers. Skinks and geckos lose their tails when attacked, which lets them escape with their lives.

CONSERVATION WATCH

Of the 4,560 lizard species, 179 appear on the IUCN Red List. The endangered Fiji banded iguana lives on the islands of Fiji. Introduced predators, such as mongooses and cats, are a major threat to its survival.

Ex	11
Cr	22
En	16
Vu	72
Other	58

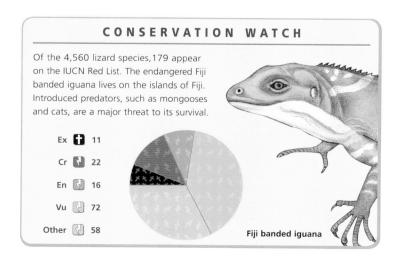

Fiji banded iguana

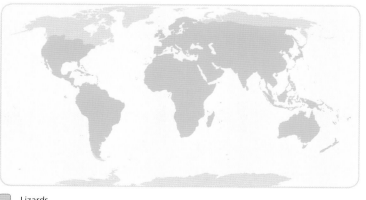

☐ Lizards

Lizards can be found on almost all continents and islands. They are missing from Antarctica and some regions of North America, Europe, and Asia.

Iguanas

Iguanas live mainly in the tropical and subtropical parts of the Americas. All are diurnal, and most have camouflaging scales. Most species have a fold of skin called a dewlap underneath their heads and necks. Many have raised scales forming a crest along their backs. Young iguanas usually feed on insects and other small animals, but adults are often herbivores that eat flowers, fruit, and leaves. Most iguanas dwell on land, either on the ground or among rocks. Some live almost exclusively in trees and come down from the branches only to lay eggs. The marine iguana is the only lizard that spends large amounts of time in the sea. It dives to depths of 30 feet (9 m) and grazes on marine algae or submerged plants. A gland in its nose removes excess salt from its body in the form of salt crystals.

West Indian iguana
Iguana delicatissima
Males have head-pushing competitions to win the right to mate with females.

Merrem's Madagascar swift
Oplurus cyclurus
This iguana lives in forested regions of Madagascar.

Leopard lizard
Gambelia sila
It often lives in abandoned burrows of ground squirrels.

Chuckwalla
Sauromalus obesus
Lives in the southwestern deserts of North America

Collared lizard
Crotaphytus collaris
When scared, it rises up on its back legs to run faster.

Desert spiny lizard
Sceloporus magister

Rhinoceros iguana
Cyclura cornuta
Bacteria in its stomach help to digest food.

Black iguana
Ctenosaura similis
By basking in sunlight, this iguana lightens its color from dark (left) to lighter (top).

Green iguana
Iguana iguana
Can grow as long as 6½ feet (2 m), including its tail

Geckos and chameleons

Geckos and chameleons are both easy to recognize. The large eyes of chameleons are covered by skin; only the pupil can be seen. Their eyes can move in different directions from each other. This helps chameleons judge distances, so they can aim their tongues precisely to catch prey. Most eat insects and other invertebrates, but larger species will also eat small birds and mammals. Unusual for lizards, geckos are mainly nocturnal. Large eyes help them hunt prey in poor light. Their feet have special toe pads that stick to surfaces to help them climb— some can run up smooth surfaces, such as glass, where there is nothing to cling to. Geckos can be found on all continents except Antarctica. Most chameleons live in forests in the African highlands or on the island of Madagascar.

Common leopard gecko
Eublepharis macularius
This species has clawed toes, rather than toe pads.

Burton's snake-lizard
Lialis burtonis
Snake lizards are related to geckos; they have tiny back legs that look like flaps and no front legs.

Common wall gecko
Tarentola mauritanica

Madagascar day gecko
Phelsuma madagascariensis
Unlike most geckos, it is active during the day.

Northern leaf-tailed gecko
Saltuarius cornutus

Knysna dwarf chameleon
Bradypodion damaranum
This chameleon gives birth to live young; it does not lay eggs.

Kuhl's flying gecko
Ptychozoon kuhli
Males are aggressive toward other males that come into their territories.

Lesser chameleon
Furcifer minor
Unlike many lizards, it does not lose its tail when threatened.

Parson's chameleon
Calumma parsoni

Jackson's chameleon
Chamaeleo jacksonii
Males have three horns and use these to fight each other.

FAST FACT
The amazing tongues of chameleons are incredibly long and fast. They can travel at speeds faster than 16 feet (5 m) per second, reaching prey a body length away in less than one-hundredth of a second.

Horned leaf chameleon
Brookesia superciliaris

Skinks

Skinks make up the largest of the lizard families. They are found throughout the world, except for the polar regions, but are more common in warmer areas. They range in length from 1 to 26 inches (2.5 to 67 cm), and almost all are covered by smooth overlapping scales. Skinks tend to be drab gray or brown in color. This provides good camouflage in the leaf litter, rock crevices, or rotting logs where they often live. Many skinks have either small or no limbs; limbless species usually live in burrows. Some species can climb trees. Like many lizards, skinks readily lose their tails to save themselves when attacked. This is called autotomy. The tail almost always grows back. Skinks themselves prey on insects and other small animals, such as spiders. They actively forage for food, using mostly sight and smell.

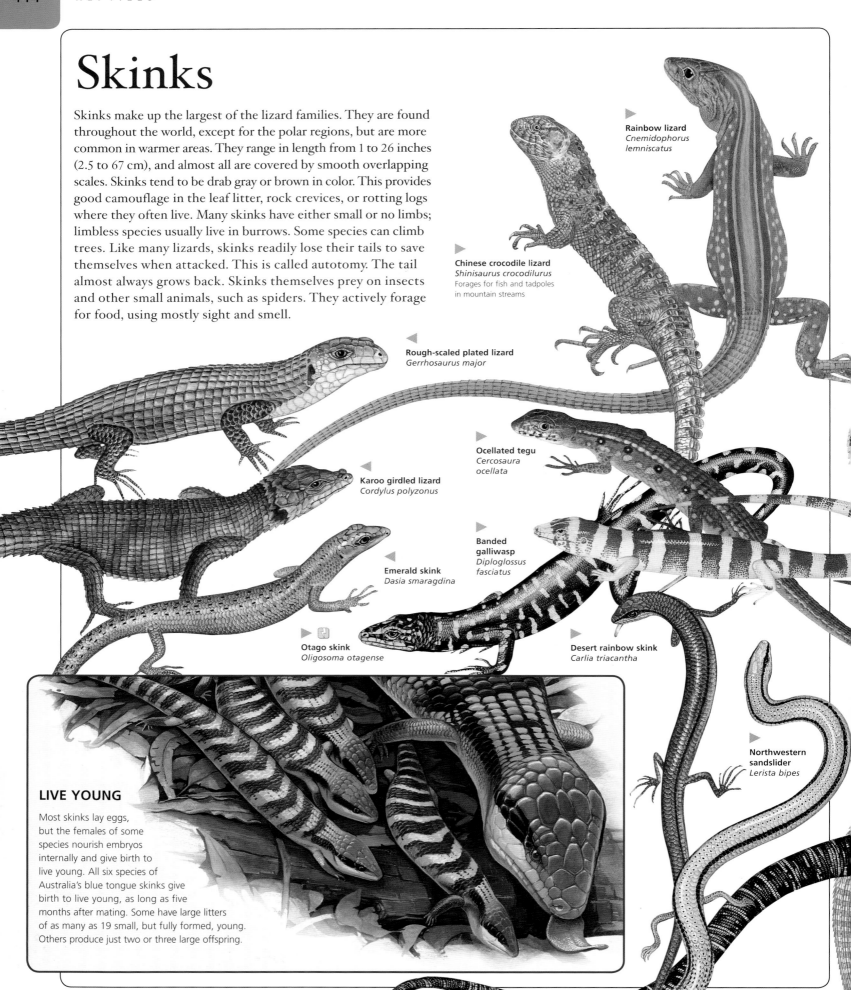

Rainbow lizard
Cnemidophorus lemniscatus

Chinese crocodile lizard
Shinisaurus crocodilurus
Forages for fish and tadpoles in mountain streams

Rough-scaled plated lizard
Gerrhosaurus major

Ocellated tegu
Cercosaura ocellata

Karoo girdled lizard
Cordylus polyzonus

Banded galliwasp
Diploglossus fasciatus

Emerald skink
Dasia smaragdina

Otago skink
Oligosoma otagense

Desert rainbow skink
Carlia triacantha

Northwestern sandslider
Lerista bipes

LIVE YOUNG

Most skinks lay eggs, but the females of some species nourish embryos internally and give birth to live young. All six species of Australia's blue tongue skinks give birth to live young, as long as five months after mating. Some have large litters of as many as 19 small, but fully formed, young. Others produce just two or three large offspring.

Monitors

Monitors are found in Africa, Asia, Australia, and the Pacific Islands. They can be as small as 8 inches (20 cm) in length and half an ounce (14 g) in weight, or as large as the Komodo dragon, which reaches 10 feet (3 m) and 365 pounds (166 kg). Komodos are the world's largest lizards; they are predators that pounce on large mammal prey. Monitors have long necks, thick skin, and whiplike tails. Their forked tongues flick in and out of their mouths, "tasting" the air for chemical signals. These signals tell them the location of food, possible mates, or predators. Related to monitors are lacterids, which include the sawtail, wall, and tiger lizards. Lacterids are small lizards with tails that can be twice as long as their bodies. They are found in Africa, Europe, and Asia, where they live either on the ground or in trees.

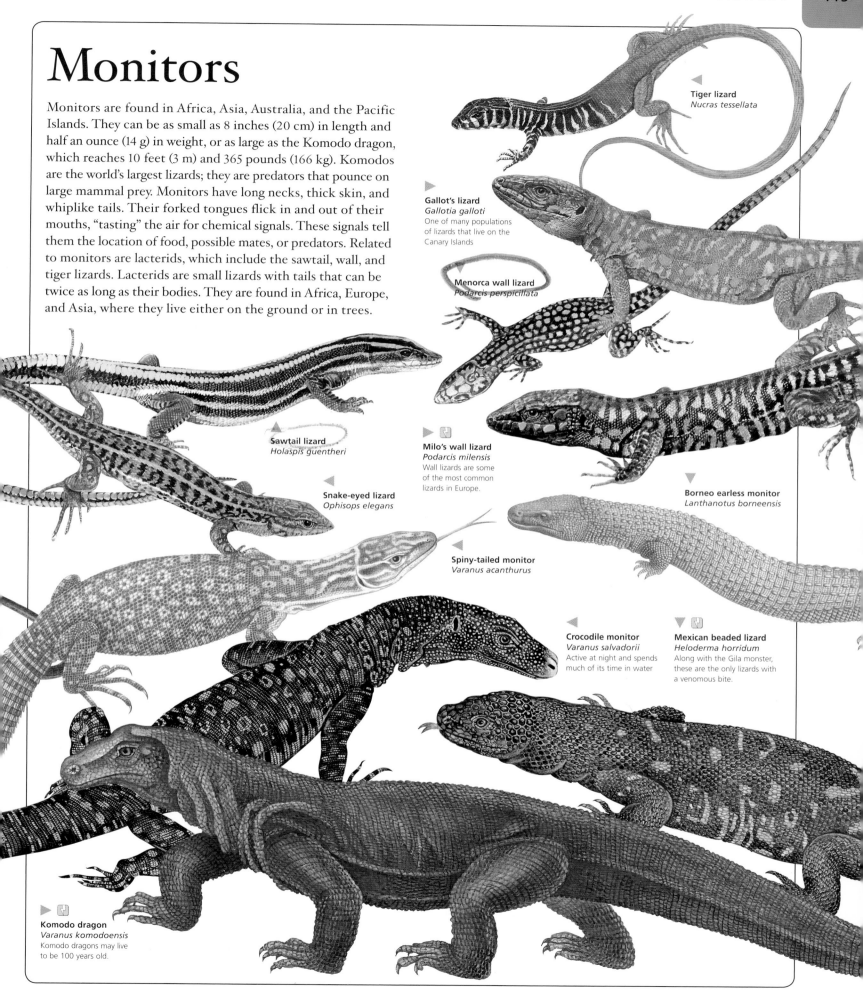

Tiger lizard
Nucras tessellata

Gallot's lizard
Gallotia galloti
One of many populations of lizards that live on the Canary Islands

Menorca wall lizard
Podarcis perspicillata

Sawtail lizard
Holaspis guentheri

Snake-eyed lizard
Ophisops elegans

Milo's wall lizard
Podarcis milensis
Wall lizards are some of the most common lizards in Europe.

Borneo earless monitor
Lanthanotus borneensis

Spiny-tailed monitor
Varanus acanthurus

Crocodile monitor
Varanus salvadorii
Active at night and spends much of its time in water

Mexican beaded lizard
Heloderma horridum
Along with the Gila monster, these are the only lizards with a venomous bite.

Komodo dragon
Varanus komodoensis
Komodo dragons may live to be 100 years old.

Anoles and agamids

Anoles and their relatives are small lizards with bodies that range in length from 1 to 4½ inches (2.5 to 12 cm). Most eat insects and other small animals. Tree-dwelling varieties have special sticky pads on their feet that make them good climbers. All lose their tails if they are grasped by predators. Anoles are found in South and Central America. One species, the green anole, lives in the southeastern United States. It can change color from bright green to dark brown, depending on light and temperature. Agamids, or chisel-toothed lizards, live in Africa, Asia, and Australia. They range in length from 1 inch to 4½ feet (2 cm to 1.4 m). Agamids have large heads, notched tongues, and well-developed limbs. They can live in environments from deserts to tropical forests. Some even live partly in fresh water.

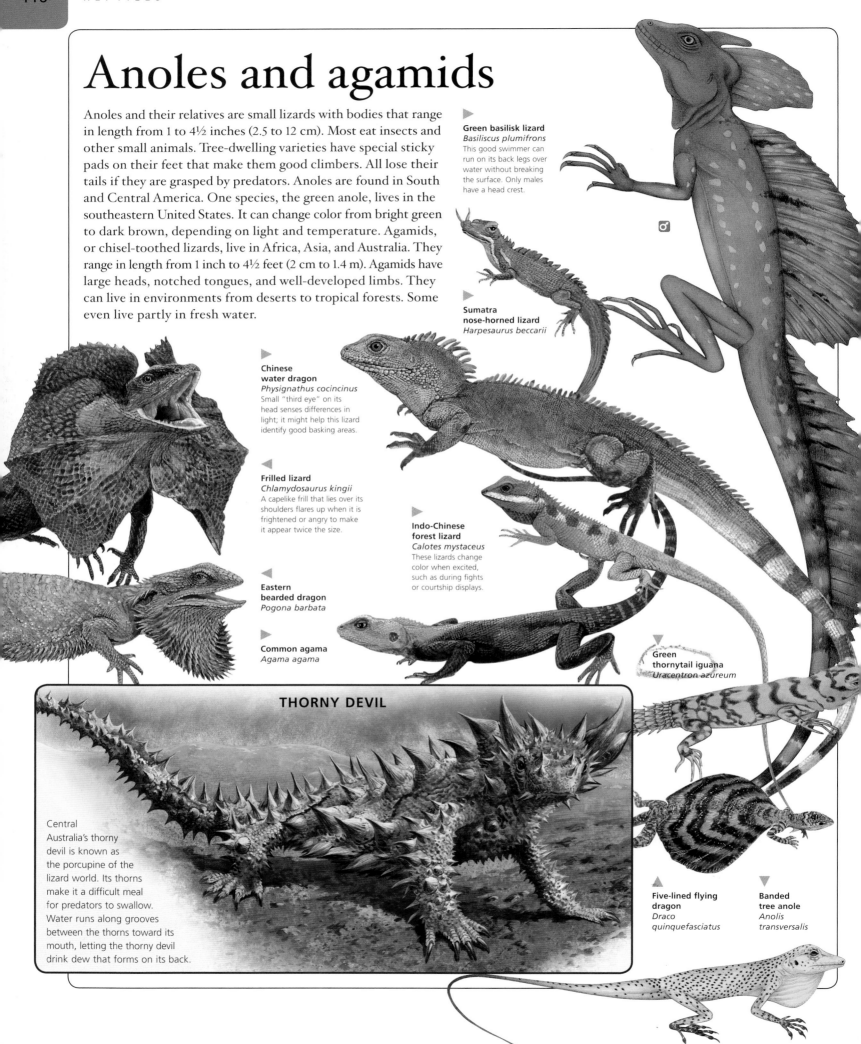

Green basilisk lizard
Basiliscus plumifrons
This good swimmer can run on its back legs over water without breaking the surface. Only males have a head crest.

Sumatra nose-horned lizard
Harpesaurus beccarii

Chinese water dragon
Physignathus cocincinus
Small "third eye" on its head senses differences in light; it might help this lizard identify good basking areas.

Frilled lizard
Chlamydosaurus kingii
A capelike frill that lies over its shoulders flares up when it is frightened or angry to make it appear twice the size.

Eastern bearded dragon
Pogona barbata

Common agama
Agama agama

Indo-Chinese forest lizard
Calotes mystaceus
These lizards change color when excited, such as during fights or courtship displays.

Green thornytail iguana
Uracentron azureum

THORNY DEVIL

Central Australia's thorny devil is known as the porcupine of the lizard world. Its thorns make it a difficult meal for predators to swallow. Water runs along grooves between the thorns toward its mouth, letting the thorny devil drink dew that forms on its back.

Five-lined flying dragon
Draco quinquefasciatus

Banded tree anole
Anolis transversalis

1 SUBORDER • 17 FAMILIES • 438 GENERA • 2,955 SPECIES

Snakes

A parrot snake in the rain forest of Costa Rica opens its mouth wide to startle a predator. The fangs are located at the back of its mouth and are used to pierce prey that it catches.

There are almost 3,000 species of snakes. They range from tiny burrowing blind snakes just 4 inches (10 cm) long to huge constrictors more than 30 feet (9 m) in length. Snakes evolved from lizards. As their bodies became long and narrow, so did their internal organs. The left lung is either missing or extremely small in all species. Snakes have no limbs, but some species still show signs of the limbs of their ancestors. Without limbs, snakes developed new ways of moving. They use special belly scales called scutes and tiny muscles attached to their ribs to move across surfaces. On the ground, they follow scent trails to mates and prey. All snakes are carnivores. The prey they eat depends on their size. Whereas some lizards tear prey apart with their teeth, snakes swallow their food whole.

CONSERVATION WATCH

There are 2,955 species of snakes, of which 79 appear on the IUCN Red List. Wagner's viper, which is found among rocks and grass in the high mountains around Lake Urmia, in northwest Iran and Turkey, is endangered. Its numbers have been reduced mainly by overenthusiastic reptile collectors.

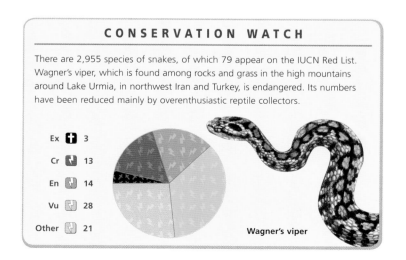

Ex   3
Cr   13
En   14
Vu   28
Other   21

Wagner's viper

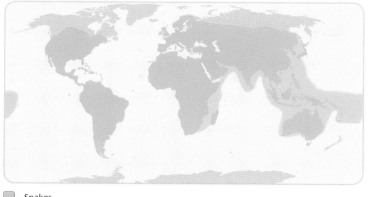

Snakes

Snakes are found on all landmasses except Antarctica and some islands, such as New Zealand, Ireland, and Iceland. Most snake species live in tropical or temperate regions.

Colubrid snakes

More than half of all snake species are colubrid snakes. They live on all continents except Antarctica. Colubrids are found in almost all habitats and are usually the most common snakes in areas where snakes occur. Some live mostly in fresh water and eat fish. Others spend much of their lives in trees and hunt small mammals or birds. Many live in grass or leaf litter on the ground and eat frogs, small reptiles, or large insects and spiders. Most colubrids produce venom, but they are often thought of as harmless snakes. Venom trickles down grooves on large fangs at the back of the mouth, so that only about half of it enters a wound during a bite. Their venom is not injected, as it is in snakes that are considered more dangerous. However, some colubrids have been known to kill humans with their venom.

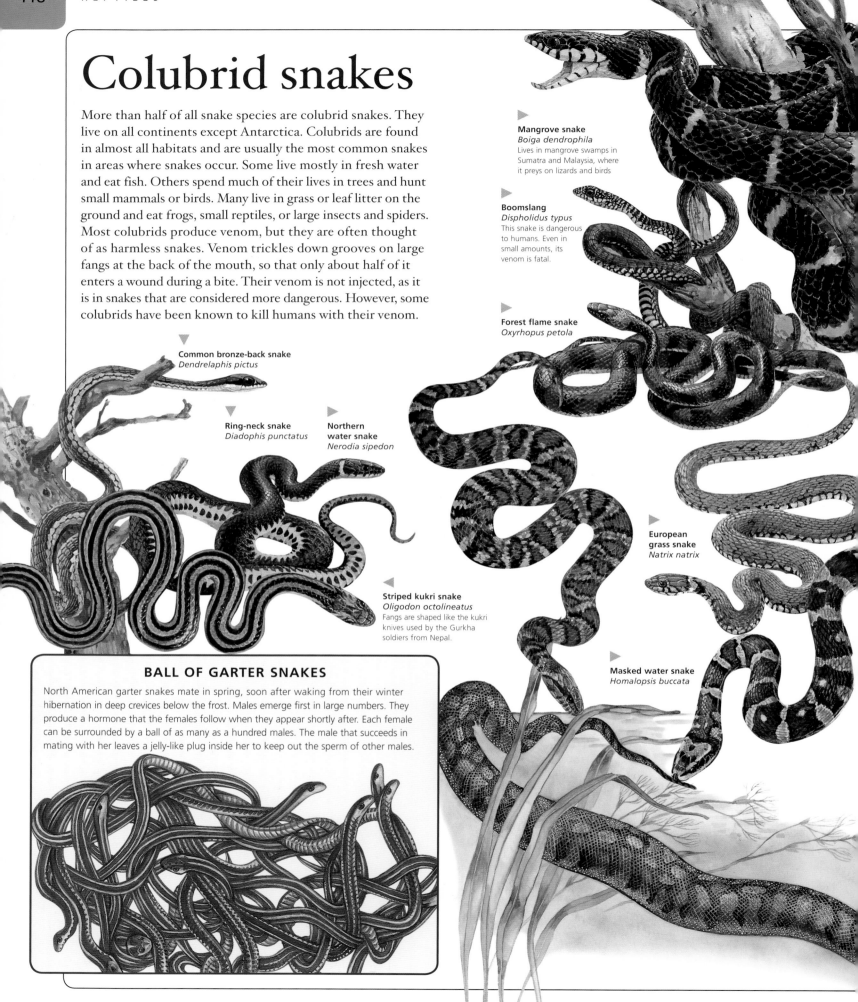

Mangrove snake
Boiga dendrophila
Lives in mangrove swamps in Sumatra and Malaysia, where it preys on lizards and birds

Boomslang
Dispholidus typus
This snake is dangerous to humans. Even in small amounts, its venom is fatal.

Forest flame snake
Oxyrhopus petola

Common bronze-back snake
Dendrelaphis pictus

Ring-neck snake
Diadophis punctatus

Northern water snake
Nerodia sipedon

European grass snake
Natrix natrix

Striped kukri snake
Oligodon octolineatus
Fangs are shaped like the kukri knives used by the Gurkha soldiers from Nepal.

Masked water snake
Homalopsis buccata

BALL OF GARTER SNAKES

North American garter snakes mate in spring, soon after waking from their winter hibernation in deep crevices below the frost. Males emerge first in large numbers. They produce a hormone that the females follow when they appear shortly after. Each female can be surrounded by a ball of as many as a hundred males. The male that succeeds in mating with her leaves a jelly-like plug inside her to keep out the sperm of other males.

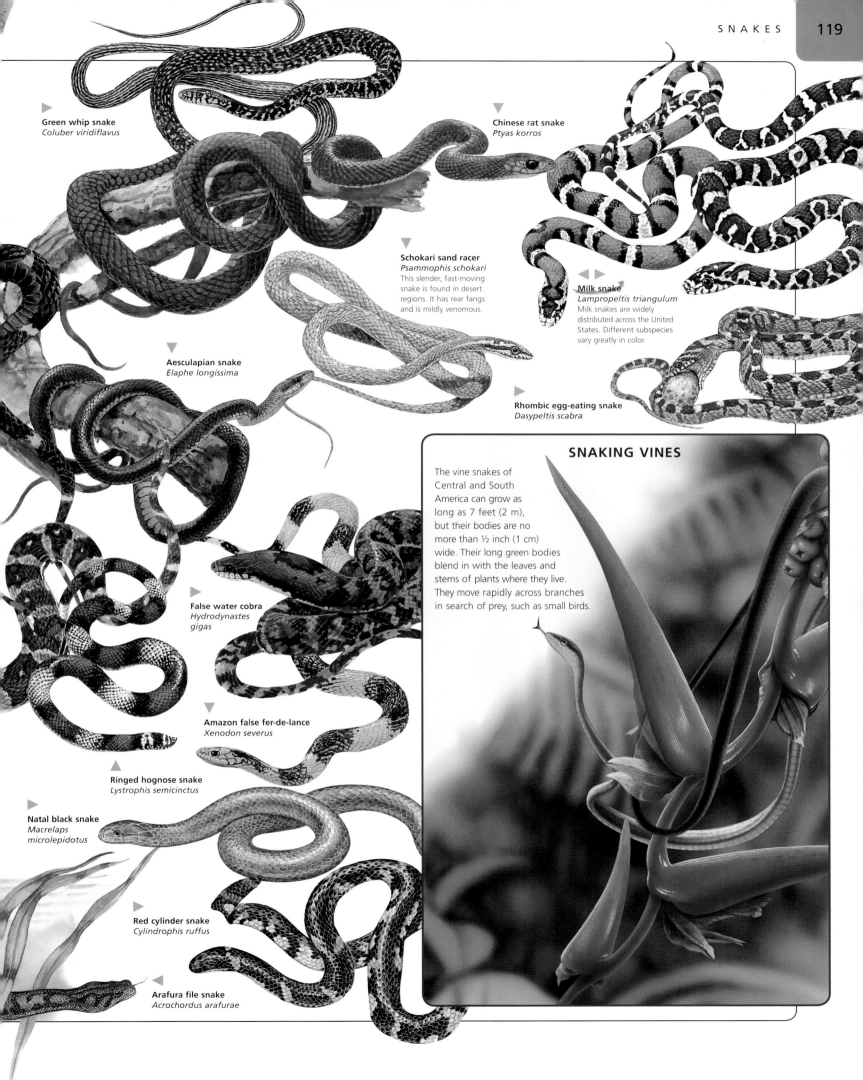

Green whip snake
Coluber viridiflavus

Chinese rat snake
Ptyas korros

Schokari sand racer
Psammophis schokari
This slender, fast-moving snake is found in desert regions. It has rear fangs and is mildly venomous.

Milk snake
Lampropeltis triangulum
Milk snakes are widely distributed across the United States. Different subspecies vary greatly in color.

Aesculapian snake
Elaphe longissima

Rhombic egg-eating snake
Dasypeltis scabra

False water cobra
Hydrodynastes gigas

Amazon false fer-de-lance
Xenodon severus

Ringed hognose snake
Lystrophis semicinctus

Natal black snake
Macrelaps microlepidotus

Red cylinder snake
Cylindrophis ruffus

Arafura file snake
Acrochordus arafurae

SNAKING VINES

The vine snakes of Central and South America can grow as long as 7 feet (2 m), but their bodies are no more than ½ inch (1 cm) wide. Their long green bodies blend in with the leaves and stems of plants where they live. They move rapidly across branches in search of prey, such as small birds.

Pythons and boas

Pythons and boas belong to the boid family. It has many small species but also includes the largest snakes. The longest snakes on record are Asia's reticulated python and South America's anaconda, which spends much of its time in the Amazon River. Individuals from both species can grow longer than 30 feet (9 m). Pythons are found mostly in Asia, Africa, and Australia. All species lay eggs. Unlike most reptiles, they protect their eggs. Females make nests and then coil around their developing broods. After hatching, the young snakes are left to look after themselves. Pythons and boas are not venomous. They kill by coiling their bodies around their prey, then constricting, or squeezing, until it suffocates. Boas occur mainly throughout the Americas. They do not lay eggs but give birth to live young.

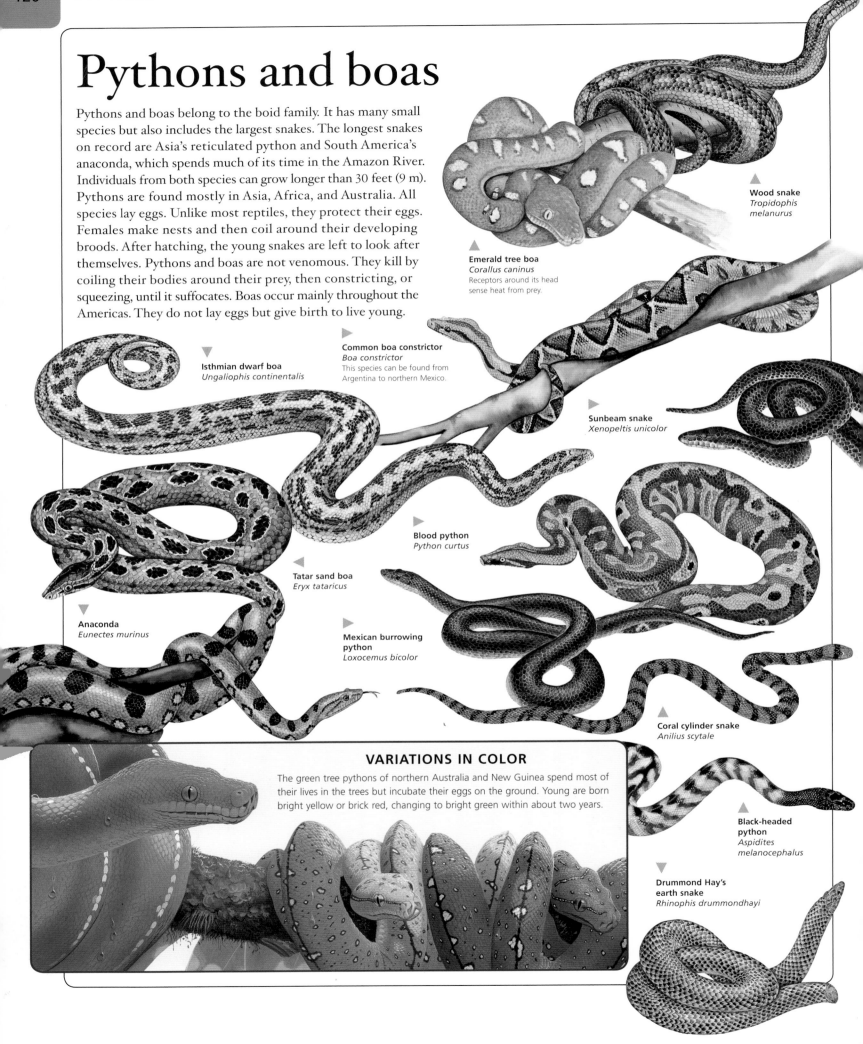

Wood snake
Tropidophis melanurus

Emerald tree boa
Corallus caninus
Receptors around its head sense heat from prey.

Isthmian dwarf boa
Ungaliophis continentalis

Common boa constrictor
Boa constrictor
This species can be found from Argentina to northern Mexico.

Sunbeam snake
Xenopeltis unicolor

Blood python
Python curtus

Tatar sand boa
Eryx tataricus

Anaconda
Eunectes murinus

Mexican burrowing python
Loxocemus bicolor

Coral cylinder snake
Anilius scytale

Black-headed python
Aspidites melanocephalus

Drummond Hay's earth snake
Rhinophis drummondhayi

VARIATIONS IN COLOR

The green tree pythons of northern Australia and New Guinea spend most of their lives in the trees but incubate their eggs on the ground. Young are born bright yellow or brick red, changing to bright green within about two years.

Adders and vipers

The viper family includes rattlesnakes and adders. All have large, hollow fangs located at the front of the mouth that swing forward to inject potent venom when they bite. The fangs are tucked away at other times. Vipers and adders occur throughout the Americas, Africa, Europe, and Asia. Instead of stalking prey, they ambush it. Their bodies are often patterned in shades of brown and green that blend in with their surroundings. This allows them to remain unseen as they lie coiled up beside a trail used by small mammals, or in the branches of a fruit tree where birds gather. They wait for prey to come within range before they strike with lightning speed. Some lure prey into range by wriggling their tails to look like a worm.

Massasauga
Sistrurus catenatus
A small North American rattlesnake

Mojave rattlesnake
Crotalus scutulatus
This rattlesnake can be recognized by the black and white rings on its thick tail.

Copperhead
Agkistrodon contortix

Cantil
Agkistrodon bilineatus

Western diamondback rattlesnake
Crotalus atrox

Adder
Vipera berus

Lichtenstein's night adder
Causus lichtensteinii

Yellow-blotched palm pit viper
Bothriechis aurifer

Fea viper
Azemiops feae

Jararacussu
Bothrops jararacussu
Like that of other vipers, its venom destroys the muscle tissue of its victims.

Bushmaster
Lachesis muta
The largest venomous snake in the Americas

Malayan pit viper
Calloselasma rhodostoma

ATTACK AND DEFENSE

THE HUNTERS AND THE HUNTED

Many snakes are aggressive predators with venomous bites. But snakes are often preyed on, too, especially by mammals and birds. Camouflage helps them hide from predators. Many tree snakes have long, slender heads and necks that blend in with their habitat. A cobra may use a threat display when challenged. To appear larger than its actual size, it raises half its body off the ground and flattens the ribs in its neck to form a hoodlike shape. A spitting cobra (left) avoids a fight that could injure its mouth by spitting poison at an attacker's eyes.

A venomous Florida cottonmouth reveals its startling white mouth. This warns potential predators to stay away.

The mild venom of this grass snake can paralyze a small fish, making it easier for the snake to swallow.

Cobras

Cobras belong to the elapid family, a venomous group that also includes kraits, sea snakes, mambas, coral snakes, and death adders. Elapids have hollow fangs located at the front of the mouth. They are fixed to the upper jawbone like normal teeth. They need to be small enough for the snake to close its mouth over them. Elapid venom acts on prey's nerves to stop the heart beating and damage the lungs. These snakes are found in Australia, Africa, South and Central America, and southeast North America. Many species live in burrows or leaf litter. Mambas and tree cobras live in trees. Sea snakes are found mainly in tropical parts of the Pacific and Indian Oceans. They have flattened bodies that are so well adapted to life in the water that it is almost impossible for them to move on land.

King cobra
Ophiophagus hannah

Black mamba
Dendroaspis polylepis
The fastest-moving snake, it has been recorded at speeds as fast as 12½ miles per hour (20 km/h).

Monocled cobra
Naja kaouthia
Markings on the back of the hood are thought to discourage predators attacking from behind.

Common death adder
Acanthophis antarcticus

Eastern coral snake
Micrurus fulvius
This venomous snake confuses would-be predators by moving its tail in the same way as it moves its head.

Taipan
Oxyuranus scutellatus

Arizona coral snake
Micruroides euryxanthus

Tiger snake
Notechis scutatus

Blue-lipped sea krait
Laticauda laticaudata

Western brown snake
Pseudonaja nuchalis

Mulga snake
Pseudechis australis

Turtle-headed sea snake
Emydocephalus annulatus

FAST FACT
Central Australia's fierce snake has the most poisonous venom of any snake. It is about 500 times more potent than that of an eastern diamondback rattlesnake. The venom in one bite could kill 250,000 mice.

Male green and black poison frogs make trilling calls to attract females. Males fight with each other for territories, which they defend during the breeding season.

AMPHIBIAN SKIN

Poison gland

Chromatophore

Epidermis

Mucus gland

Unlike reptiles, amphibians do not have protective scales to cover their skin. Many amphibian species can breathe through their skin, even those that have lungs. They have mucus glands that keep the skin moist. Some species can produce substances that kill bacteria or fungi, which are common in moist environments. Poison glands make them bad-tasting or even toxic to other animals. Special cells called chromatophores produce bright colors as a warning to potential predators.

Salamanders are often preyed on by birds. The red salamander's bright color warns these predators that it is poisonous.

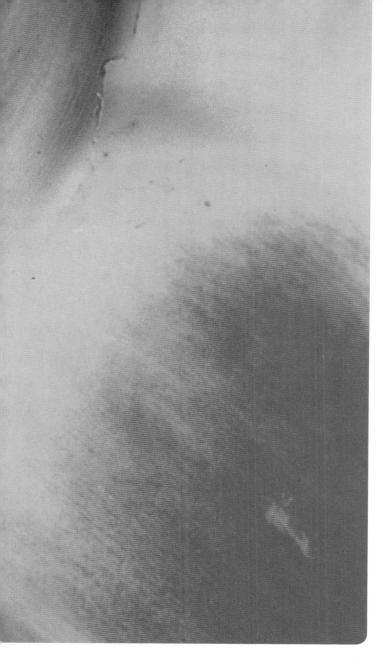

There are three main groups of amphibians: salamanders; caecilians; and frogs and toads. Most species live in water when young and on land as adults. Amphibians are cold-blooded: Their body temperature is controlled largely by their environment. They can also alter their temperature through behavior. Amphibians are usually active at night, but only when the conditions are moist enough to prevent their bodies from losing too much water by evaporation. As adults, amphibians eat small animals, such as insects and worms. They catch prey mostly by waiting until it comes within reach. Their young usually eat different food. Tadpoles, for example, are often plant-eaters, but become carnivores as frogs. Because they are relatively small, amphibians are often preyed on by larger animals. Many species have poison glands in their skin that produce bad-tasting or poisonous substances to protect them from predators. Some salamanders lose their tails when grasped. If threatened, frogs often lie motionless on their backs and play dead until a predator passes. To frighten away predators, toads may puff up, making themselves look larger. Some frogs can even scream loudly, to scare off would-be attackers and warn other frogs. Male and female amphibians usually live apart. To find each other to breed, salamanders leave scent trails. Male frogs and toads call and croak to attract females. Some amphibians actively care for their young, protecting their eggs until they hatch.

HOW AMPHIBIANS REPRODUCE

Amphibian eggs lack shells. To stay moist, eggs are usually placed in or near water. Embryos are surrounded by protective jelly-like membranes. Most frogs' eggs contain just enough yolk for embryos to grow into free-swimming larvae; the eggs of some species nourish embryos through the tadpole stage, too.

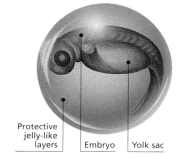

Protective jelly-like layers

Embryo

Yolk sac

As a larva, the warty newt lives in water and breathes with its feathery gills.

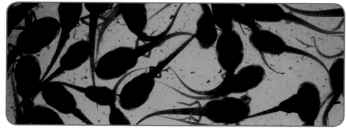

Many tadpoles move into shallow water on sunny days to control body temperature.

— 2 ORDERS • 16 FAMILIES • 93 GENERA • 621 SPECIES —

Salamanders and Caecilians

Salamanders, their relatives, and caecilians all have long tails as adults. Most salamanders have four limbs, but a few have only two. They look like lizards but are easily distinguished because they lack scales. Caecilians look like worms. They do not have limbs and almost always live underground. They dig with their strong, bullet-shaped heads to create burrows. Salamanders are secretive animals. Although they are common, they are rarely seen. All are carnivores that eat mostly insects, worms, and other small animals. They breathe through the skin, although many also breathe through lungs. Species often develop in water as larvae but live on land as adults. A few always live in water. Caecilians reproduce by internal fertilization, and most species give birth to live young. Adults eat earthworms and insects.

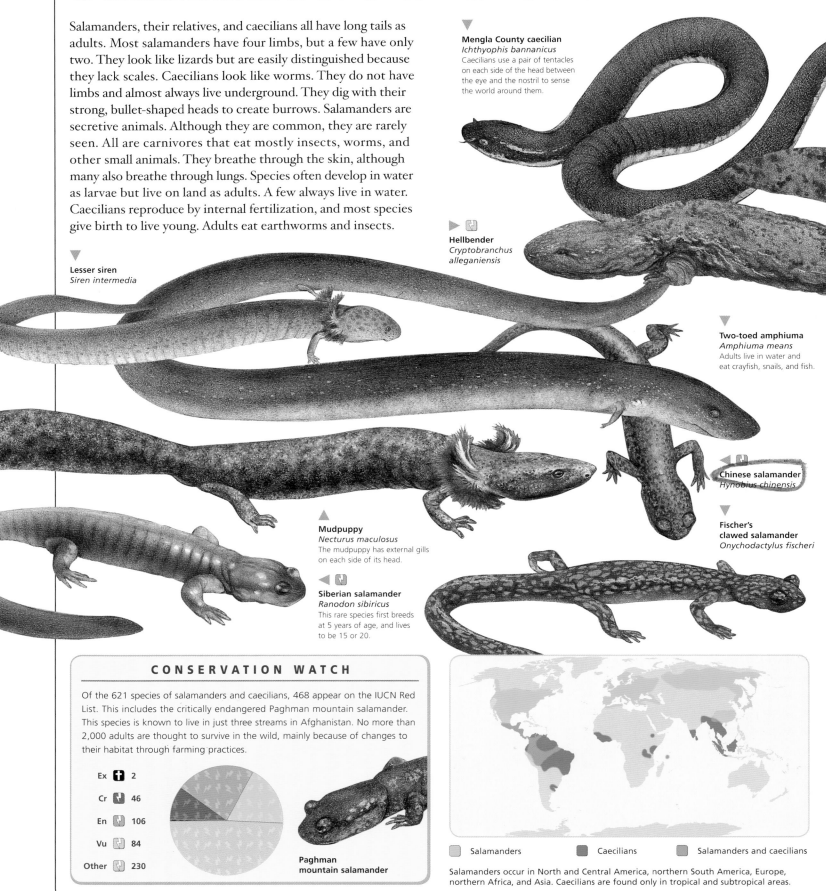

Mengla County caecilian
Ichthyophis bannanicus
Caecilians use a pair of tentacles on each side of the head between the eye and the nostril to sense the world around them.

Hellbender
Cryptobranchus alleganiensis

Lesser siren
Siren intermedia

Two-toed amphiuma
Amphiuma means
Adults live in water and eat crayfish, snails, and fish.

Chinese salamander
Hynobius chinensis

Mudpuppy
Necturus maculosus
The mudpuppy has external gills on each side of its head.

Fischer's clawed salamander
Onychodactylus fischeri

Siberian salamander
Ranodon sibiricus
This rare species first breeds at 5 years of age, and lives to be 15 or 20.

CONSERVATION WATCH

Of the 621 species of salamanders and caecilians, 468 appear on the IUCN Red List. This includes the critically endangered Paghman mountain salamander. This species is known to live in just three streams in Afghanistan. No more than 2,000 adults are thought to survive in the wild, mainly because of changes to their habitat through farming practices.

Ex	🕱	2
Cr		46
En		106
Vu		84
Other		230

Paghman mountain salamander

Salamanders · Caecilians · Salamanders and caecilians

Salamanders occur in North and Central America, northern South America, Europe, northern Africa, and Asia. Caecilians are found only in tropical and subtropical areas.

Tiger salamander
Ambystoma tigrinum
Spends most of its adult life
in underground burrows

**Japanese
firebelly newt**
Cynops pyrrhogaster
Markings on the belly may
take the form of spots,
blotches, or wavy lines.

Blue-spotted salamander
Ambystoma laterale
The blue spots on its sides and
tail provide camouflage.

**European
fire salamander**
Salamandra salamandra

Red-backed salamander
Plethodon cinereus

Vietnam warty newt
Paramesotriton deloustali
Adults live mainly in water;
they are aggressive during
the breeding season.

**Jackson's
mushroomtongue
salamander**
*Bolitoglossa
jacksoni*

Slimy salamander
Plethodon glutinosus

Common newt
Triturus vulgaris

Four-toed salamander
Hemidactylium scutatum

Chinese giant salamander
Andrias davidianus
The largest salamander: Some
individuals grow as long as
6 feet (1.8 m). It lacks eyelids.

**California
giant salamander**
Dicamptodon ensatus

1 ORDER • 28 FAMILIES • 338 GENERA • 4,937 SPECIES

Frogs and Toads

Anurans—frogs and toads—make up the largest amphibian order. They have long back legs, short bodies, and moist skin. Most have no tail. Their skeletons are adapted for jumping. The smallest anuran is Brazil's Izecksohn's toad, which is less than ½ inch (1 cm) long. Africa's goliath frog, at 12 inches (30 cm) long and weighing more than 7 pounds (3 kg), is the largest. Frogs and toads capture insects and other small animals by flicking out their long, sticky tongues. They blink their eyes once food is inside the mouth; the movement pushes food down the throat. Frogs are indicators of environmental pollution. Since the 1970s, there has been growing evidence worldwide that frog populations are disappearing. Many species have become extinct, even in apparently pristine areas.

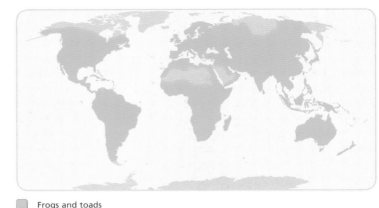

☐ Frogs and toads

Frogs and toads are found on all continents except Antarctica. More than 80 percent of anuran species live in the tropics.

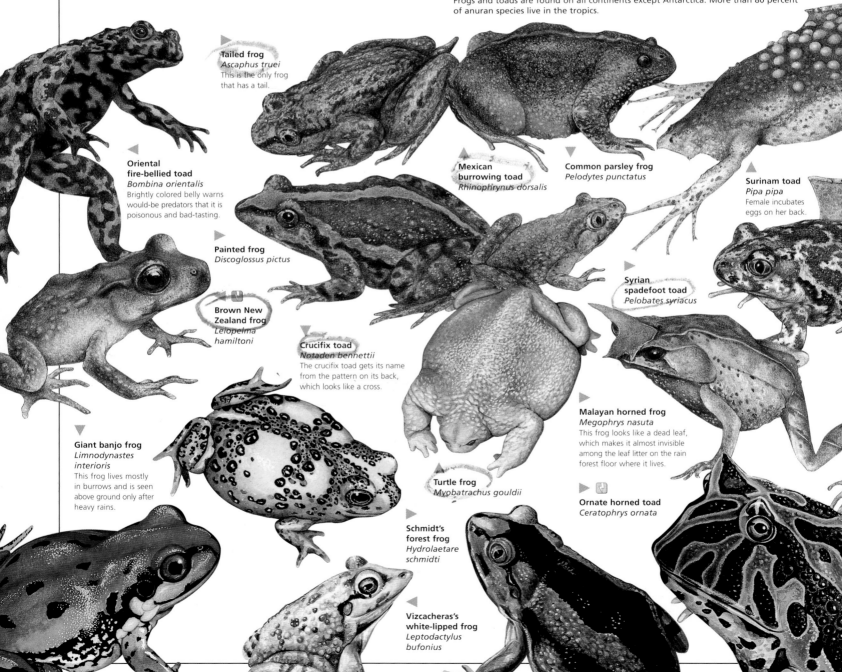

Tailed frog
Ascaphus truei
This is the only frog that has a tail.

Oriental fire-bellied toad
Bombina orientalis
Brightly colored belly warns would-be predators that it is poisonous and bad-tasting.

Mexican burrowing toad
Rhinophrynus dorsalis

Common parsley frog
Pelodytes punctatus

Surinam toad
Pipa pipa
Female incubates eggs on her back.

Painted frog
Discoglossus pictus

Brown New Zealand frog
Leiopelma hamiltoni

Crucifix toad
Notaden bennettii
The crucifix toad gets its name from the pattern on its back, which looks like a cross.

Syrian spadefoot toad
Pelobates syriacus

Giant banjo frog
Limnodynastes interioris
This frog lives mostly in burrows and is seen above ground only after heavy rains.

Turtle frog
Myobatrachus gouldii

Malayan horned frog
Megophrys nasuta
This frog looks like a dead leaf, which makes it almost invisible among the leaf litter on the rain forest floor where it lives.

Ornate horned toad
Ceratophrys ornata

Schmidt's forest frog
Hydrolaetare schmidti

Vizcacheras's white-lipped frog
Leptodactylus bufonius

STAGES OF LIFE

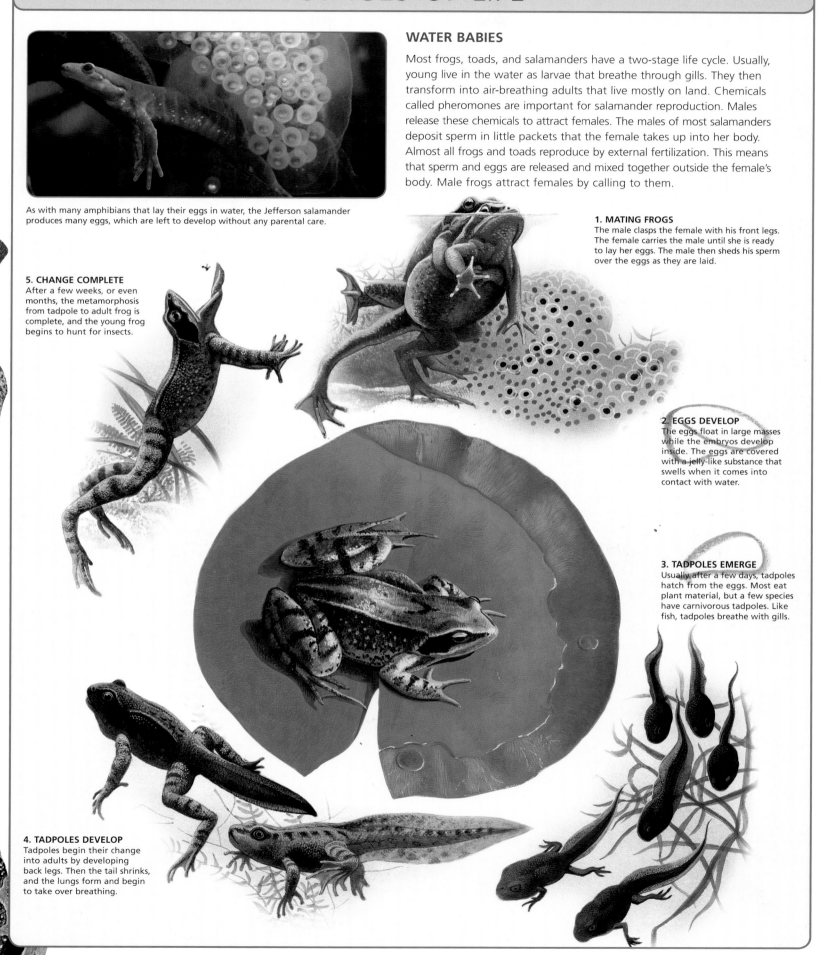

WATER BABIES

Most frogs, toads, and salamanders have a two-stage life cycle. Usually, young live in the water as larvae that breathe through gills. They then transform into air-breathing adults that live mostly on land. Chemicals called pheromones are important for salamander reproduction. Males release these chemicals to attract females. The males of most salamanders deposit sperm in little packets that the female takes up into her body. Almost all frogs and toads reproduce by external fertilization. This means that sperm and eggs are released and mixed together outside the female's body. Male frogs attract females by calling to them.

As with many amphibians that lay their eggs in water, the Jefferson salamander produces many eggs, which are left to develop without any parental care.

1. MATING FROGS
The male clasps the female with his front legs. The female carries the male until she is ready to lay her eggs. The male then sheds his sperm over the eggs as they are laid.

5. CHANGE COMPLETE
After a few weeks, or even months, the metamorphosis from tadpole to adult frog is complete, and the young frog begins to hunt for insects.

2. EGGS DEVELOP
The eggs float in large masses while the embryos develop inside. The eggs are covered with a jelly-like substance that swells when it comes into contact with water.

3. TADPOLES EMERGE
Usually, after a few days, tadpoles hatch from the eggs. Most eat plant material, but a few species have carnivorous tadpoles. Like fish, tadpoles breathe with gills.

4. TADPOLES DEVELOP
Tadpoles begin their change into adults by developing back legs. Then the tail shrinks, and the lungs form and begin to take over breathing.

Frogs and toads

The largest family of anurans is the New World frogs. Many species develop entirely in the egg and hatch as miniature adults. Some frogs in this family are adapted to burrowing, others for life in trees. The hylid family, or tree frogs, are all similar in shape. Their toes are enlarged at the tips and are sticky to aid in climbing. Toads belong to the bufonid family. They tend to be short-legged, and their bodies can be covered in wartlike glands. They do not have teeth. The ranid family, or "true frogs," look like typical frogs with smooth, moist skin and bulging eyes. They live near ponds and other bodies of water. Their relatives in Asia and Africa are the racophorid tree frog family. This includes flying frogs that glide on huge webbed feet. Another related family are known as squeakers, because some have high-pitched calls.

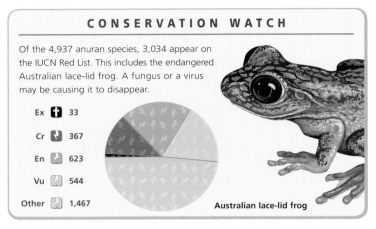

CONSERVATION WATCH

Of the 4,937 anuran species, 3,034 appear on the IUCN Red List. This includes the endangered Australian lace-lid frog. A fungus or a virus may be causing it to disappear.

Ex 🕆 33
Cr 📊 367
En 📊 623
Vu 📊 544
Other 📊 1,467

Australian lace-lid frog

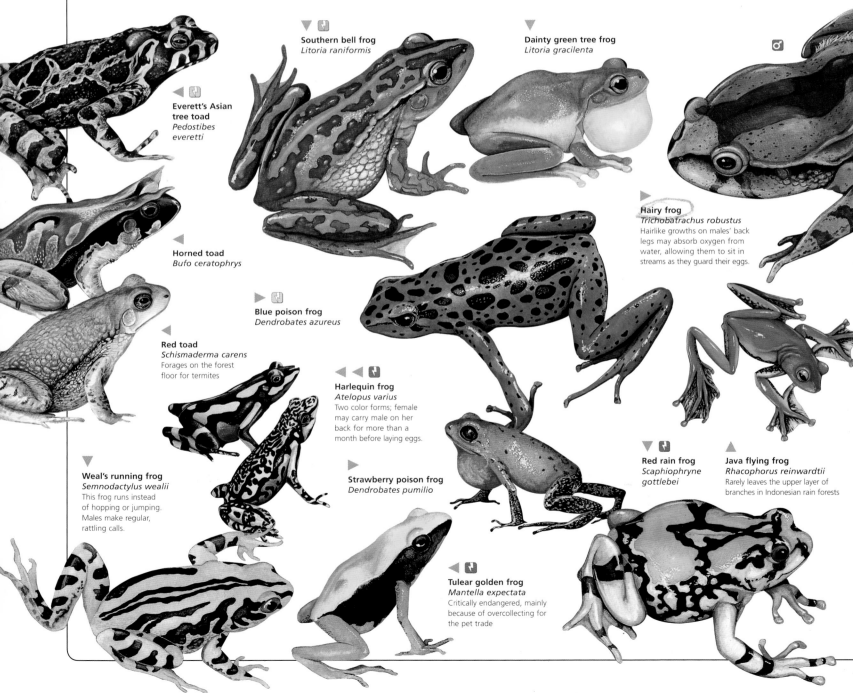

Southern bell frog
Litoria raniformis

Dainty green tree frog
Litoria gracilenta

Everett's Asian tree toad
Pedostibes everetti

Hairy frog
Trichobatrachus robustus
Hairlike growths on males' back legs may absorb oxygen from water, allowing them to sit in streams as they guard their eggs.

Horned toad
Bufo ceratophrys

Blue poison frog
Dendrobates azureus

Red toad
Schismaderma carens
Forages on the forest floor for termites

Harlequin frog
Atelopus varius
Two color forms; female may carry male on her back for more than a month before laying eggs.

Weal's running frog
Semnodactylus wealii
This frog runs instead of hopping or jumping. Males make regular, rattling calls.

Strawberry poison frog
Dendrobates pumilio

Red rain frog
Scaphiophryne gottlebei

Java flying frog
Rhacophorus reinwardtii
Rarely leaves the upper layer of branches in Indonesian rain forests

Tulear golden frog
Mantella expectata
Critically endangered, mainly because of overcollecting for the pet trade

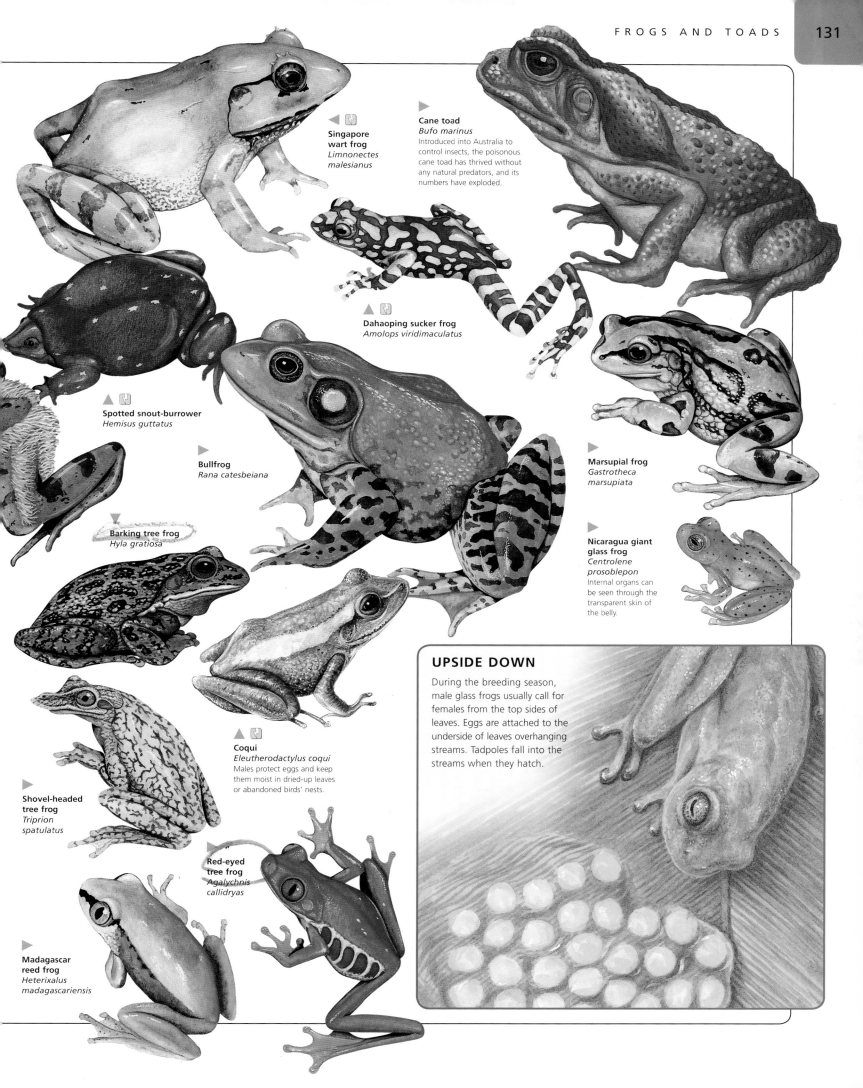

◀ Singapore wart frog
Limnonectes malesianus

▶ Cane toad
Bufo marinus
Introduced into Australia to control insects, the poisonous cane toad has thrived without any natural predators, and its numbers have exploded.

▲ Dahaoping sucker frog
Amolops viridimaculatus

▲ Spotted snout-burrower
Hemisus guttatus

▶ Bullfrog
Rana catesbeiana

▶ Marsupial frog
Gastrotheca marsupiata

▼ Barking tree frog
Hyla gratiosa

▶ Nicaragua giant glass frog
Centrolene prosoblepon
Internal organs can be seen through the transparent skin of the belly.

▲ Coqui
Eleutherodactylus coqui
Males protect eggs and keep them moist in dried-up leaves or abandoned birds' nests.

▶ Shovel-headed tree frog
Triprion spatulatus

Red-eyed tree frog
Agalychnis callidryas

▶ Madagascar reed frog
Heterixalus madagascariensis

UPSIDE DOWN

During the breeding season, male glass frogs usually call for females from the top sides of leaves. Eggs are attached to the underside of leaves overhanging streams. Tadpoles fall into the streams when they hatch.

Butterflyfish live in large groups called schools around the coral reefs that fringe islands in the Pacific Ocean. They have a varied diet that includes algae and small animals.

FISH ANATOMY

Many fish have streamlined, torpedo-shaped bodies that let them move easily through water. Some have bodies that are designed for camouflage or for attracting attention. Their skin is usually protected by bony scales. There are four main kinds of scales. The most common interlock like roof tiles. They can have a rough surface (ctenoid) or smoother (cycloid). A few primitive fish have scales like armor (ganoid). Sharks have hollow, toothlike scales (placoid), with an outer layer of enamel.

To avoid attention from predators, the skin of a freshwater leaffish mimicks dead leaves lying on the water's surface.

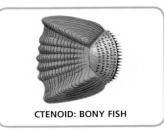

CTENOID: BONY FISH

CYCLOID: BONY FISH

GANOID: ARMORED FISH

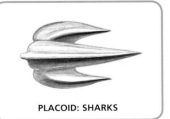

PLACOID: SHARKS

More than half of all vertebrate animals alive today are fish. At least 25,000 fish species have been identified, but there are probably thousands more still to be discovered. There are three main groups of fish: jawless fish (hagfish and lampreys), cartilaginous fish (sharks and rays), and bony fish (lobe-finned fish and ray-finned fish). They are found in almost every watery habitat, from polar seas to tropical ponds. Fish can be as small as tiny gobies, which grow to be just ⅔ inch (1 cm) long, or as large as whale sharks, which reach 59 feet (18 m) in length. Some fish are vibrantly colored. Others can be silvery-blue, mottled green, or colored and shaded to blend in with their environment. Many fish eat algae or insect larvae and other small animals. However, some fish are fierce predators that hunt large sea mammals. Almost all fish have fins, which they use to swim. Some species have fins adapted for "flying" briefly above water; a few can even "walk," using their fins like feet. Fish have the same basic senses as other vertebrate animals: sight, smell, hearing, touch, and taste. In fish, however, these senses are adapted to work in water. Although they do not have noses, they have nostrils that are highly sensitive to chemicals in the water. Many fish have an additional sense called the lateral line. This allows them to feel tiny movements and pressure changes in the water around them. The lateral line helps fish find food and avoid obstacles, even when swimming in murky water or darkness.

HOW FISH REPRODUCE

Most bony fish lay a large number of eggs. These are fertilized by the male's sperm outside the female's body in the surrounding water. The larvae that hatch from these eggs usually look very different from their adult parents. All male cartilaginous fish, such as sharks, place their sperm inside the female's body. The young of these fish develop inside their mother's body, or in hard shell cases. They are born looking like miniature copies of their parents.

The male gold-specs jawfish incubates eggs in his mouth to keep them safe.

Each shark's egg contains one embryo.

Mandarinfish swim together to mate.

2 CLASSES • 2 ORDERS • 2 FAMILIES • 105 SPECIES

Jawless Fish

Hagfish and lampreys, or jawless fish, were among the first fish. Most early species became extinct about 360 million years ago, but these two small groups have survived. Hagfish and lampreys have no jaws or scales. Their skeletons are not made of bone but of cartilage—the same kind of flexible material that supports human ears. Their bodies are shaped like those of eels, and they often lack paired fins. Hagfish produce enormous amounts of slime from mucus glands in their skin. This probably makes them too slippery for predators to bite firmly. They eat the flesh of dead or dying fish and invertebrates. Adult lampreys are parasites that attach themselves to larger fish, from which they suck body fluids. Young lampreys spend their first few years as larvae that feed by filtering small food particles from the water.

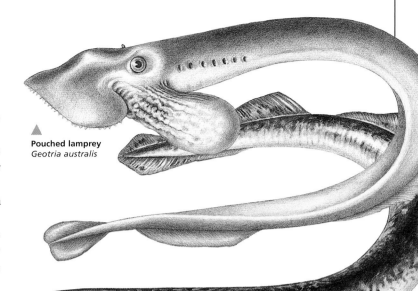

▲
Pouched lamprey
Geotria australis

▲
Sea lamprey
Petromyzon marinus
Sea lamprey live in rivers as larvae, swim into the sea to live as adults, then migrate back to rivers to breed once and die.

◄
Pacific lamprey
Lampetra tridentata
Migrates around the Pacific, attached to whales and large fish

FAST FACT
To feed, a hagfish attaches itself to dead animals with its mouth and ties itself into a knot. By pulling the knot along its slippery, slimy body to its head, it gains enough leverage to tear off pieces of flesh.

▼
Atlantic hagfish
Myxine glutinosa
Lampreys and hagfish both have porelike gill openings.

▲
European river lamprey
Lampetra fluviatilis
Unlike most lampreys, the river lamprey has sharp teeth.

CONSERVATION WATCH

Of the 105 jawless fish species, 12 appear on the IUCN Red List. The brook lamprey is listed as vulnerable, mostly because of water pollution. It is also threatened by the building of dams. This freshwater species occurs naturally only in Greece.

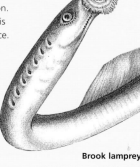

Ex 🕆 0
Cr 🗇 0
En 🗇 1
Vu 🗇 2
Other 🗇 9

Brook lamprey

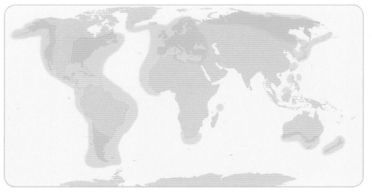

☐ Jawless fish

Jawless fish are found in shallow, temperate waters worldwide, and cool, deep waters in the tropics. Hagfish live only in salt water. Lampreys are found also in fresh water.

2 SUBCLASSES • 12 ORDERS • 47 FAMILIES • 160 GENERA • 999 SPECIES

Cartilaginous Fish

The gray reef shark is well camouflaged. To animals below, its white belly seems to disappear into the light above. From above, its dark back blends into the ocean's depths.

Sharks, rays, and their relatives are cartilaginous fish: They have skeletons of cartilage, not bone. Sharks have existed for about 400 million years; the first rays appeared about 200 million years ago. Most cartilaginous fish live in saltwater habitats. They have strong jaws and feed on other animals. They fertilize their eggs internally, with the male depositing sperm inside the female. Males have firm rods called claspers that look like fins running along the body behind their pectoral fins. They use these to guide sperm into the female. Unlike most fish, cartilaginous fish produce only small numbers of eggs. Some lay eggs with large amounts of yolk that nourish the developing young for months before they hatch. For most of this group, the young are nourished inside their mother's body for long periods before birth.

CONSERVATION WATCH

Of the 999 species of cartilaginous fish, 277 appear on the IUCN Red List. Europe's once common blue skate is endangered because too many have been fished for food.

Ex	🌳	0
Cr	🌳	9
En	🌳	19
Vu	🌳	38
Other	🌳	211

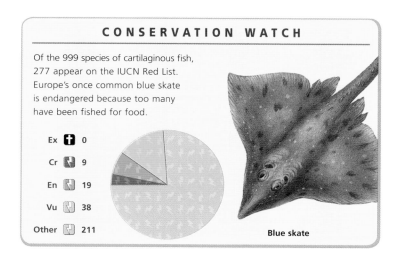

Blue skate

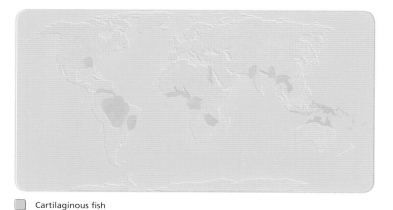

☐ Cartilaginous fish

Cartilaginous fish are found throughout the oceans. Some live in estuaries and freshwater rivers and lakes. Rays and skates live mostly on the bottom of oceans and seas.

Sharks

Sharks play a critical role in marine environments because they are apex predators. This means they are at, or near, the top of the food chain. If too many sharks are fished or killed by pollution, all species further down the food chain are affected, with some populations swelling and others declining. Most sharks are strong, agile swimmers. They generally eat fish and other small animals, but the largest sharks also hunt sea turtles and mammals, such as seals. Sharks have good eyesight and a keen sense of smell. Many can detect tiny amounts of blood in the ocean. They are also sensitive to sound waves traveling through water. Most sharks have a lateral line system, which detects movement in water. Some species have special organs called ampullae of Lorenzi around the head. These detect weak electrical fields that come from prey.

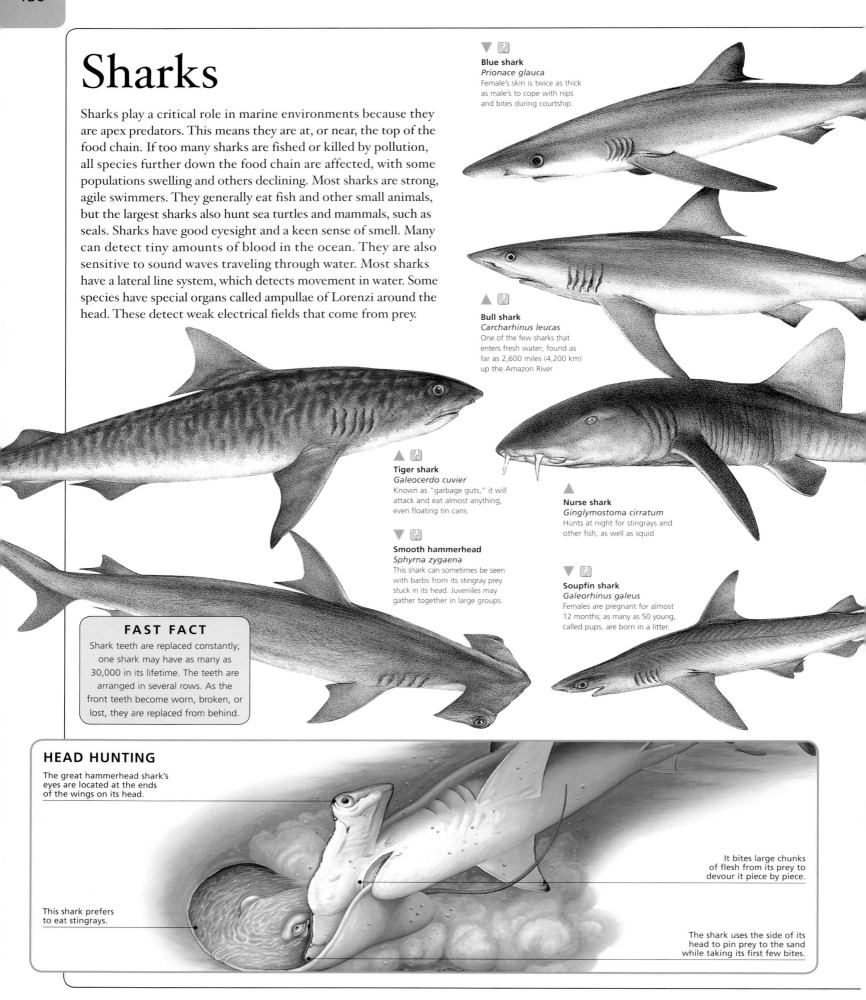

Blue shark
Prionace glauca
Female's skin is twice as thick as male's to cope with nips and bites during courtship.

Bull shark
Carcharhinus leucas
One of the few sharks that enters fresh water; found as far as 2,600 miles (4,200 km) up the Amazon River

Tiger shark
Galeocerdo cuvier
Known as "garbage guts," it will attack and eat almost anything, even floating tin cans.

Nurse shark
Ginglymostoma cirratum
Hunts at night for stingrays and other fish, as well as squid

Smooth hammerhead
Sphyrna zygaena
This shark can sometimes be seen with barbs from its stingray prey stuck in its head. Juveniles may gather together in large groups.

Soupfin shark
Galeorhinus galeus
Females are pregnant for almost 12 months; as many as 50 young, called pups, are born in a litter.

FAST FACT

Shark teeth are replaced constantly; one shark may have as many as 30,000 in its lifetime. The teeth are arranged in several rows. As the front teeth become worn, broken, or lost, they are replaced from behind.

HEAD HUNTING

The great hammerhead shark's eyes are located at the ends of the wings on its head.

This shark prefers to eat stingrays.

It bites large chunks of flesh from its prey to devour it piece by piece.

The shark uses the side of its head to pin prey to the sand while taking its first few bites.

Great white shark
Carcharodon carcharias
Sometimes leap clear of the water to snatch their prey of seals, fish, turtles, or squid

Angel shark
Squatina squatina
Often rests on bottom of ocean, covered in sand with just its eyes protruding

Shortfin mako
Isurus oxyrinchus
Makos hunt fast-swimming fish, such as tuna and swordfish.

Longnose sawshark
Pristiophorus cirratus

Sharpnose sevengill shark
Heptranchias perlo
Usually found living near the ocean floor, as deep as 3,300 feet (1,000 m) below the surface

Bramble shark
Echinorhinus brucus
This shark's name comes from the unusual thorny scales all over its body. Embryos eat each other while still inside their mother; only two ever survive to be born.

Spotted ratfish
Hydrolagus colliei
One of the chimeras, a group of mostly deepwater fish that is related to sharks and rays.

Spiny dogfish
Squalus acanthias
Forms large schools of individuals of the same size, age, and often sex; spines on the dorsal fins are used against predators.

Whale shark
Rhincodon typus
Tiny animals are filtered from the water's surface through its huge open mouth.

Rays

Rays and their relatives, the skates, are related to sharks. Their distinctive body shape—flattened from top to bottom—suits life on the ocean floor, where most of these fish are found. They have large pectoral fins that extend from near their snouts to the base of their tails. These fins join the body, and often the head, to form a disk that can be triangular, round, or shaped like a diamond. The mouth is underneath the disk and the eyes are on top. Rays and skates also have two openings, called spiracles, located near the front of the head. The spiracles are often mistaken for eyes, but rays and skates use them to breathe. Water is taken in through the spiracles and then passes across the gills. This process allows rays and skates to breathe even when their mouths are buried in sediment. Their teeth are used for crushing prey.

Manta
Manta birostris
Mantas regularly go to "cleaning stations" where small fish remove their external parasites. Their fins can extend 29 feet (8.8 m) from tip to tip.

Marbled electric ray
Torpedo marmorata
Stuns or kills prey with an electric shock produced by organs near its eyes

Largetooth sawfish
Pristis pristis
As many as 20 pairs of needle-like teeth line its long, flat snout. This saw is slashed at fish and squid to stun and kill them.

Atlantic guitarfish
Rhinobatos lentiginosus
The guitarfish looks like a cross between a shark and a ray. It often buries itself in the top layer of mud or sand along beaches.

Thornback ray
Raja clavata

MANTA RAY FEEDING

Some rays, such as mantas, live in the open ocean. Mantas feed on small animals called zooplankton. They use two special fins on either side of the head to guide zooplankton into the mouth, where they are filtered from the water and swallowed. Groups of feeding mantas may be seen swimming in large loops in surface waters rich with zooplankton.

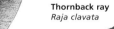

FAST FACT
Devil fish are some of the largest fish on Earth. The devil fish may reach widths of 23 feet (7 m) and weigh as much as 2,200 pounds (1,000 kg). Despite their size, some can leap clear of the water.

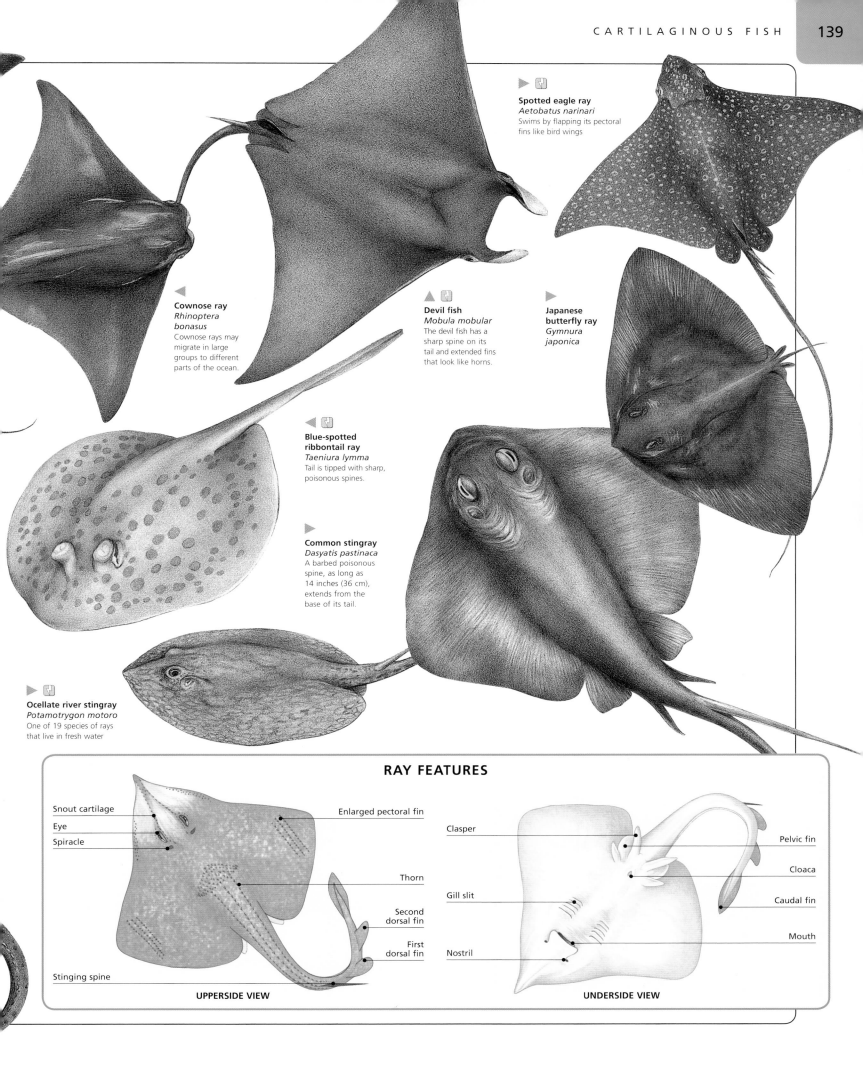

Spotted eagle ray
Aetobatus narinari
Swims by flapping its pectoral
fins like bird wings

Cownose ray
*Rhinoptera
bonasus*
Cownose rays may
migrate in large
groups to different
parts of the ocean.

Devil fish
Mobula mobular
The devil fish has a
sharp spine on its
tail and extended fins
that look like horns.

**Japanese
butterfly ray**
*Gymnura
japonica*

**Blue-spotted
ribbontail ray**
Taeniura lymma
Tail is tipped with sharp,
poisonous spines.

Common stingray
Dasyatis pastinaca
A barbed poisonous
spine, as long as
14 inches (36 cm),
extends from the
base of its tail.

Ocellate river stingray
Potamotrygon motoro
One of 19 species of rays
that live in fresh water

RAY FEATURES

Snout cartilage

Eye

Spiracle

Enlarged pectoral fin

Thorn

Second
dorsal fin

First
dorsal fin

Stinging spine

UPPERSIDE VIEW

Clasper

Gill slit

Nostril

Pelvic fin

Cloaca

Caudal fin

Mouth

UNDERSIDE VIEW

2 CLASSES • 48 ORDERS • 455 FAMILIES • 3,080 GENERA • 24,673 SPECIES

Bony Fish

Red lionfish are aggressive predators that hide by day and hunt by night. They stalk small fish and shrimp, which they corner by stretching out their pectoral fins like fans.

Lobe-finned and ray-finned fish are the two bony fish classes. Their fins are supported by complex muscles and bones, giving them more control when they swim than other fish. Many can move backward as well as forward, and some can hover. Increasing or decreasing the air in a swim bladder, a gas-filled sac inside the body, changes buoyancy and gives them even more control over their movement.

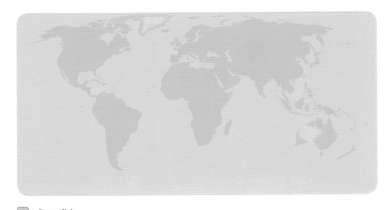

☐ Bony fish

Bony fish are found in almost every available water habitat in the world. Some even live in waterways that have dried up. Species are most numerous and diverse near coastlines.

BONY FISH FEATURES

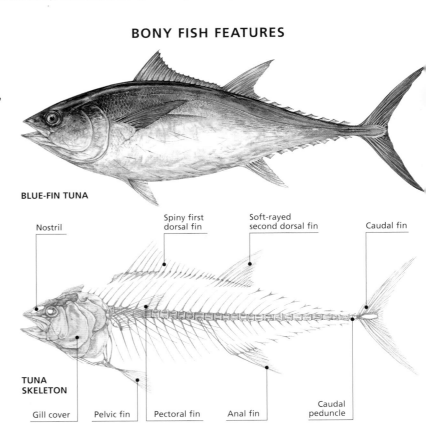

BLUE-FIN TUNA

Nostril

Spiny first dorsal fin

Soft-rayed second dorsal fin

Caudal fin

TUNA SKELETON

Gill cover   Pelvic fin   Pectoral fin   Anal fin   Caudal peduncle

Primitive fish

Lungfish and coelacanths are lobe-finned fish, an ancient class that has fleshy fins. Their fins have bones and muscles that are more like the limbs of a land-dwelling vertebrate than the raylike fins of most other living fish. Lungfish live in fresh water in the tropics. Most species survive dry seasons inside burrows, in cocoons made of dried mucus. Most bony fish are ray-finned fish. Sturgeons and paddlefish are among the most primitive of these, with scales that look like armor. Gars probably look similar to early fish, with their interlocking scales. They are aggressive predators with long rows of sharp teeth. Another primitive group includes the freshwater bonytongues, featherbacks, and elephantfish. The unusual, toothlike bones on their tongues bite against teeth on the roofs of their mouths.

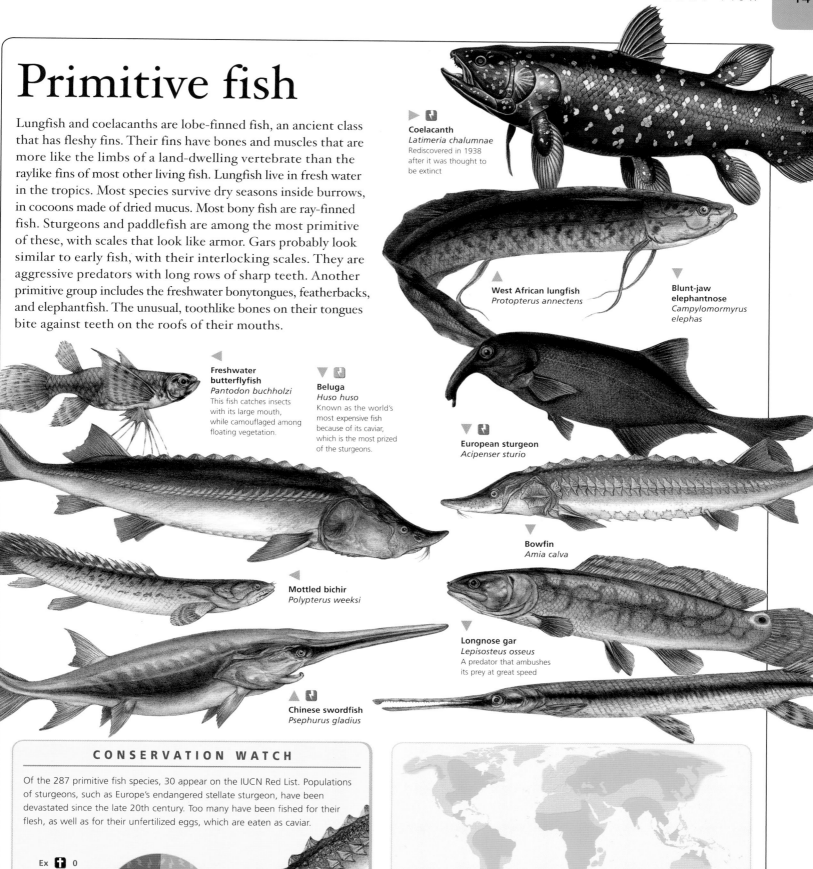

Coelacanth
Latimeria chalumnae
Rediscovered in 1938 after it was thought to be extinct

West African lungfish
Protopterus annectens

Blunt-jaw elephantnose
Campylomormyrus elephas

Freshwater butterflyfish
Pantodon buchholzi
This fish catches insects with its large mouth, while camouflaged among floating vegetation.

Beluga
Huso huso
Known as the world's most expensive fish because of its caviar, which is the most prized of the sturgeons.

European sturgeon
Acipenser sturio

Mottled bichir
Polypterus weeksi

Bowfin
Amia calva

Longnose gar
Lepisosteus osseus
A predator that ambushes its prey at great speed

Chinese swordfish
Psephurus gladius

CONSERVATION WATCH

Of the 287 primitive fish species, 30 appear on the IUCN Red List. Populations of sturgeons, such as Europe's endangered stellate sturgeon, have been devastated since the late 20th century. Too many have been fished for their flesh, as well as for their unfertilized eggs, which are eaten as caviar.

Ex 0
Cr 8
En 12
Vu 7
Other 4

Stellate sturgeon

Primitive fish

Lungfish live in Africa, South America, and Australia. Coelacanths survive in just two ocean areas. Gars, sturgeons, and bonytongues occur in temperate and tropical regions.

Eels

There are 900 species of eels and their relatives, the eel-like fish. All begin life as leptocephalus larvae. These larvae are see-through, shaped like a ribbon, and drift on ocean currents for as long as three years. They then change into a small version of their adult form. Most live in the oceans or around the mouths of rivers. The largest group—the true eels—includes moray, conger, and freshwater eels. They have long bodies, and most have no pelvic or pectoral fins. As adults, many eel-like fish look different from true eels. Tarpons and bonefish have forked tails and large, metallic scales. Deep-sea swallowers do not have scales. They have enormous mouths and expandable stomachs that allow them to gulp down large, but infrequent, meals.

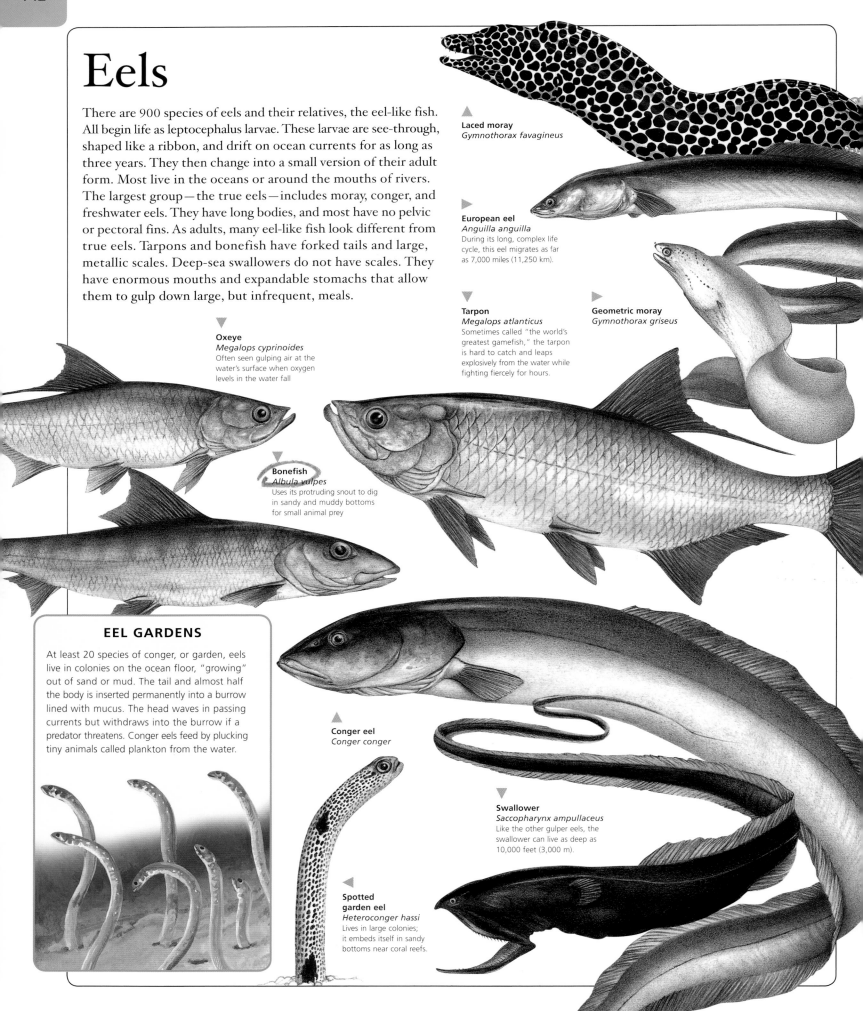

Laced moray
Gymnothorax favagineus

European eel
Anguilla anguilla
During its long, complex life cycle, this eel migrates as far as 7,000 miles (11,250 km).

Tarpon
Megalops atlanticus
Sometimes called "the world's greatest gamefish," the tarpon is hard to catch and leaps explosively from the water while fighting fiercely for hours.

Geometric moray
Gymnothorax griseus

Oxeye
Megalops cyprinoides
Often seen gulping air at the water's surface when oxygen levels in the water fall

Bonefish
Albula vulpes
Uses its protruding snout to dig in sandy and muddy bottoms for small animal prey

EEL GARDENS

At least 20 species of conger, or garden, eels live in colonies on the ocean floor, "growing" out of sand or mud. The tail and almost half the body is inserted permanently into a burrow lined with mucus. The head waves in passing currents but withdraws into the burrow if a predator threatens. Conger eels feed by plucking tiny animals called plankton from the water.

Conger eel
Conger conger

Spotted garden eel
Heteroconger hassi
Lives in large colonies; it embeds itself in sandy bottoms near coral reefs.

Swallower
Saccopharynx ampullaceus
Like the other gulper eels, the swallower can live as deep as 10,000 feet (3,000 m).

Sardines

Sardines and their relatives are called clupeoids. This order includes some of the most important commercial fish, such as herrings, pilchards, anchovies, and shads, as well as sardines. They have streamlined bodies, large silver scales, and forked tails. Most form large schools in the ocean, near coastlines. Some travel in huge numbers on migrations that can cover thousands of miles and take several years. Most clupeoids feed by filtering small animals called zooplankton from the water. This group experiences "boom–bust" population cycles, based on availability of food. Their numbers may crash, with many dying at once. But these fish reproduce quickly from a young age, so their numbers bounce back when conditions are good.

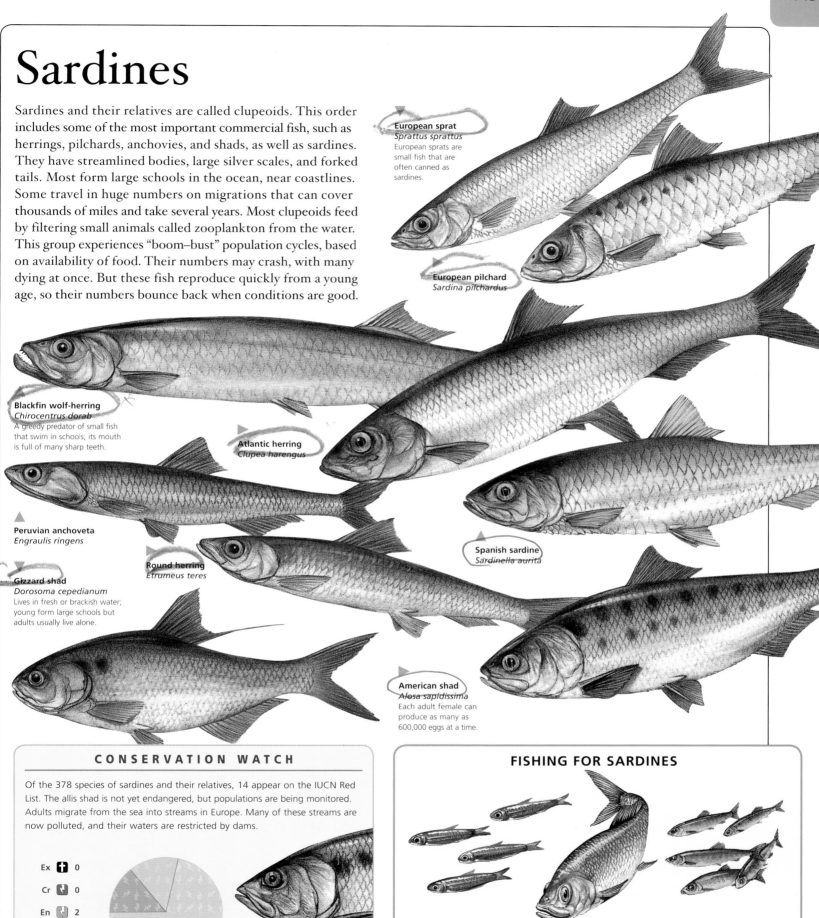

European sprat
Sprattus sprattus
European sprats are small fish that are often canned as sardines.

European pilchard
Sardina pilchardus

Blackfin wolf-herring
Chirocentrus dorab
A greedy predator of small fish that swim in schools; its mouth is full of many sharp teeth.

Atlantic herring
Clupea harengus

Peruvian anchoveta
Engraulis ringens

Round herring
Etrumeus teres

Gizzard shad
Dorosoma cepedianum
Lives in fresh or brackish water; young form large schools but adults usually live alone.

Spanish sardine
Sardinella aurita

American shad
Alosa sapidissima
Each adult female can produce as many as 600,000 eggs at a time.

CONSERVATION WATCH

Of the 378 species of sardines and their relatives, 14 appear on the IUCN Red List. The allis shad is not yet endangered, but populations are being monitored. Adults migrate from the sea into streams in Europe. Many of these streams are now polluted, and their waters are restricted by dams.

Ex	0
Cr	0
En	2
Vu	2
Other	10

Allis shad

FISHING FOR SARDINES

ANCHOVIES
Six different species fished commercially

PACIFIC HERRING
Both eggs and flesh used for food

SARDINES
Oily fish, harvested commercially as pilchards

Catfish

Catfish and their relatives are the most common fish in freshwater habitats worldwide. More than 7,000 species belong to this group. When they face danger, most species produce chemicals from special skin cells, warning other fish nearby of the threat. They also have a set of bones that enhances their hearing. The largest order of catfish includes the goldfish, minnows, and many other fish that are kept as pets in aquariums around the world. Another order, the characins, includes piranhas, which are famous for eating the flesh of animals that stray into the South American rivers where they live. The harmless tetras also belong to this order. True catfish are easily identified by the tentacle-like barbels around their mouths, which they use to find food.

CONSERVATION WATCH

Of the 7,023 species of catfish and their relatives, 70 appear on the IUCN Red List. Like freshwater fish elsewhere, Asia's endangered tricolor sharkminnow is threatened by the destruction of its habitat caused by clearing for agriculture and the expansion of cities.

Ex   1
Cr   10
En   8
Vu   22
Other   29

Tricolor sharkminnow

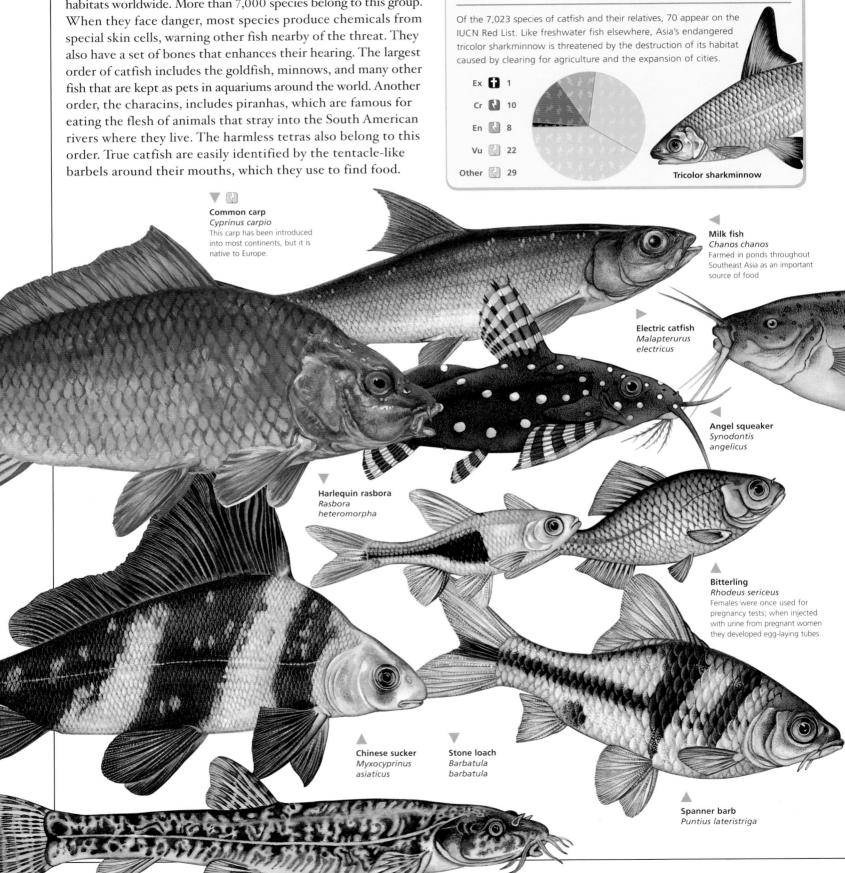

Common carp
Cyprinus carpio
This carp has been introduced into most continents, but it is native to Europe.

Milk fish
Chanos chanos
Farmed in ponds throughout Southeast Asia as an important source of food

Electric catfish
Malapterurus electricus

Angel squeaker
Synodontis angelicus

Harlequin rasbora
Rasbora heteromorpha

Bitterling
Rhodeus sericeus
Females were once used for pregnancy tests; when injected with urine from pregnant women they developed egg-laying tubes.

Chinese sucker
Myxocyprinus asiaticus

Stone loach
Barbatula barbatula

Spanner barb
Puntius lateristriga

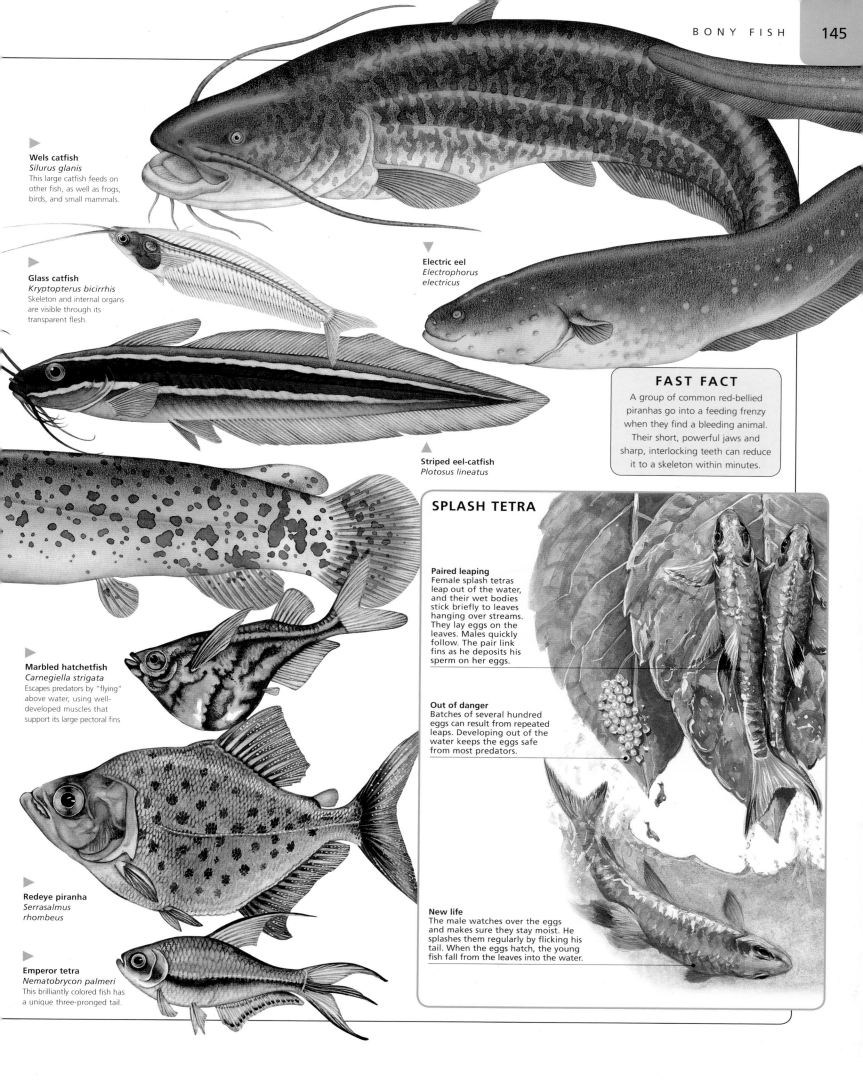

Wels catfish
Silurus glanis
This large catfish feeds on other fish, as well as frogs, birds, and small mammals.

Glass catfish
Kryptopterus bicirrhis
Skeleton and internal organs are visible through its transparent flesh.

Electric eel
Electrophorus electricus

Striped eel-catfish
Plotosus lineatus

Marbled hatchetfish
Carnegiella strigata
Escapes predators by "flying" above water, using well-developed muscles that support its large pectoral fins

Redeye piranha
Serrasalmus rhombeus

Emperor tetra
Nematobrycon palmeri
This brilliantly colored fish has a unique three-pronged tail.

FAST FACT

A group of common red-bellied piranhas go into a feeding frenzy when they find a bleeding animal. Their short, powerful jaws and sharp, interlocking teeth can reduce it to a skeleton within minutes.

SPLASH TETRA

Paired leaping
Female splash tetras leap out of the water, and their wet bodies stick briefly to leaves hanging over streams. They lay eggs on the leaves. Males quickly follow. The pair link fins as he deposits his sperm on her eggs.

Out of danger
Batches of several hundred eggs can result from repeated leaps. Developing out of the water keeps the eggs safe from most predators.

New life
The male watches over the eggs and makes sure they stay moist. He splashes them regularly by flicking his tail. When the eggs hatch, the young fish fall from the leaves into the water.

Salmon

Salmon and their relatives are mostly carnivores, or meat-eaters. Their large mouths and sharp teeth are well designed for catching food. Streamlined bodies and strong tails make them fast, powerful swimmers. They are divided into three orders. One includes the pikes and pickerels, fierce freshwater predators that ambush prey. Another order includes the smelts, which are abundant along ocean coastlines in the Northern Hemisphere. Trout and salmon are in the third order, which also includes whitefish, graylings, and chars. Salmon are strong swimmers. Many make long, difficult migrations to breed. Although salmon and trout are native to the Northern Hemisphere, many species have been introduced around the world, because they are so exciting to catch and good to eat.

CONSERVATION WATCH

Of the 502 species of salmon and their relatives, 67 appear on the IUCN Red List. The critically endangered apache trout, which lives in rivers and streams in the southwestern United States, has been threatened by overfishing. Competition from introduced species has also reduced the trout's numbers:

Ex   5
Cr   8
En   6
Vu   22
Other   26

Apache trout

Atlantic salmon
Salmo salar

European smelt
Osmerus eperlanus

Capelin
Mallotus villosus
Most produce eggs or sperm only once and then die.

Cutthroat trout
Oncorhynchus clarki
Adults migrate from the sea into streams to breed; young fish enter the sea after about two years.

Sea trout
Salmo trutta trutta

Chain pickerel
Esox niger

Mudminnow
Umbra krameri

Alaska blackfish
Dallia pectoralis
Can breathe oxygen from the air so it can survive in stagnant Arctic ponds during summer

Ayu
Plecoglossus altivelis

California slickhead
Alepocephalus tenebrosus

Northern pike
Esox lucius

Sockeye salmon
Oncorhynchus nerka

Cherry salmon
Oncorhynchus masou

Golden trout
Oncorhynchus aguabonita

Lake trout
Salvelinus namaycush
Females are mated with brook trout males in commercial hatcheries to produce fast-growing fish called splakes.

FAST FACT

Salmon probably rely on their sense of smell to find their way back to the streams where they were born. Each waterway has its own distinctive odor, created by the surrounding soil and plants.

Huchen
Hucho hucho

Grayling
Thymallus thymallus
Females lay their eggs in nests dug by males in streams and lakes in northern Europe.

Cisco
Coregonus artedi
Lives in deep, clean, cold waters of North American lakes and rivers

SALMON LIFE CYCLE

Sockeye salmon start their lives in rivers. They hatch with yolk sacs attached. A few days later, they become fry. As parr, they stay in fresh water for several years before becoming smolt that live in salt water. They live at sea as adults, returning to fresh water to breed.

Eggs are laid in gravel nests.

Free-swimming fry

Just-hatched young (with yolk sac attached) are called alevin.

Parr live in fresh water.

Salmon breed and lay eggs in rivers. When breeding, the male sockeye salmon turns a brilliant red color.

Pink salmon
Oncorhynchus gorbuscha
Female uses her tail to make a deep gravel nest in a streambed; she guards eggs for several weeks but dies after spawning.

Rainbow trout
Oncorhynchus mykiss

Seagoing adults

Smolt

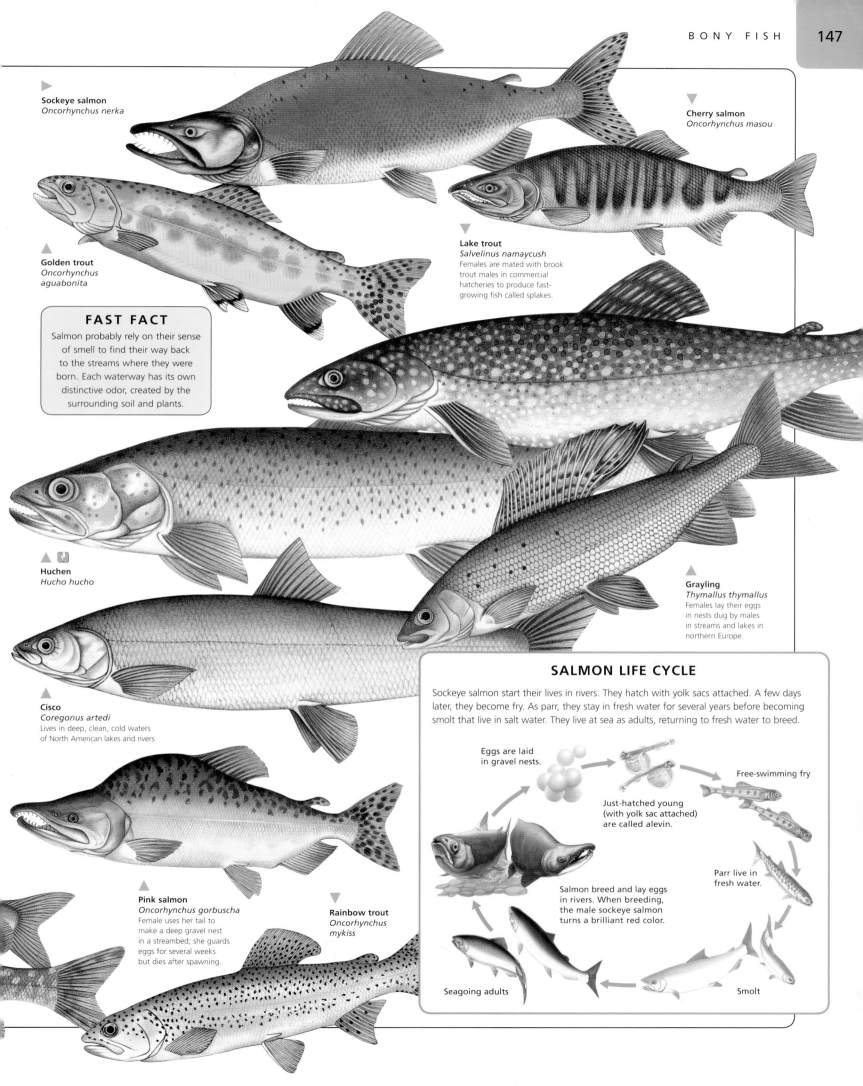

Cod and anglerfish

Most cod and anglerfish live on or near the bottom of seas and oceans. They tend to be most active at night, or live in dark habitats such as underwater caves or the deep sea. Some exceptions include commercially important species—such as haddock, hake, and cod—which form large schools that swim in the open ocean. Some can produce noise with special muscles found on the swim bladder. They may use noises for courting mates or sending distress messages to warn other fish of danger. Many cod are strong swimmers that actively hunt for prey. Anglerfish tend to be slow-moving fish that prefer to wait for food to come to them. Other fish that live in the deep sea are the dragonfish, lizardfish, lanternfish, and beardfish. These have adapted in different ways to life in the dark ocean depths.

Hatchetfish
Argyropelecus olfersi
Mouth and eyes are directed upward because it always attacks its prey from below.

Pacific viperfish
Chauliodus macouni

Oarfish
Regalecus glesne

Stout beardfish
Polymixia nobilis
Sensory barbels hang from the chins of all beardfish.

Metallic lanternfish
Myctophum affine
Head and underside are covered with flashing light organs.

Northern pearleye
Benthalbella dentata
This fish has both male and female sex organs.

American anglerfish
Lophius americanus
A spine on the front of its head forms a "fishing pole" that anglerfish use to catch other fish.

Atlantic cod
Gadus morhua

Starry handfish
Halieutaea stellata

Trout perch
Percopsis omiscomaycus

Haddock
Melanogrammus aeglefinus

European hake
Merluccius merluccius

CLEVER CAMOUFLAGE

Because most anglerfish are predators that ambush prey, they do not need smooth, streamlined bodies. Instead, their colors and shapes are similar to their surroundings. The sargassumfish blends in with sargassum weed. The roughbar frogfish looks like a rock.

SARGASSUMFISH   **ROUGHBAR FROGFISH**

Onion-eye grenadier
Macrourus berglax
Fished commercially; scales are so tough they can dull knives in processing plants.

Burbot
Lota lota

DEEP-SEA FISH

EXPLORING THE DEEP

Deep-sea fish live in a world with no light, where the pressure of the surrounding water pushes in on their bodies. In the darkness, many produce their own light, by a process called bioluminescence. Because it would be difficult to find a member of the opposite sex in the dark, deep-sea fish are often hermaphrodites—they have both male and female sex organs. This means they can play either role when they get the rare opportunity to mate. If necessary, they can even fertilize their own eggs. Prey is also in short supply in the ocean depths. Most deep-sea fish have long teeth, big mouths, and stomachs that can stretch to enormous proportions so that their bodies can cope with even the largest prey.

Deep-sea dragonfish stay hidden in the complete darkness of the ocean depths during the day, but swim upward at night for a better chance of finding prey.

Patterns created by flashing light organs on the bodies of lanternfish may help these fish stay in position within their deep-sea schools.

Tube worms

Eelpout

UNDERWATER HOT SPRINGS
In 1977, scientists were exploring the floor of the Pacific Ocean in a deepwater craft called *Alvin*. At 8,000 feet (2,440 m) below the surface, not far from the Galápagos Islands, they discovered a new habitat: an underwater hot spring called a hydrothermal vent. These vents are surrounded by unusual deep-sea life, such as a fish called an eelpout that eats giant tube worms.

15 ORDERS • 269 FAMILIES • 2,289 GENERA • 13,262 SPECIES

Spiny-rayed Fish

The leafy seadragon, which occurs along the Australian coastline, has frilled, leafy fins that look like the seaweeds and seagrasses among which it lives.

The largest group of bony fish, spiny-rayed fish, show almost every variation on the basic fish body plan. Some are flat, for life on the ocean floor. Bullet-shaped bodies make others among the fastest swimming marine animals. Special fins help a few to glide above water. For others, lightweight, overlapping scales have developed into hard body armor. Spiny-rays usually have flexible mouths that can protrude a long way, letting them eat a huge range of foods.

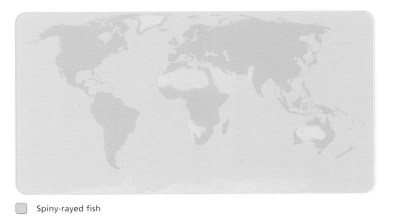

Spiny-rayed fish

Spiny-rayed fish occur almost worldwide. They are found in both fresh and salt water.

SPINY-RAYED FISH FEATURES

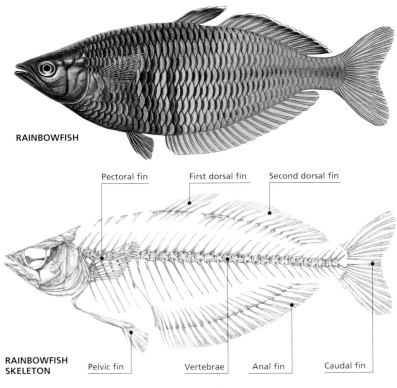

RAINBOWFISH

Pectoral fin   First dorsal fin   Second dorsal fin

RAINBOWFISH
SKELETON

Pelvic fin   Vertebrae   Anal fin   Caudal fin

Spiny-rayed fish

Killifish are some of the best known spiny-rayed fish, because they are among the most popular aquarium fish in the world. They include guppies, mollies, and swordtails. Most killifish occur in the fresh or slightly salty water of rivers and estuaries. Relatives of killifish include silversides. Most silversides live in coastal waters around the world and may form dense schools near the surface over coral reefs. There are also many species that live in fresh water. Silversides are common in the streams, lakes, and swamps of Australia and New Guinea. In contrast, squirrelfish and their relatives live only in salt water. Almost all of this group avoid bright sunlight. They live in deep water, shelter in caves, or hide in other dark places during the day. They become active only at night.

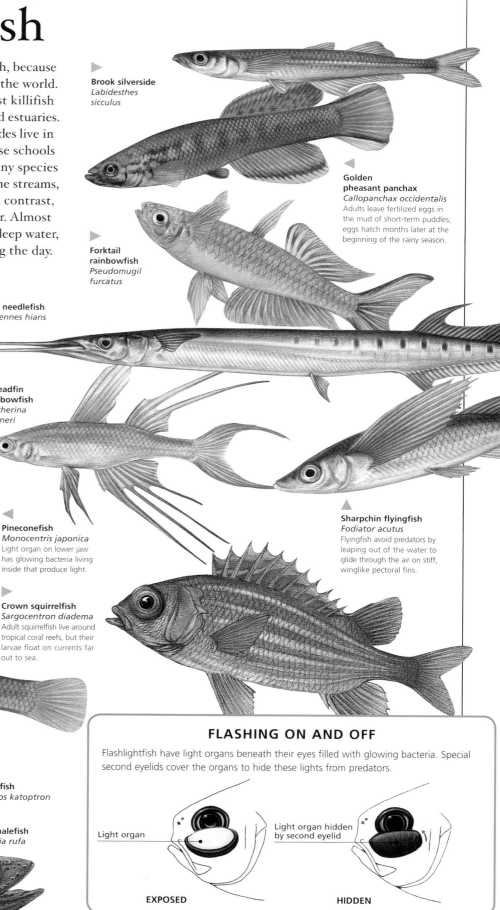

Brook silverside
Labidesthes sicculus

Golden pheasant panchax
Callopanchax occidentalis
Adults leave fertilized eggs in the mud of short-term puddles; eggs hatch months later at the beginning of the rainy season.

Forktail rainbowfish
Pseudomugil furcatus

Saberfin killie
Terranatos dolichopterus

Flat needlefish
Ablennes hians

Threadfin rainbowfish
Iriatherina werneri

Sharpchin flyingfish
Fodiator acutus
Flyingfish avoid predators by leaping out of the water to glide through the air on stiff, winglike pectoral fins.

Pineconefish
Monocentris japonica
Light organ on lower jaw has glowing bacteria living inside that produce light.

Crown squirrelfish
Sargocentron diadema
Adult squirrelfish live around tropical coral reefs, but their larvae float on currents far out to sea.

Guppy
Poecilia reticulata
The guppy is one of the few spiny-rays that gives birth to live young.

Splitfin flashlightfish
Anomalops katoptron

Velvet whalefish
Barbourisia rufa

FLASHING ON AND OFF

Flashlightfish have light organs beneath their eyes filled with glowing bacteria. Special second eyelids cover the organs to hide these lights from predators.

Light organ

Light organ hidden by second eyelid

EXPOSED

HIDDEN

Spiny-rayed fish

The perchlike order of spiny-rayed fish includes snappers, drums, and groupers, which feed millions of people worldwide. Adults live in schools in coastal waters or around reefs. Many larvae travel on ocean currents, eating plankton. Cichlids, such as angelfish, are a family of perchlike fish that lives mainly in fresh water. Their elaborate courtship displays involve body and fin movements. The sexes of many cichlids are distinguished by different colors and patterns. Another perchlike family, damselfish, also show complex courtship behavior. Some males rise and fall rapidly in the water to attract females. Seahorses belong to a separate order. They have remarkable breeding habits. The female lays her eggs into a pouch on the male's belly, where he incubates them. When the young are mature, he releases them from the pouch one at a time.

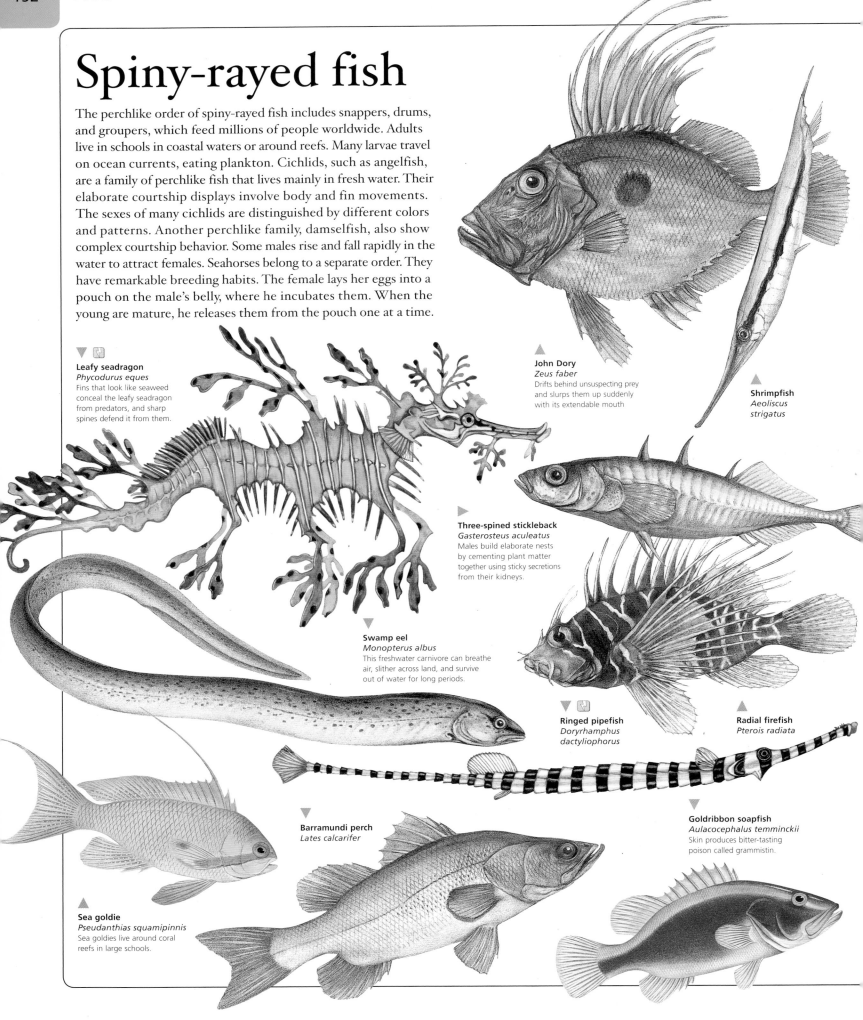

Leafy seadragon
Phycodurus eques
Fins that look like seaweed conceal the leafy seadragon from predators, and sharp spines defend it from them.

John Dory
Zeus faber
Drifts behind unsuspecting prey and slurps them up suddenly with its extendable mouth

Shrimpfish
Aeoliscus strigatus

Three-spined stickleback
Gasterosteus aculeatus
Males build elaborate nests by cementing plant matter together using sticky secretions from their kidneys.

Swamp eel
Monopterus albus
This freshwater carnivore can breathe air, slither across land, and survive out of water for long periods.

Ringed pipefish
Doryrhamphus dactyliophorus

Radial firefish
Pterois radiata

Barramundi perch
Lates calcarifer

Goldribbon soapfish
Aulacocephalus temminckii
Skin produces bitter-tasting poison called grammistin.

Sea goldie
Pseudanthias squamipinnis
Sea goldies live around coral reefs in large schools.

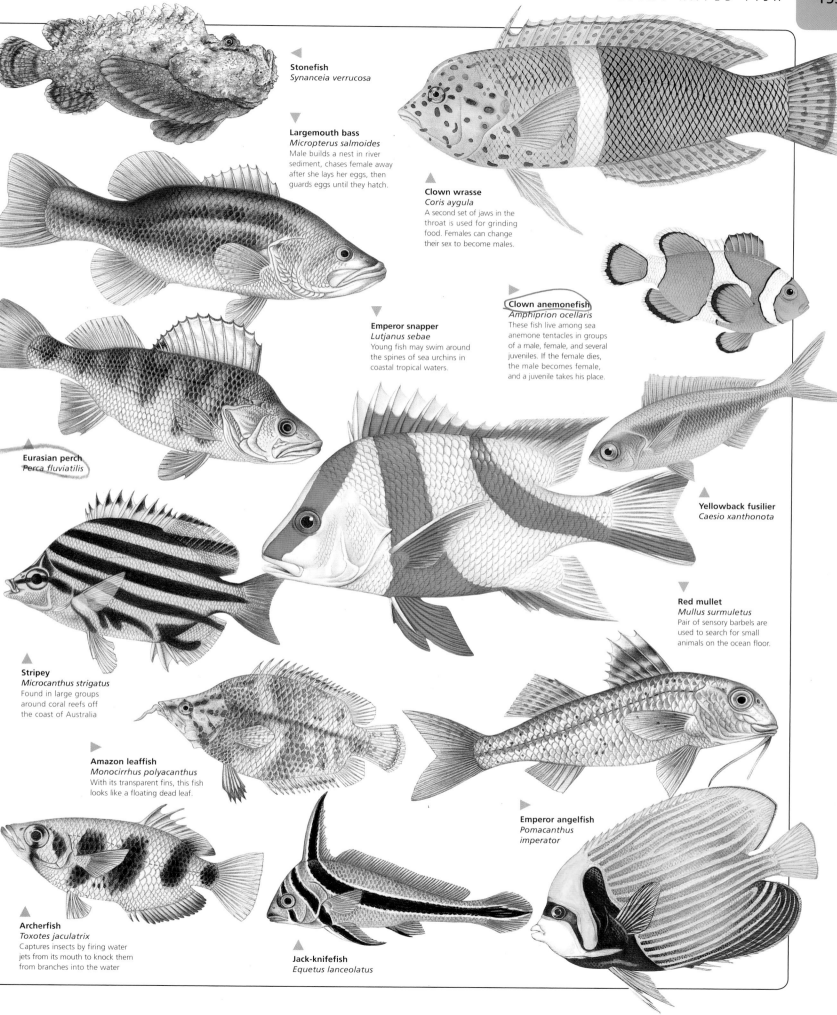

Stonefish
Synanceia verrucosa

Largemouth bass
Micropterus salmoides
Male builds a nest in river
sediment, chases female away
after she lays her eggs, then
guards eggs until they hatch.

Clown wrasse
Coris aygula
A second set of jaws in the
throat is used for grinding
food. Females can change
their sex to become males.

Clown anemonefish
Amphiprion ocellaris
These fish live among sea
anemone tentacles in groups
of a male, female, and several
juveniles. If the female dies,
the male becomes female,
and a juvenile takes his place.

Emperor snapper
Lutjanus sebae
Young fish may swim around
the spines of sea urchins in
coastal tropical waters.

Eurasian perch
Perca fluviatilis

Yellowback fusilier
Caesio xanthonota

Red mullet
Mullus surmuletus
Pair of sensory barbels are
used to search for small
animals on the ocean floor.

Stripey
Microcanthus strigatus
Found in large groups
around coral reefs off
the coast of Australia

Amazon leaffish
Monocirrhus polyacanthus
With its transparent fins, this fish
looks like a floating dead leaf.

Emperor angelfish
*Pomacanthus
imperator*

Archerfish
Toxotes jaculatrix
Captures insects by firing water
jets from its mouth to knock them
from branches into the water

Jack-knifefish
Equetus lanceolatus

Spiny-rayed fish

Spiny-rayed fish have adapted to many different habitats and ways of life. Tuna and their relatives, such as mackerel and billfish, are agile predators of the open water. Their streamlined bodies are perfectly designed for speed; many are among the fastest swimming animals in the oceans. Flatfish, such as flounders and soles, have bodies that are compressed sideways so they seem to disappear into the ocean floor. They wait there for prey to come to them. Flatfish are the chameleons of the fish world; some species can modify the color of their skin to match their surroundings perfectly. Gobies, such as mudskippers, are shaped like lizards and live among sediment on the ocean floor. Most gobies are tiny, and many live in cooperative relationships with other animals, such as corals, mollusks, and crustaceans.

CONSERVATION WATCH

Of the 13,262 species of spiny-rayed fish, 683 appear on the IUCN Red List. Too many of the critically endangered jewfish have been taken by anglers and spear fishers. Another threat is the destruction of the mangrove habitats where the young fish live.

Ex   69
Cr   90
En   71
Vu   234
Other   219

Jewfish

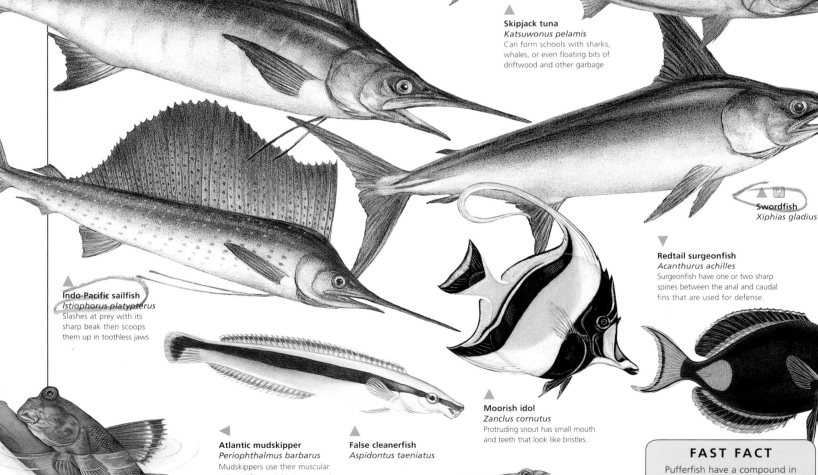

Blue marlin
Makaira nigricans
Upper jaw forms a long slender bill.

Skipjack tuna
Katsuwonus pelamis
Can form schools with sharks, whales, or even floating bits of driftwood and other garbage

Swordfish
Xiphias gladius

Indo-Pacific sailfish
Istiophorus platypterus
Slashes at prey with its sharp beak then scoops them up in toothless jaws

Redtail surgeonfish
Acanthurus achilles
Surgeonfish have one or two sharp spines between the anal and caudal fins that are used for defense.

Moorish idol
Zanclus cornutus
Protruding snout has small mouth and teeth that look like bristles.

Atlantic mudskipper
Periophthalmus barbarus
Mudskippers use their muscular tails and fins to "skip" over mud at low tide. Some can even climb trees, using a suction cup on the belly formed by the pelvic fins.

False cleanerfish
Aspidontus taeniatus

Viviparous blenny
Zoarces viviparus

FAST FACT
Pufferfish have a compound in their bodies called tetrodotoxin, which is a poison more powerful than cyanide. These fish release the poison into the water when threatened by a predator.

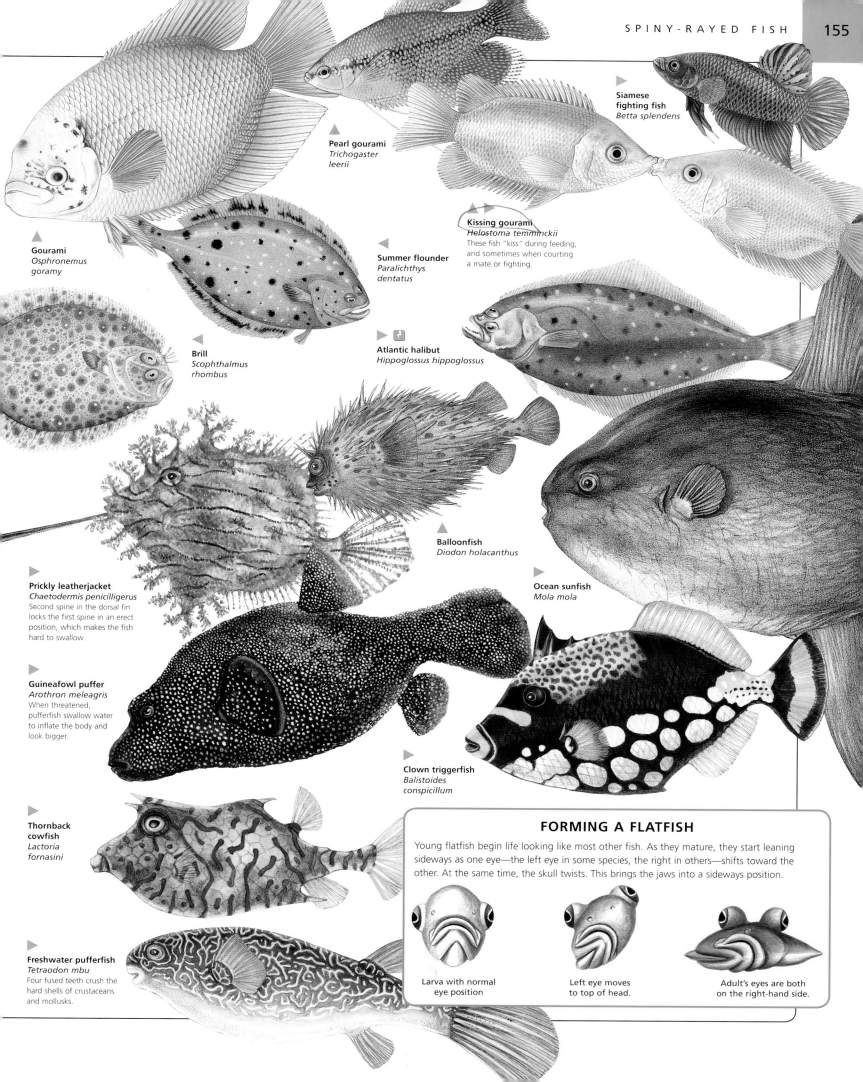

Siamese fighting fish
Betta splendens

Pearl gourami
Trichogaster leerii

Gourami
Osphronemus goramy

Kissing gourami
Helostoma temminckii
These fish "kiss" during feeding, and sometimes when courting a mate or fighting.

Summer flounder
Paralichthys dentatus

Brill
Scophthalmus rhombus

Atlantic halibut
Hippoglossus hippoglossus

Balloonfish
Diodon holacanthus

Prickly leatherjacket
Chaetodermis penicilligerus
Second spine in the dorsal fin locks the first spine in an erect position, which makes the fish hard to swallow.

Ocean sunfish
Mola mola

Guineafowl puffer
Arothron meleagris
When threatened, pufferfish swallow water to inflate the body and look bigger.

Clown triggerfish
Balistoides conspicillum

Thornback cowfish
Lactoria fornasini

FORMING A FLATFISH

Young flatfish begin life looking like most other fish. As they mature, they start leaning sideways as one eye—the left eye in some species, the right in others—shifts toward the other. At the same time, the skull twists. This brings the jaws into a sideways position.

Larva with normal eye position

Left eye moves to top of head.

Adult's eyes are both on the right-hand side.

Freshwater pufferfish
Tetraodon mbu
Four fused teeth crush the hard shells of crustaceans and mollusks.

The purple jellyfish can grow as wide as 1½ feet (45 cm). It provides a temporary home to fish and young crabs as it floats on the ocean's currents.

KINDS OF INVERTEBRATES

There are at least 1.3 million known species of invertebrates. Most are small, but a few can be enormous. The giant squid can grow as large as a whale. Invertebrates are divided into more than 30 groups, known as phyla. All lack vertebrae, or backbones, but have few other common features. The largest phylum, arthropods, contains insects, spiders, and crustaceans.

BEETLE
Insect

EARTHWORM
Segmented worm

SPIDER
Arachnid

SNAIL
Mollusk

SHRIMP
Crustacean

ANEMONE
Cnidarian

SPONGE
Poriferan

SEA URCHIN
Echinoderm

This brightly colored nudibranch, or sea slug, belongs to the mollusk phylum.

Just a fraction of all known species—fewer than 50,000—are vertebrates, such as mammals, reptiles, amphibians, and fish. The rest are invertebrates, including sponges, worms, snails, spiders, and insects. The first invertebrates appeared in Earth's oceans more than 650 million years ago. This was many millions of years before the first vertebrates appeared. Today, most invertebrates still live in the oceans, but they can be found in almost every habitat worldwide. Invertebrates differ from vertebrates in that they have no backbone. In fact, they have no bones at all. Invertebrate bodies are usually supported by some sort of skeleton. Some species have a hard casing called an exoskeleton on the outside of their bodies, with the soft tissues contained inside. Others have hard materials scattered through their bodies to provide support. Invertebrates have two basic body plans. Jellyfish and sea anemones have a circular body plan with a mouth at the center. This is known as radial symmetry. Others, such as worms and insects, have bilateral symmetry, meaning they have a distinct head and identical left and right sides. Young invertebrates often look very different from their parents and must go through a change called a metamorphosis to reach their adult form. This may be a simple, gradual change or a complete transformation. Many invertebrates, from prawns and lobsters to honeybees, provide humans with food. Some species can be a source of lifesaving medicines, whereas others are pests or parasites.

Azure snout weevils, like most insects, reproduce through internal fertilization.

INVERTEBRATE REPRODUCTION

Most invertebrates reproduce sexually. Eggs are fertilized inside the female by sperm from the male. The female usually lays huge numbers of fertilized eggs. Some invertebrates develop from unfertilized eggs. Others reproduce by "budding": breaking off a piece of their own bodies to create copies of themselves. Eggs and young are generally left to develop unprotected.

SHALL WE DANCE?
Jumping spiders perform a courtship "dance" before mating. Males begin the dance by waving their pedipalps.

SHAKY START
If a female responds, the dance continues with limb shaking and tapping before mating occurs.

7 CLASSES • 27 ORDERS • 127 FAMILIES • >11,000 SPECIES

Sponges and Squirts

People once thought that sponges were plants, not animals. Sponges have a simple structure. They have no tissues or organs, such as a stomach or heart. Instead, different cells are specialized for functions like collecting or digesting food. Sponges are found mostly in the oceans. They range in shape from bushes, vases, barrels, and balls to shapeless masses. Sea squirts are known as tunicates. Most adults live attached to the seafloor and are simple baglike creatures that filter food particles from the water. Sea squirts are linked to vertebrates; this can best be seen in sea squirt larvae. Shaped like tadpoles, they have a flexible rod in their backs called a notochord. Vertebrate embryos share this feature, but their notochords are replaced with backbones as they become adults.

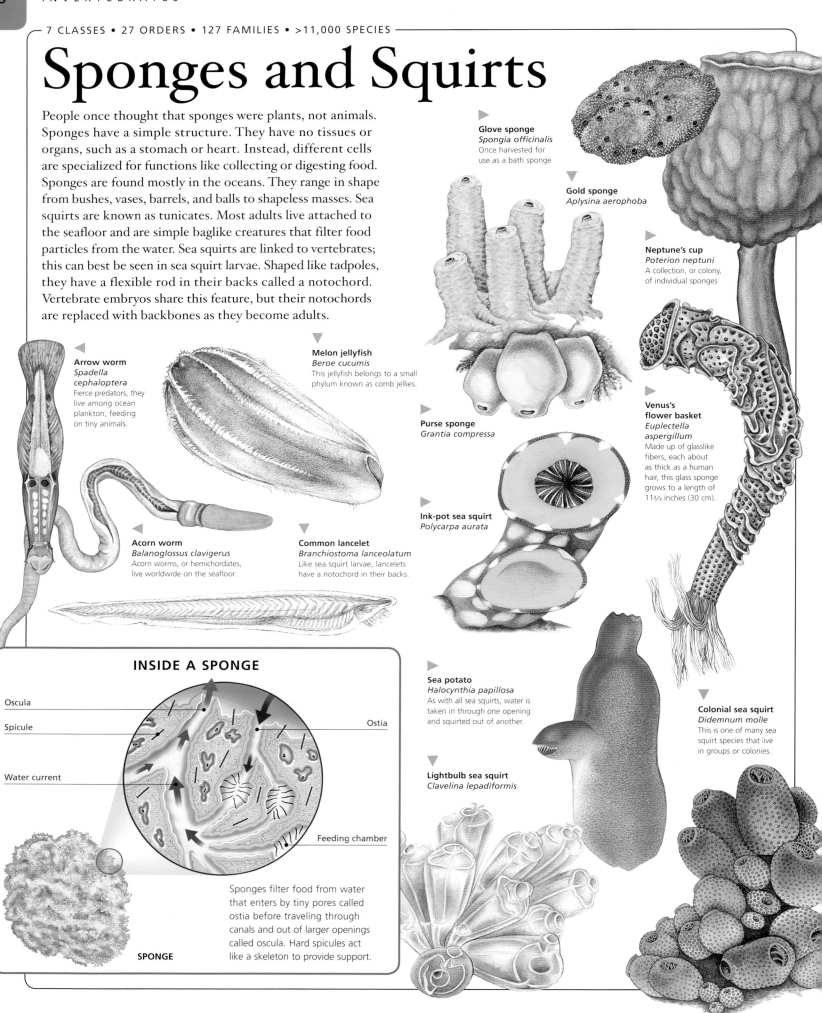

Glove sponge
Spongia officinalis
Once harvested for use as a bath sponge

Gold sponge
Aplysina aerophoba

Neptune's cup
Poterion neptuni
A collection, or colony, of individual sponges

Arrow worm
Spadella cephaloptera
Fierce predators, they live among ocean plankton, feeding on tiny animals.

Melon jellyfish
Beroe cucumis
This jellyfish belongs to a small phylum known as comb jellies.

Acorn worm
Balanoglossus clavigerus
Acorn worms, or hemichordates, live worldwide on the seafloor.

Common lancelet
Branchiostoma lanceolatum
Like sea squirt larvae, lancelets have a notochord in their backs.

Purse sponge
Grantia compressa

Ink-pot sea squirt
Polycarpa aurata

Venus's flower basket
Euplectella aspergillum
Made up of glasslike fibers, each about as thick as a human hair, this glass sponge grows to a length of 11⅔ inches (30 cm).

Sea potato
Halocynthia papillosa
As with all sea squirts, water is taken in through one opening and squirted out of another.

Colonial sea squirt
Didemnum molle
This is one of many sea squirt species that live in groups or colonies.

Lightbulb sea squirt
Clavelina lepadiformis

INSIDE A SPONGE

Oscula

Spicule

Water current

Ostia

Feeding chamber

SPONGE

Sponges filter food from water that enters by tiny pores called ostia before traveling through canals and out of larger openings called oscula. Hard spicules act like a skeleton to provide support.

10 CLASSES • 76 ORDERS • 675 FAMILIES • >45,000 SPECIES

Worms

There are three main kinds of worms: flatworms, roundworms, and segmented worms. Flatworms can be as small as microscopic species found in water or as large as 100-foot (30-m) tapeworms living as parasites inside humans. Because they are flat and thin, gases such as carbon dioxide and oxygen pass through their skin, so they do not need organs for breathing. Roundworms have long, slender bodies. Most are microscopic, so it is hard to imagine they are some of the most abundant animals. Many live in water or soil; others are parasites in plants or animals. Segmented worms look different from other worms. Their long bodies are made of ringlike sections called segments. Each has its own organs for breathing, moving, and getting rid of waste. Other body parts, such as the nervous and digestive systems, are shared.

CONSERVATION WATCH

Of the more than 45,000 species of flatworms, roundworms, and segmented worms, just 11 appear on the IUCN Red List. The medicinal leech is near threatened in its natural habitat, mainly because too many have been collected in past centuries for medical use.

Ex 🕆 2
Cr 2
En 0
Vu 4
Other 3

Medicinal leech

Intestinal roundworm
Ascaris lumbricoides

Shovel-headed garden worm
Bipalium kewense
This flatworm has spread throughout the world in soil and on plants, from its usual habitat in Southeast Asia's rain forests.

Ragworm
Nereis diversicolor

Human whipworm
Trichuris trichiura
This roundworm is found living in the intestines of about 400 million people worldwide. Its eggs are spread in human feces.

Caenorhabditis elegans
Normally found living in soil, it grows to a length of just ⅟₂₅ inch (1 mm).

Polystoma integerrimum

Medicinal leech
Hirudo medicinalis
This segmented worm sucks the blood of warm-blooded animals; it has been used extensively in medicine.

Palolo worm
Eunice viridis
Lives in burrows near coral reefs; once a year rear portions break off, rise to the surface, and shed sperm and eggs.

Night crawler
Lumbricus terrestris
These earthworms loosen and fertilize the soil where they live.

Water bear
Macrobiotus hufelandi

Goblet worm
Loxosoma harmeri
This solitary species uses its mucus-covered tentacles to trap food.

MINOR GROUPS

Minor invertebrate phyla have small numbers of species or are found in unusual habitats. Some, such as goblet worms, velvet worms, and the spiny-crown worm, are called "worms" but are not really worms. Other small groups include gastrotrichs, rotifers, and water bears.

Velvet worm
Peripatopsis capensis
Velvet worms live in leaf litter, soil, and under rocks; they capture insects and other prey by squirting sticky threads from slime glands.

Rotifer
Philodina roseola

Spiny-crown worm
Echinoderes sp.

Gastrotrich
Chaetonotus maximus
There are about 430 species of gastrotrich. These are microscopic animals that can be found in lakes, ponds, and coastal sands.

4 CLASSES • 27 ORDERS • 236 FAMILIES • >9,000 SPECIES

Corals and Jellyfish

Corals and jellyfish are known as cnidarians. This phylum also includes sea anemones and hydras. Most cnidarians live in the seas and oceans. All eat other animals and use stinging cells to capture their prey as well as to deter predators. Cnidarians occur in two forms. Some, such as sea anemones and corals, are polyps. Polyps are shaped like cylinders. They have a mouth surrounded by tentacles at one end of their bodies; they attach themselves to a surface with the other end. Other cnidarians, such as jellyfish, are medusae. They have an umbrella shape and swim or float freely in the water with their mouths and tentacles hanging downward. Although there are cnidarians that exist only as a medusa or as a polyp, many species alternate between the two forms during their life cycles.

CONSERVATION WATCH

Small changes in the surrounding water caused by environmental stresses like global warming can weaken coral reefs. This makes them vulnerable to predators, such as the crown-of-thorns starfish.

Ex	✚	0
Cr		0
En		0
Vu		2
Other		1

Crown-of-thorns starfish

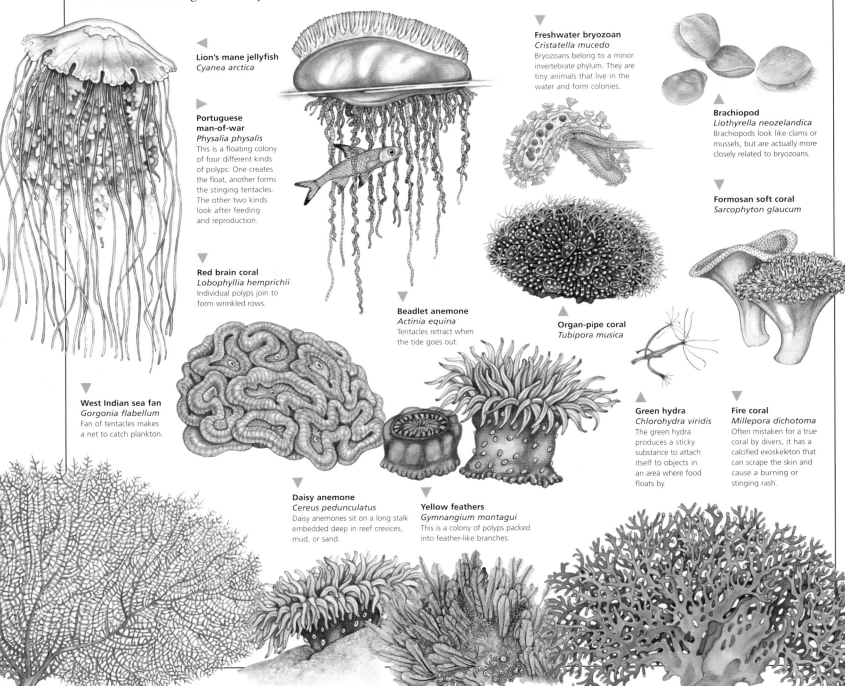

Lion's mane jellyfish
Cyanea arctica

Portuguese man-of-war
Physalia physalis
This is a floating colony of four different kinds of polyps: One creates the float, another forms the stinging tentacles. The other two kinds look after feeding and reproduction.

Red brain coral
Lobophyllia hemprichii
Individual polyps join to form wrinkled rows.

West Indian sea fan
Gorgonia flabellum
Fan of tentacles makes a net to catch plankton.

Beadlet anemone
Actinia equina
Tentacles retract when the tide goes out.

Daisy anemone
Cereus pedunculatus
Daisy anemones sit on a long stalk embedded deep in reef crevices, mud, or sand.

Yellow feathers
Gymnangium montagui
This is a colony of polyps packed into feather-like branches.

Freshwater bryozoan
Cristatella mucedo
Bryozoans belong to a minor invertebrate phylum. They are tiny animals that live in the water and form colonies.

Brachiopod
Liothyrella neozelandica
Brachiopods look like clams or mussels, but are actually more closely related to bryozoans.

Formosan soft coral
Sarcophyton glaucum

Organ-pipe coral
Tubipora musica

Green hydra
Chlorohydra viridis
The green hydra produces a sticky substance to attach itself to objects in an area where food floats by.

Fire coral
Millepora dichotoma
Often mistaken for a true coral by divers, it has a calcified exoskeleton that can scrape the skin and cause a burning or stinging rash.

7 CLASSES • 20 ORDERS • 185 FAMILIES • 75,000 SPECIES

Mollusks

Most mollusks are found in the oceans, but many live in fresh water and in moist conditions on land. Mollusk bodies have a well-defined head region, a muscular foot that may produce mucus, and an area for organs, such as the stomach. Many have a hard shell of calcium carbonate made by a special skin layer called the mantle, which covers the body. Mollusks mostly have separate sexes. Some release eggs and sperm into the sea, while others reproduce internally. Squid, octopuses, nautiluses, and cuttlefish form a class called cephalopods. This means "head foot." Their foot lies close to the head and is modified to form arms and tentacles. Nautiluses have a large shell; squid and cuttlefish have a shrunken shell located inside the body; octopuses have lost their shell entirely. They are intelligent and show complex behavior.

Long-finned squid
Loligo vulgaris
Squid have eight arms and two long tentacles, all with suckers.

Flying squid
Ommastrephes sagittatus

Giant squid
Architeuthis dux
One of the largest invertebrates ever to have lived, the giant squid may reach a weight of almost a ton (900 kg).

Lesser cuttlefish (dwarf bobtail)
Sepiola rondeleti

Common cuttlefish
Sepia officinalis

Deep-sea vampire squid
Vampyroteuthis infernalis

Common octopus
Octopus vulgaris
Can change color to match its surroundings

Common nautilus
Nautilus pompilius
Much of the shell is filled with gas, and the nautilus controls its buoyancy by adding or removing liquid.

Blue-ringed octopus
Hapalochlaena sp.
Most cephalopods move by jet propulsion: They squirt water out of their bodies to swim forward or backward.

Musky octopus
Eledone moschata
Like most octopuses, it crawls over rocks using its eight arms.

Paper nautilus
Argonauta argo
The paper nautilus is really an octopus. The female produces a fragile shell to protect her eggs.

Mollusks

There are seven classes of mollusks, including bivalves, chitons, gastropods, and tusk shells. Bivalves, such as oysters, clams, and mussels, have a two-part hinged shell and a tiny head. Most bivalves burrow into sediment. Others attach themselves to a firm surface. Some bivalves are parasites that live in other aquatic animals. Gastropods are the largest mollusk group and include snails, slugs, and limpets. Gastropod means "belly foot." Most species have a spiral shell, although some have no shell. Chitons are oval in shape, with a row of eight flexible, interlocking plates on the upper shell. They can curl tightly into a ball when they are threatened. Tusk shells have a long, tubelike shell that is open at both ends. The larger end contains the foot, head, and tentacles; the smaller end admits water to breathe and removes waste.

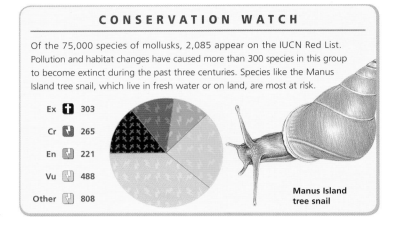

CONSERVATION WATCH

Of the 75,000 species of mollusks, 2,085 appear on the IUCN Red List. Pollution and habitat changes have caused more than 300 species in this group to become extinct during the past three centuries. Species like the Manus Island tree snail, which live in fresh water or on land, are most at risk.

Ex	✝	303
Cr	⚐	265
En	⚐	221
Vu	⚐	488
Other	⚐	808

Manus Island tree snail

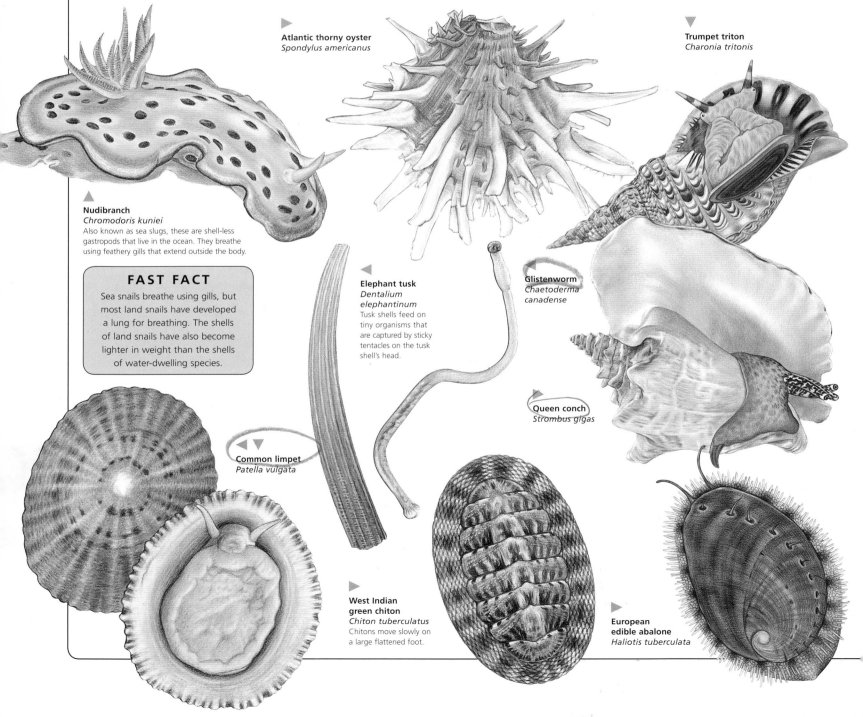

Atlantic thorny oyster
Spondylus americanus

Trumpet triton
Charonia tritonis

Nudibranch
Chromodoris kuniei
Also known as sea slugs, these are shell-less gastropods that live in the ocean. They breathe using feathery gills that extend outside the body.

FAST FACT

Sea snails breathe using gills, but most land snails have developed a lung for breathing. The shells of land snails have also become lighter in weight than the shells of water-dwelling species.

Elephant tusk
Dentalium elephantinum
Tusk shells feed on tiny organisms that are captured by sticky tentacles on the tusk shell's head.

Glistenworm
Chaetoderma canadense

Queen conch
Strombus gigas

Common limpet
Patella vulgata

West Indian green chiton
Chiton tuberculatus
Chitons move slowly on a large flattened foot.

European edible abalone
Haliotis tuberculata

Freshwater pearl mussel
Margaritana margaritifera

Spiny cockle
Acanthocardia aculeata
Like most bivalves, it burrows
into shallow sand or mud.

Nut shell
Nucula nucleus

Pen shell
Pinna nobilis

Flat oyster
Ostrea edulis

Giant tiger snail
Achatina achatina
This land snail can grow as
long as 12 inches (31 cm);
it is one of the largest snails.

Chocolate arion
Arion rufus

Escargot
Helix pomatia
The escargot has been eaten by
humans since prehistoric times.

Gray garden slug
Deroceras reticulatus

Blue sea slug
Glaucus atlanticus
Feeds on the Portuguese
man-of-war, eating its
poisonous stinging cells
to use as its own defense

Common egg cowrie
Ovula ovum

GIANT CLAM

Giant clams are the largest bivalves,
reaching 700 pounds (320 kg) in
weight. They live embedded in the
seafloor around tropical coral reefs
in the Indian and Pacific Oceans.
Giant clams filter feed on plankton,
but most of their nourishment comes
from algae living in their soft tissues.
The algae are protected by living
in the clams. Adult clams cannot
move once they have settled. They
reproduce by expelling clouds of
sperm and eggs, which mix with
those of nearby clams. Larvae then
develop from the fertilized eggs
and live floating in ocean currents
until they settle and become adults.

22 CLASSES • 110 ORDERS • 2,120 FAMILIES • >1.1 MILLION SPECIES

Arthropods

Some spiders, such as this pink-toed tarantula, breathe using book lungs. Book lungs work like gills and are made up of stacked leaves of tissue.

Three-quarters of all animal species are arthropods, which means "jointed feet." All have appendages, such as limbs or antennae, with joints. Arthropods have an exoskeleton, a tough but flexible covering that encloses their soft body parts. Their bodies are divided into segments. In most cases, these segments are arranged into distinct body regions called tagma. For many, these consist of the head, abdomen, and an area in between called the thorax. The first arthropods appeared in the oceans, but they are now found in almost every habitat on Earth.

KINDS OF ARTHROPODS

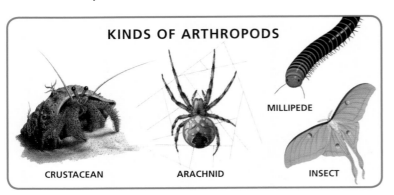

CRUSTACEAN

ARACHNID

MILLIPEDE

INSECT

ARTHROPOD ANATOMY

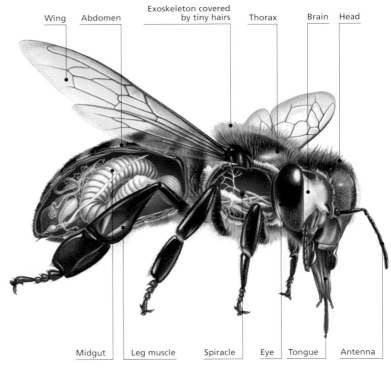

Wing Abdomen Exoskeleton covered by tiny hairs Thorax Brain Head

Midgut Leg muscle Spiracle Eye Tongue Antenna

Arachnids

Spiders, scorpions, daddy longlegs, mites, and ticks are arachnids. All but a small number live on land, and most are predators that eat other invertebrates. Arachnids are unable to swallow solid food. They liquefy their prey by squirting it with digestive juices, then they suck it up into their mouths. Arachnids have a two-part body: the abdomen and a single section composed of the head and thorax, called the cephalothorax. They have eight jointed limbs and a number of simple eyes that only detect variations in light. Spiders are the best known arachnids. They are noted for having silk glands. These produce webs and protective egg cases. Most spiders are venomous and inject poison into prey or enemies through fanglike mouthparts called chelicerae. The venom of only 30 out of 40,000 species can cause illness in humans.

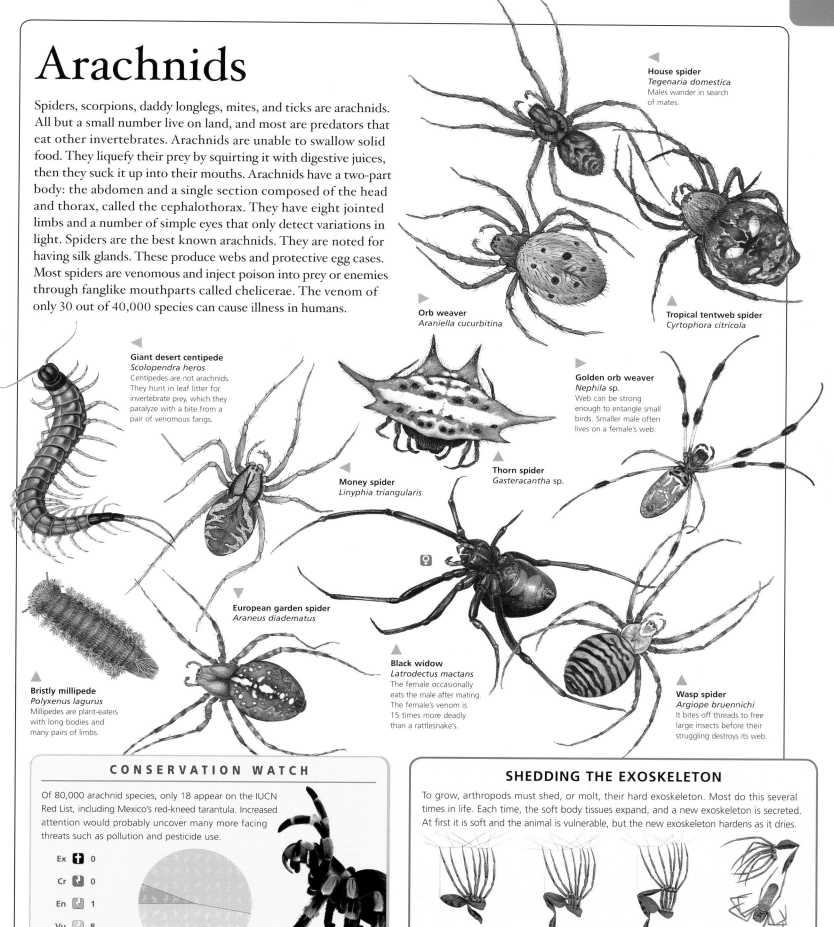

House spider
Tegenaria domestica
Males wander in search of mates.

Orb weaver
Araniella cucurbitina

Tropical tentweb spider
Cyrtophora citricola

Giant desert centipede
Scolopendra heros
Centipedes are not arachnids. They hunt in leaf litter for invertebrate prey, which they paralyze with a bite from a pair of venomous fangs.

Golden orb weaver
Nephila sp.
Web can be strong enough to entangle small birds. Smaller male often lives on a female's web.

Money spider
Linyphia triangularis

Thorn spider
Gasteracantha sp.

European garden spider
Araneus diadematus

Bristly millipede
Polyxenus lagurus
Millipedes are plant-eaters with long bodies and many pairs of limbs.

Black widow
Latrodectus mactans
The female occasionally eats the male after mating. The female's venom is 15 times more deadly than a rattlesnake's.

Wasp spider
Argiope bruennichi
It bites off threads to free large insects before their struggling destroys its web.

CONSERVATION WATCH

Of 80,000 arachnid species, only 18 appear on the IUCN Red List, including Mexico's red-kneed tarantula. Increased attention would probably uncover many more facing threats such as pollution and pesticide use.

Ex	⬥	0
Cr	⬥	0
En	⬥	1
Vu	⬥	8
Other	⬥	8

Red-kneed tarantula

SHEDDING THE EXOSKELETON

To grow, arthropods must shed, or molt, their hard exoskeleton. Most do this several times in life. Each time, the soft body tissues expand, and a new exoskeleton is secreted. At first it is soft and the animal is vulnerable, but the new exoskeleton hardens as it dries.

Exoskeleton splits from head.

Exoskeleton tears apart.

Fragile limbs are drawn out.

New exoskeleton needs time to dry.

Arachnids

Arachnids have two pairs of appendages near the mouth. The first pair are the chelicerae, which work like fangs. The second pair are pedipalps, sometimes called pincers. These may be used like antennae to sense the surrounding environment. The pedipalps of scorpions and some other arachnids have developed into large claws. Scorpions also have a stinger at the tip of their tails. Most species hide in crevices or burrows during the day and hunt at night. Although scorpions and spiders are the best known arachnids, the most abundant and varied are the mites and ticks. They occur in almost every habitat, from polar caps to deserts, and from hot springs to ocean depths. Some are parasites, feeding on the fluids of other animals or plants. Many spread bacteria that cause disease in other living things.

Zebra jumping spider
Salticus scenicus
Stalks prey, then leaps as far as 50 times its own body length to capture it

Malaysian trapdoor spider
Liphistius malayanus
This spider is a protected species; it has not changed in four million years.

Hooded tick spider
Ricinoides sjoestedti
Its hood can be lowered over its mouth.

Whip-spider
Phrynichus sp.
Whip-spiders do not have venomous fangs, but many capture prey using large pedipalps known as whips.

Fat-tailed scorpion
Androctonus australis
Found throughout Africa and Asia, this is one of the most deadly scorpions. Its sting kills several people every year.

Short-tailed whip-scorpion
Schizomus crassicaudatus

Book scorpion
Chelifer cancroides
Does not have a tail stinger like a true scorpion; it belongs to a group that has venom glands in their pedipalps.

Whip-scorpion
Thelyphonus caudatus
Female whip-scorpions lay eggs into a sac on their bodies and carry them until they hatch.

SCORPION COURTSHIP

Males and females of some scorpion species grasp each other using their pedipalps. They then "dance" around each other to find a level piece of ground where they can mate.

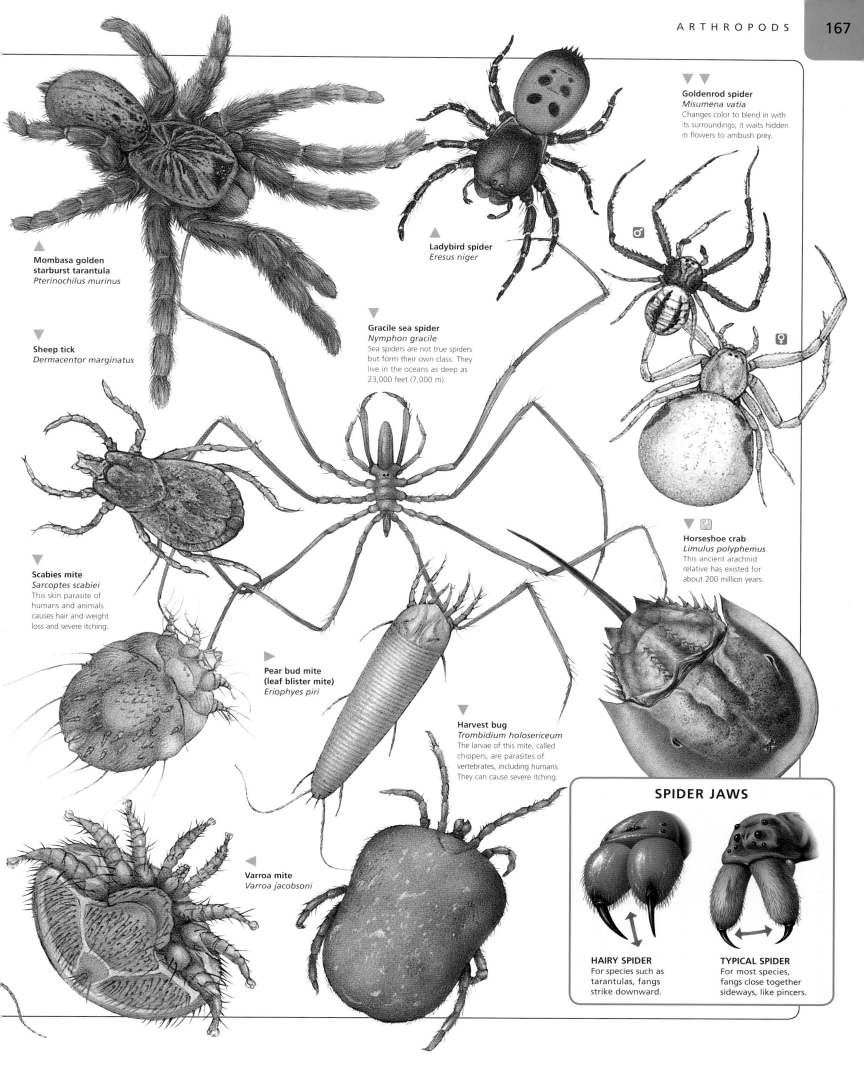

Mombasa golden starburst tarantula
Pterinochilus murinus

Sheep tick
Dermacentor marginatus

Ladybird spider
Eresus niger

Goldenrod spider
Misumena vatia
Changes color to blend in with its surroundings; it waits hidden in flowers to ambush prey.

Gracile sea spider
Nymphon gracile
Sea spiders are not true spiders but form their own class. They live in the oceans as deep as 23,000 feet (7,000 m).

Scabies mite
Sarcoptes scabiei
This skin parasite of humans and animals causes hair and weight loss and severe itching.

Pear bud mite (leaf blister mite)
Eriophyes piri

Horseshoe crab
Limulus polyphemus
This ancient arachnid relative has existed for about 200 million years.

Harvest bug
Trombidium holosericeum
The larvae of this mite, called chippers, are parasites of vertebrates, including humans. They can cause severe itching.

Varroa mite
Varroa jacobsoni

SPIDER JAWS

HAIRY SPIDER
For species such as tarantulas, fangs strike downward.

TYPICAL SPIDER
For most species, fangs close together sideways, like pincers.

Crabs and crayfish

Crabs and crayfish are crustaceans. This group ranges from waterfleas less than 1/100 inch (0.25 mm) in length to giant spider crabs with limbs 12 feet (3.7 m) long. A few crustacean species have adapted to life on land, but most live in salt or fresh water. Their bodies are similar to those of other arthropods, with a segmented body, jointed limbs, and a hard exoskeleton that must be shed to allow the body to grow. The head usually has two pairs of antennae; well-developed eyes, often on stalks; and three pairs of biting mouthparts. The front legs of many species have become claws that are used to collect food, fight off predators, or communicate with each other. Some females lay their eggs in water and leave them to develop on their own. Many, however, keep their eggs on their bodies until they hatch.

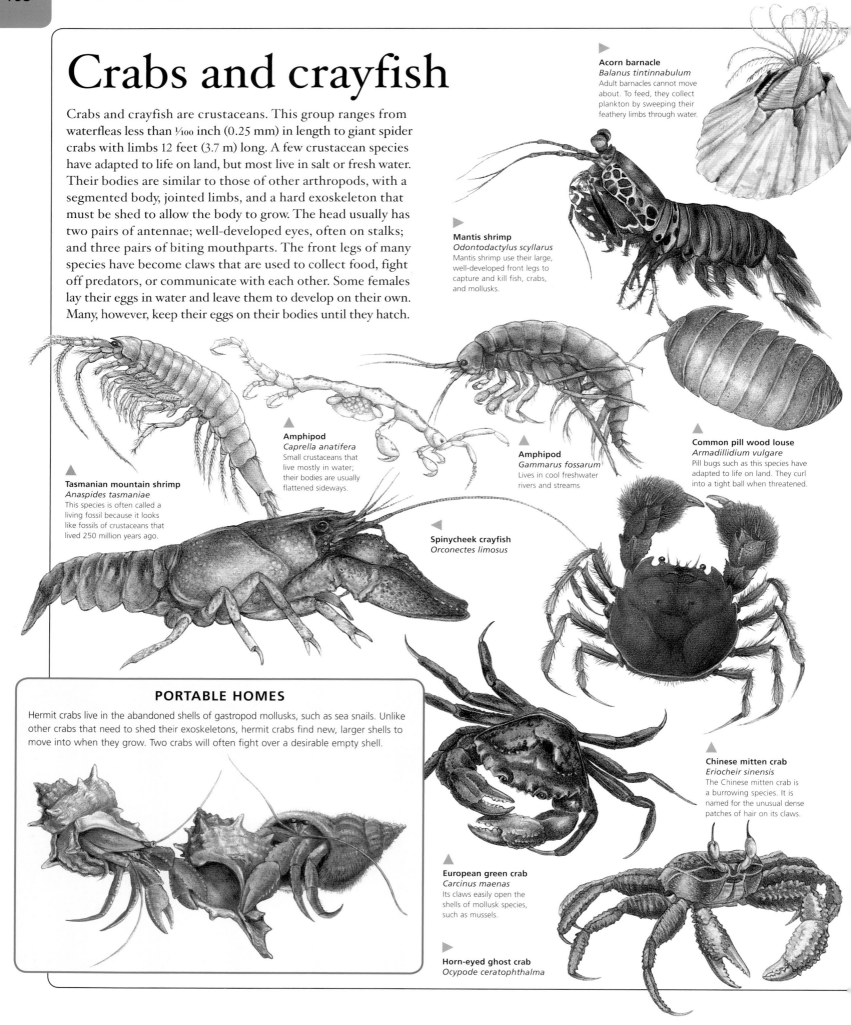

Acorn barnacle
Balanus tintinnabulum
Adult barnacles cannot move about. To feed, they collect plankton by sweeping their feathery limbs through water.

Mantis shrimp
Odontodactylus scyllarus
Mantis shrimp use their large, well-developed front legs to capture and kill fish, crabs, and mollusks.

Amphipod
Caprella anatifera
Small crustaceans that live mostly in water; their bodies are usually flattened sideways.

Amphipod
Gammarus fossarum
Lives in cool freshwater rivers and streams

Common pill wood louse
Armadillidium vulgare
Pill bugs such as this species have adapted to life on land. They curl into a tight ball when threatened.

Tasmanian mountain shrimp
Anaspides tasmaniae
This species is often called a living fossil because it looks like fossils of crustaceans that lived 250 million years ago.

Spinycheek crayfish
Orconectes limosus

Chinese mitten crab
Eriocheir sinensis
The Chinese mitten crab is a burrowing species. It is named for the unusual dense patches of hair on its claws.

PORTABLE HOMES

Hermit crabs live in the abandoned shells of gastropod mollusks, such as sea snails. Unlike other crabs that need to shed their exoskeletons, hermit crabs find new, larger shells to move into when they grow. Two crabs will often fight over a desirable empty shell.

European green crab
Carcinus maenas
Its claws easily open the shells of mollusk species, such as mussels.

Horn-eyed ghost crab
Ocypode ceratophthalma

Copepod
Cyclops strenuus
Huge numbers of copepods are found in the oceans. They are an important link in many marine food chains.

Mystarocarid
Derocheilocaris remanei
Lives among sand grains in the intertidal zone, where the ocean meets the land

Freshwater fish louse
Argulus foliaceus
Feeds on the skin or in the gills of freshwater fish; it often causes tissue damage.

Ostracod
Candona suburbana

Cleaner shrimp
Lysmata amboinensis
Feeds on parasites that it picks from the tissues of fish

Black tiger prawn
Penaeus monodon

Spiny lobster
Palinurus vulgaris
This species lacks the large claws found on true lobsters.

Tadpole shrimp
Triops cancriformis
The tadpole shrimp is one of the oldest known living animal species; fossil records show it has not changed for about 220 million years.

Giant water flea
Leptodora kindtii
Water fleas use their leaflike limbs to gather food, swim, and breathe.

Cephalocarid
Hutchinsoniella macracantha
Most cephalocarids, such as this one, are no bigger than a sesame seed.

Atlantic lobster (American lobster)
Homarus americanus
Fished commercially, this lobster is greenish when alive but turns red when cooked.

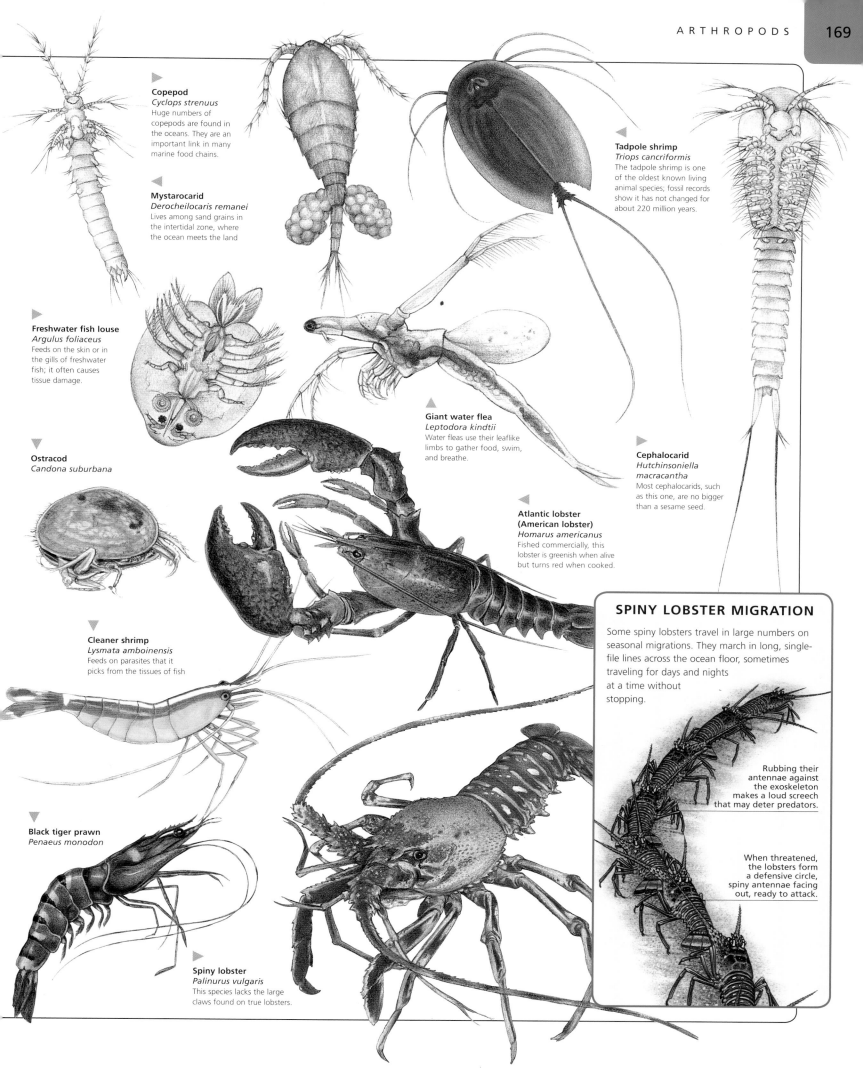

SPINY LOBSTER MIGRATION

Some spiny lobsters travel in large numbers on seasonal migrations. They march in long, single-file lines across the ocean floor, sometimes traveling for days and nights at a time without stopping.

Rubbing their antennae against the exoskeleton makes a loud screech that may deter predators.

When threatened, the lobsters form a defensive circle, spiny antennae facing out, ready to attack.

29 ORDERS • 949 FAMILIES • >1 MILLION SPECIES

Insects

Most insects, such as this two-spotted lady beetle, are less than 2 inches (5 cm) long. Their size allows them to live in an enormous variety of habitats and develop into many different forms.

In many ways, insects are the most successful animals ever to have lived. More than half of all known animal species are insects. More than a million species have been discovered, but there may be as many as 30 million. There are also many more individuals than in other kinds of animals. The success of insects is partly due to their tough, but flexible, exoskeleton. This lets them move easily, protects them, and stops them from drying out. While some insects spread disease and destroy crops, most cause no harm and play important roles in the environment. About three-quarters of all flowering plants are pollinated by insects, and many animals depend on insects for food.

KINDS OF ANTENNAE

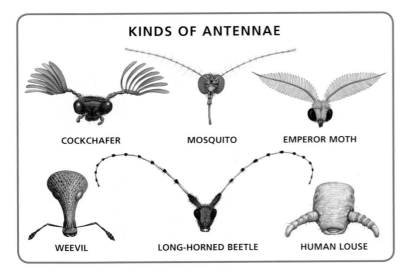

COCKCHAFER   MOSQUITO   EMPEROR MOTH

WEEVIL   LONG-HORNED BEETLE   HUMAN LOUSE

KINDS OF WINGS

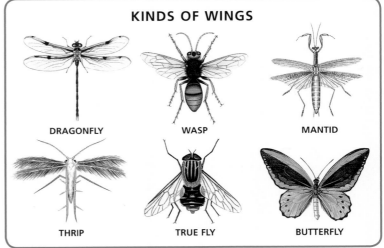

DRAGONFLY   WASP   MANTID

THRIP   TRUE FLY   BUTTERFLY

Insects

Appearing 300 million years ago, dragonflies and damselflies are among the oldest living insect orders. They have wingspans of as much as 7½ inches (19 cm) across and usually live near water. They are predators that catch other insects while flying. Mantids also prey on other insects. Some of the largest species, which are 10 inches (25 cm) in length, also catch small birds and reptiles. They sit perfectly still, waiting for prey to appear. With lightning-fast reflexes, they then pounce and grasp prey with their strong front legs. Termites and cockroaches do not hunt. Cockroaches usually eat decaying plant matter as well as bird and mammal droppings. Social termites feed on dead wood. This recycles nutrients in their natural habitats but can damage buildings in urban environments. Grasshoppers and crickets are omnivorous: They eat both plants and animals. They are not usually social, but some group together in huge swarms.

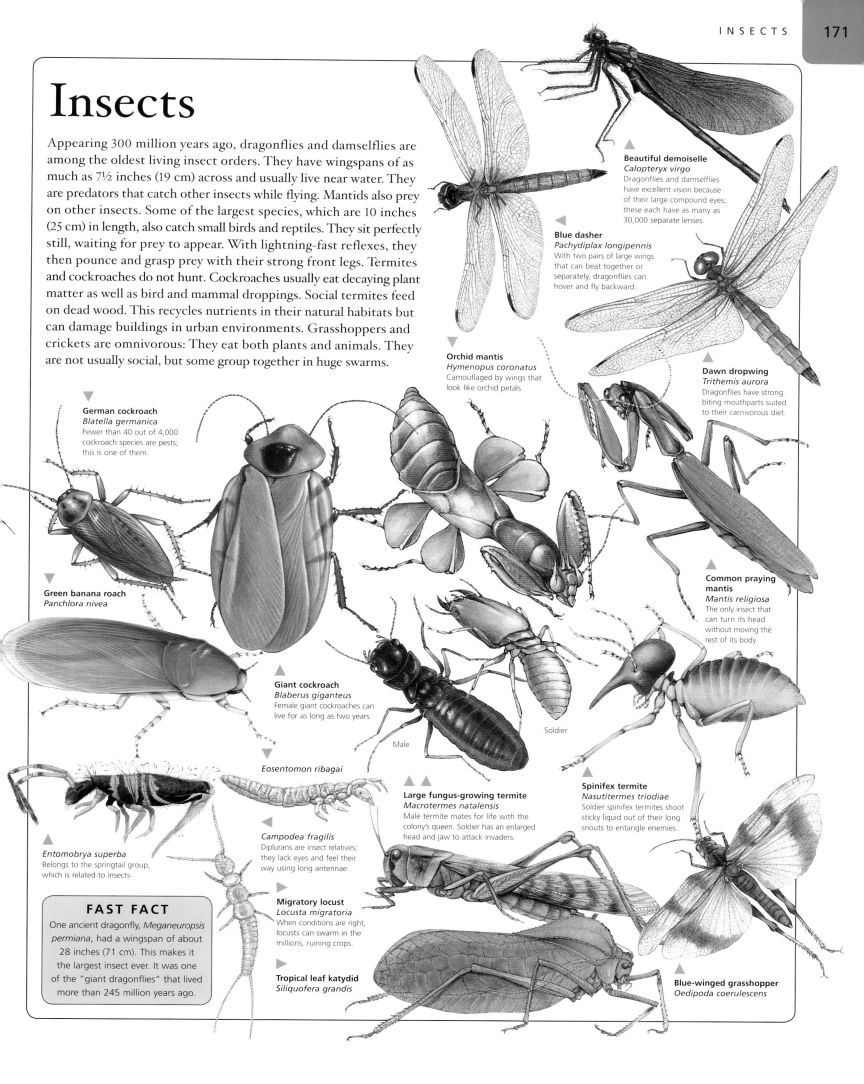

Beautiful demoiselle
Calopteryx virgo
Dragonflies and damselflies have excellent vision because of their large compound eyes; these each have as many as 30,000 separate lenses.

Blue dasher
Pachydiplax longipennis
With two pairs of large wings that can beat together or separately, dragonflies can hover and fly backward.

Orchid mantis
Hymenopus coronatus
Camouflaged by wings that look like orchid petals

Dawn dropwing
Trithemis aurora
Dragonflies have strong biting mouthparts suited to their carnivorous diet.

German cockroach
Blatella germanica
Fewer than 40 out of 4,000 cockroach species are pests; this is one of them.

Green banana roach
Panchlora nivea

Giant cockroach
Blaberus giganteus
Female giant cockroaches can live for as long as two years.

Common praying mantis
Mantis religiosa
The only insect that can turn its head without moving the rest of its body

Male

Soldier

Eosentomon ribagai

Entomobrya superba
Belongs to the springtail group, which is related to insects

Campodea fragilis
Diplurans are insect relatives; they lack eyes and feel their way using long antennae.

Large fungus-growing termite
Macrotermes natalensis
Male termite mates for life with the colony's queen. Soldier has an enlarged head and jaw to attack invaders.

Spinifex termite
Nasutitermes triodiae
Soldier spinifex termites shoot sticky liquid out of their long snouts to entangle enemies.

Migratory locust
Locusta migratoria
When conditions are right, locusts can swarm in the millions, ruining crops.

Tropical leaf katydid
Siliquofera grandis

Blue-winged grasshopper
Oedipoda coerulescens

FAST FACT

One ancient dragonfly, *Meganeuropsis permiana*, had a wingspan of about 28 inches (71 cm). This makes it the largest insect ever. It was one of the "giant dragonflies" that lived more than 245 million years ago.

Bugs

To many people, all insects are bugs. However, true bugs belong to an order of about 80,000 species called hemipterans. This includes cicadas, aphids, scale insects, and shield bugs. Many shield bugs, also known as stink bugs, have glands that produce a smelly substance when the animal is threatened. All bugs have mouthparts designed for piercing and sucking. These penetrate plant surfaces or animal skin and then inject digestive juices. This breaks down the tissues inside, so they can be sucked up as a liquid. Most bugs feed on plant sap. Others suck the blood of vertebrate animals or prey on other insects. Bugs can be found in most land habitats around the world. There are even some that have adapted to life in or on water. These include sea skaters, which are the only insects that live in the open ocean.

CONSERVATION WATCH

The IUCN has assessed fewer than 800 of all known insect species; most of these are on the Red List. Of the more than 80,000 species of bugs, 5 appear on the IUCN Red List. The unusual life cycle of periodic cicadas, which involves every adult appearing above ground at the same time, makes them vulnerable.

Ex ✝ 2
Cr 🗡 0
En 🗡 0
Vu 🗡 0
Other 🗡 3

Periodic cicada

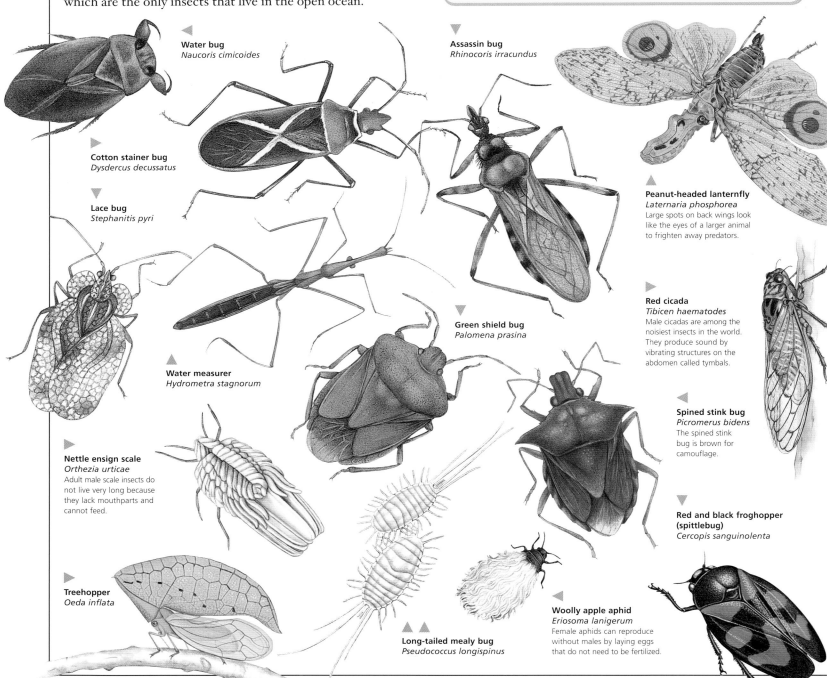

Water bug
Naucoris cimicoides

Assassin bug
Rhinocoris irracundus

Cotton stainer bug
Dysdercus decussatus

Lace bug
Stephanitis pyri

Peanut-headed lanternfly
Laternaria phosphorea
Large spots on back wings look like the eyes of a larger animal to frighten away predators.

Red cicada
Tibicen haematodes
Male cicadas are among the noisiest insects in the world. They produce sound by vibrating structures on the abdomen called tymbals.

Green shield bug
Palomena prasina

Water measurer
Hydrometra stagnorum

Nettle ensign scale
Orthezia urticae
Adult male scale insects do not live very long because they lack mouthparts and cannot feed.

Spined stink bug
Picromerus bidens
The spined stink bug is brown for camouflage.

Red and black froghopper (spittlebug)
Cercopis sanguinolenta

Treehopper
Oeda inflata

Woolly apple aphid
Eriosoma lanigerum
Female aphids can reproduce without males by laying eggs that do not need to be fertilized.

Long-tailed mealy bug
Pseudococcus longispinus

CHANGING FORMS

DRAGONFLY LIFE CYCLE

Some insects look like small versions of their parents when they hatch, but most do not. They need to go through a change called metamorphosis to become adults. For some insects, such as bugs and dragonflies, this change occurs gradually. This is called simple metamorphosis. Young dragonflies called nymphs hatch from eggs. They live underwater and do not have wings. To develop into their adult form, they molt several times. During each molt they shed their exoskeleton, growing and changing a little more each time. It can take as long as five years before they finally climb up a plant stem, molt for the last time, and emerge as fully grown adults that can fly.

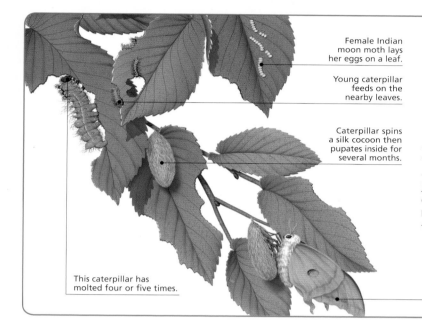

Female Indian moon moth lays her eggs on a leaf.

Young caterpillar feeds on the nearby leaves.

Caterpillar spins a silk cocoon then pupates inside for several months.

This caterpillar has molted four or five times.

A new adult moon moth hangs to stretch and dry its wings.

MOTH LIFE CYCLE

For butterflies and moths to become adults, they change completely. This is called complex metamorphosis. They hatch from eggs as soft-bodied larvae, or caterpillars. They eat and grow constantly until ready to pupate, or change into adults. During this time, their juvenile larval body parts break down and adult features grow. Finally, an adult moth emerges from the cocoon.

Female dragonfly lays her eggs in a plant below the water's surface.

Tiny nymphs hatch by chewing their way out of their egg cases.

Adult male and female dragonflies mate on plants in or near the water.

Nymphs catch and eat tadpoles and worms.

Nymph climbs out of the water for its final molt into adulthood.

Nymph swallows air to burst open its outer skeleton.

New adult dragonfly basks in the sun, extending its wings.

Beetles

About one in every four animals on Earth is a beetle. This diverse order, called coleopterans, includes glow worms and fireflies. Beetles can be found in almost every habitat, from Arctic wastelands to lush woodlands and the surface waters of lakes. Most species live in the fertile forests of the tropics. Beetles generally live on the ground, but some live in trees, in water, or underground. One of the smallest is the feather-winged beetle, which is just ¹⁄₁₀₀ inch (0.25 mm) long. The largest is the American longhorn beetle, which can grow longer than 6½ inches (17 cm). The mouthparts of beetles are adapted for biting but can be used in many different ways. Plant-eating beetles may eat roots, seeds, stems, leaves, flowers, fruit, or wood. Predatory beetles usually feed on other invertebrates.

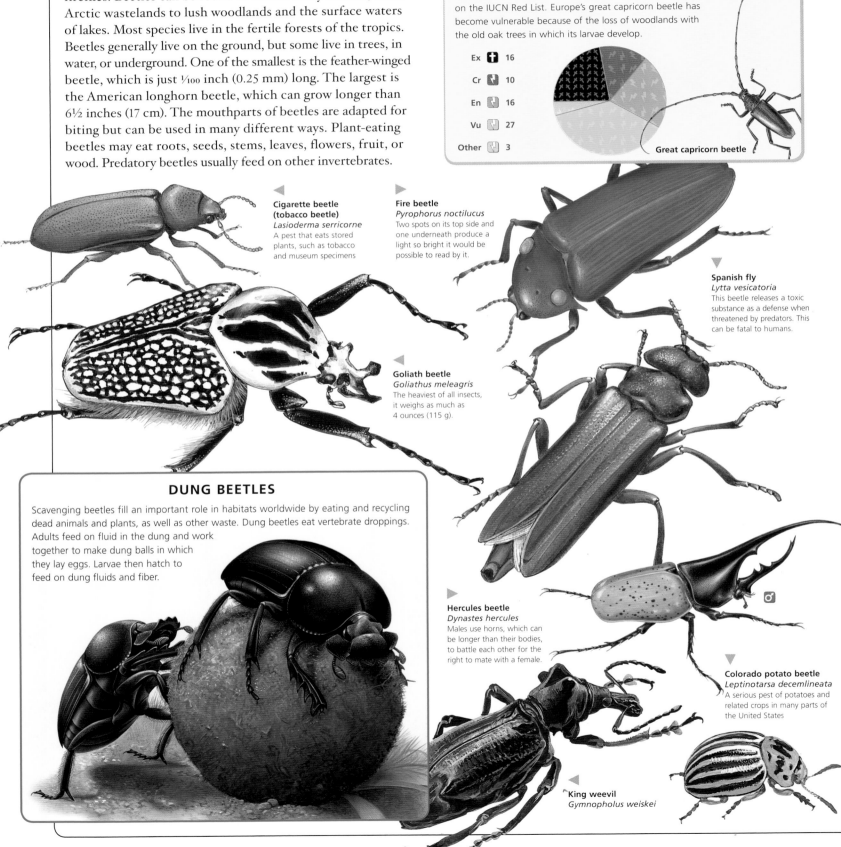

CONSERVATION WATCH

Of the more than 370,000 known beetle species, 72 appear on the IUCN Red List. Europe's great capricorn beetle has become vulnerable because of the loss of woodlands with the old oak trees in which its larvae develop.

Ex 16
Cr 10
En 16
Vu 27
Other 3

Great capricorn beetle

Cigarette beetle (tobacco beetle)
Lasioderma serricorne
A pest that eats stored plants, such as tobacco and museum specimens

Fire beetle
Pyrophorus noctilucus
Two spots on its top side and one underneath produce a light so bright it would be possible to read by it.

Spanish fly
Lytta vesicatoria
This beetle releases a toxic substance as a defense when threatened by predators. This can be fatal to humans.

Goliath beetle
Goliathus meleagris
The heaviest of all insects, it weighs as much as 4 ounces (115 g).

DUNG BEETLES

Scavenging beetles fill an important role in habitats worldwide by eating and recycling dead animals and plants, as well as other waste. Dung beetles eat vertebrate droppings. Adults feed on fluid in the dung and work together to make dung balls in which they lay eggs. Larvae then hatch to feed on dung fluids and fiber.

Hercules beetle
Dynastes hercules
Males use horns, which can be longer than their bodies, to battle each other for the right to mate with a female.

Colorado potato beetle
Leptinotarsa decemlineata
A serious pest of potatoes and related crops in many parts of the United States

King weevil
Gymnopholus weiskei

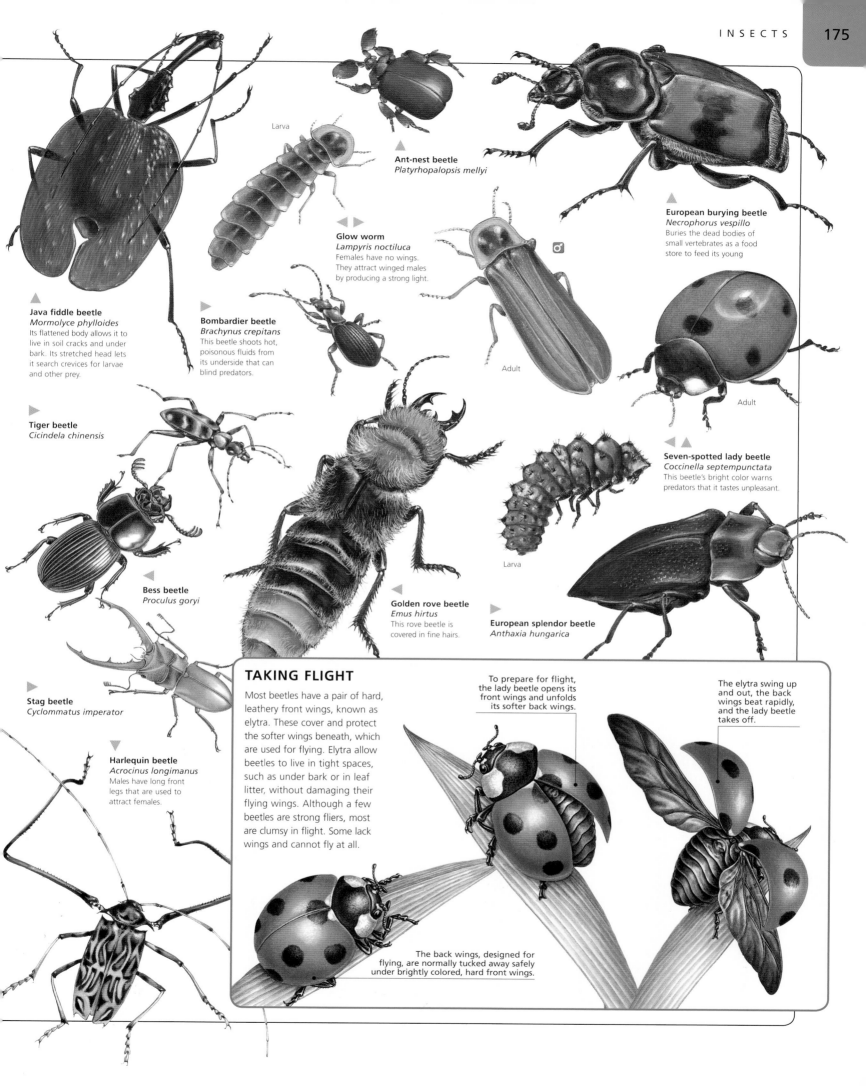

Java fiddle beetle
Mormolyce phylloides
Its flattened body allows it to
live in soil cracks and under
bark. Its stretched head lets
it search crevices for larvae
and other prey.

Larva

Ant-nest beetle
Platyrhopalopsis mellyi

Glow worm
Lampyris noctiluca
Females have no wings.
They attract winged males
by producing a strong light.

European burying beetle
Necrophorus vespillo
Buries the dead bodies of
small vertebrates as a food
store to feed its young

Adult

Adult

Bombardier beetle
Brachynus crepitans
This beetle shoots hot,
poisonous fluids from
its underside that can
blind predators.

Tiger beetle
Cicindela chinensis

Seven-spotted lady beetle
Coccinella septempunctata
This beetle's bright color warns
predators that it tastes unpleasant.

Larva

Bess beetle
Proculus goryi

Golden rove beetle
Emus hirtus
This rove beetle is
covered in fine hairs.

European splendor beetle
Anthaxia hungarica

Stag beetle
Cyclommatus imperator

Harlequin beetle
Acrocinus longimanus
Males have long front
legs that are used to
attract females.

TAKING FLIGHT

Most beetles have a pair of hard,
leathery front wings, known as
elytra. These cover and protect
the softer wings beneath, which
are used for flying. Elytra allow
beetles to live in tight spaces,
such as under bark or in leaf
litter, without damaging their
flying wings. Although a few
beetles are strong fliers, most
are clumsy in flight. Some lack
wings and cannot fly at all.

To prepare for flight,
the lady beetle opens its
front wings and unfolds
its softer back wings.

The elytra swing up
and out, the back
wings beat rapidly,
and the lady beetle
takes off.

The back wings, designed for
flying, are normally tucked away safely
under brightly colored, hard front wings.

Butterflies and moths

Butterflies and moths are lepidopterans. This means "scale wing" in Greek: Their wings and bodies are covered by tiny, colored, overlapping scales. These are actually hollow, flattened hairs. More than 85 percent of lepidopterans are moths, but butterflies are more easily recognized. Butterflies are diurnal, and their wings are often brightly colored. Moths are nocturnal and usually drab in color. Both butterflies and moths have two pairs of wings. These are linked by tiny hooks so that they beat together when flying. Almost all lepidopterans are plant-eaters. The mouthparts of most butterflies form a long tube called a proboscis. This is usually coiled up, but uncurls to feed on flower nectar. Some lack mouthparts and do not feed at all. Lepidopteran larvae are called caterpillars; most feed on plant matter.

CONSERVATION WATCH

Of the 165,000 species of lepidopterans, 284 appear on the IUCN Red List. Habitat destruction is the major threat to the vulnerable Apollo butterfly, but this species, and many others, also suffers because collectors capture too many.

Ex ✝ 27
Cr   8
En   39
Vu   130
Other 80

Apollo butterfly

European pine shoot moth
Rhyacionia buoliana
Larvae eat pine shoots; they can cause great damage to European pine forests.

Carpet moth (tapestry moth)
Trichophaga tapetzella
Larvae eat fabric made from plants, such as cotton, leaving holes in clothes and carpets.

Bent-wing ghost moth
Zelotypia stacyi

Bird-cherry ermine
Yponomeuta evonymella

Eyed hawk moth
Smerinthus ocellatus
Eye-spots on back wings look like a larger animal's eyes to scare off predators, such as birds.

Eliena skipper
Trapezites eliena

Hornet clearwing
Sesia apiformis
This moth looks like a stinging hornet to scare away predators.

Giant atlas moth
Attacus atlas
Female attracts mates with a chemical substance from a special gland in her body.

WORKING TOGETHER

The yucca moth and the yucca plant depend on each other for survival. Only yucca moths can pollinate yucca plants. They do this by laying their eggs at the base of the yucca's flowers. The moth's caterpillars hatch and feed on some, but not all, of the yucca's seeds. Those that remain grow into the next generation of plants. The caterpillars drop off the plant, pupate in soil, and emerge as the next yucca moth generation.

Silver-washed fritillary
Argynnis paphia

African monarch (lesser wanderer)
Danaus chrysippus

Dead leaf butterfly
Kallima inachus

Helena butterfly
Morpho rhetenor

Mimic
Hypolimnas misippus
Female deters predators by
mimicking the foul-tasting
African monarch; male is
camouflaged to blend in
with the ground, where
he waits for the female.

The postman
Heliconius melpomene

Large blue
Maculinea arion

Mottled umber
Erannis defoliaria
Only males can fly;
females have no wings.

African giant swallowtail
Papilio antimachus
Caterpillars of swallowtail
butterflies have a special organ
on the head that can release a
foul smell to warn off predators.

Orange-barred sulphur
Phoebis philea

Bogong moth
Agrotis infusa
Thousands migrate in summer
to the cool, high-mountain
caves of southern Australia.

**Northern jungle
queen butterfly**
Stichophthalma camadeva

BUTTERFLY OR MOTH?

Butterfly wings fold
vertically when resting.

Moth wings are held
horizontally when resting.

Butterflies have thin, threadlike
antennae with clubbed tips.

Moths have feathery or straight
antennae without clubbed tips.

Bees, wasps, and ants

Bees, wasps, ants, and sawflies are hymenopterids, a word that means "membrane wing" in Greek. Hymenopterids usually have two pairs of see-through wings. The back pair is attached to the larger front pair by tiny hooks, so that they beat together during flight. The mouthparts of adult hymenopterids are designed for biting or sucking. They may eat plants or other insects; some are parasites. Apart from sawflies, all species have a slim "waist" between the middle part of the body, the thorax, and the back part, the abdomen. The smallest species is the fairyfly wasp, which is so tiny it could fly through the eye of a needle. The largest is the spider-eating wasp, which is about 2¾ inches (7 cm) long. Although many species live alone, some live and work together in complex societies called colonies.

CONSERVATION WATCH

Of the 198,000 species of hymenopterids, 150 appear on the IUCN Red List. The red wood ant is extinct in some areas. The loss and disturbance of its woodland habitat threaten its existence in other regions.

Ex		0
Cr		3
En		0
Vu		139
Other		8

Red wood ant

Larva

Rose sawfly
Arge ochropus

Adult

Currant sawfly
Nematus ribesii
Larvae are pests that can rapidly strip currant bushes of their leaves.

Sirex parasite (saber wasp)
Rhyssa persuasoria
Female drills through wood with the long, egg-laying appendage at the tip of her abdomen. She lays eggs directly into the wood-boring larvae of other insects.

Weaver ant
Oecophylla smaragdina

Red-tailed bumblebee
Bombus lapidarius
Bumblebees are related to honeybees, but their colonies are much smaller: They consist of only a hundred or so members.

Common wasp
Vespula vulgaris

INTO THE POT

Adult potter wasps sting and paralyze caterpillars, then stash them in mud nests shaped like small pots. The female lays an egg in each nest. When the larva hatches, it eats the caterpillar.

Potter wasp
Eumenes pomiformis

Paper wasp
Polistes gallicus
Builds a nest of paper-thin six-sided cells by rolling wood particles around in its mouth with saliva

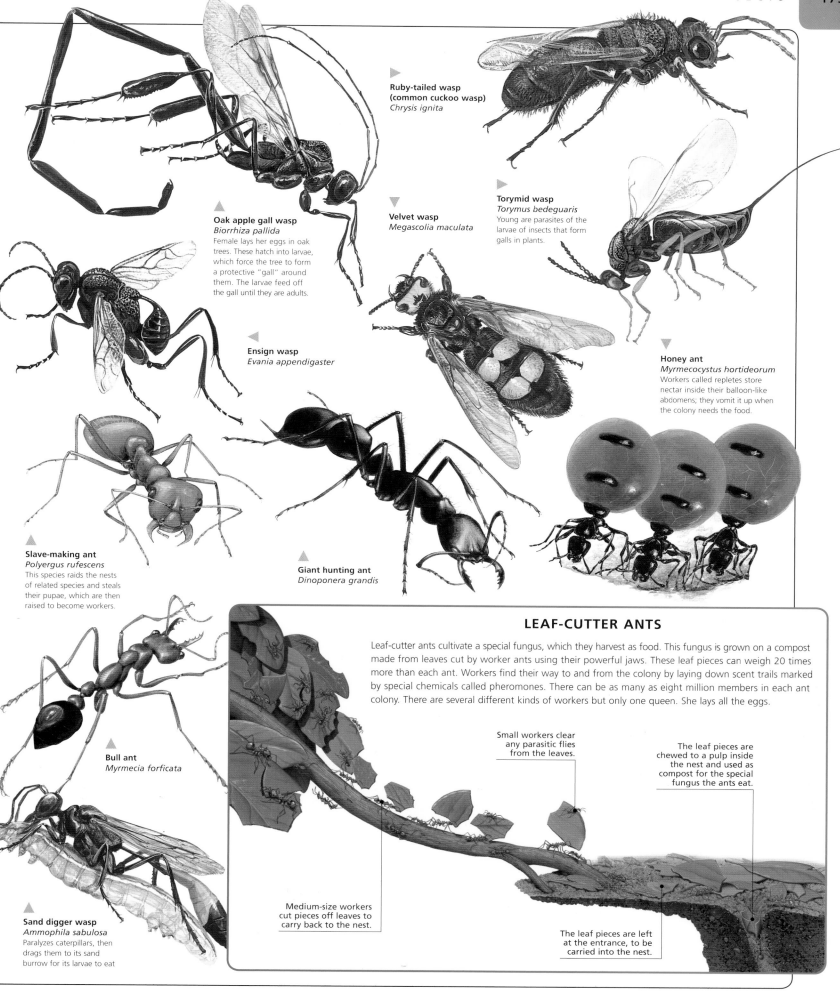

Ruby-tailed wasp (common cuckoo wasp)
Chrysis ignita

Oak apple gall wasp
Biorrhiza pallida
Female lays her eggs in oak trees. These hatch into larvae, which force the tree to form a protective "gall" around them. The larvae feed off the gall until they are adults.

Velvet wasp
Megascolia maculata

Torymid wasp
Torymus bedeguaris
Young are parasites of the larvae of insects that form galls in plants.

Ensign wasp
Evania appendigaster

Honey ant
Myrmecocystus hortideorum
Workers called repletes store nectar inside their balloon-like abdomens; they vomit it up when the colony needs the food.

Slave-making ant
Polyergus rufescens
This species raids the nests of related species and steals their pupae, which are then raised to become workers.

Giant hunting ant
Dinoponera grandis

Bull ant
Myrmecia forficata

Sand digger wasp
Ammophila sabulosa
Paralyzes caterpillars, then drags them to its sand burrow for its larvae to eat

LEAF-CUTTER ANTS

Leaf-cutter ants cultivate a special fungus, which they harvest as food. This fungus is grown on a compost made from leaves cut by worker ants using their powerful jaws. These leaf pieces can weigh 20 times more than each ant. Workers find their way to and from the colony by laying down scent trails marked by special chemicals called pheromones. There can be as many as eight million members in each ant colony. There are several different kinds of workers but only one queen. She lays all the eggs.

Small workers clear any parasitic flies from the leaves.

The leaf pieces are chewed to a pulp inside the nest and used as compost for the special fungus the ants eat.

Medium-size workers cut pieces off leaves to carry back to the nest.

The leaf pieces are left at the entrance, to be carried into the nest.

Flies

Houseflies and mosquitoes are known as dipterans. This order includes gnats, midges, blowflies, fruit flies, crane flies, hover flies, and horseflies. Most flying insects use four wings to fly, but dipterans usually fly with just their front pair. The back pair, called halteres, have become very small and look like two tiny clubs instead of wings. During flight, the halteres vibrate up and down in time with the front wings to help balance the insect. Some dipterans have lost their wings completely and cannot fly. Flies eat liquid food with mouthparts that are designed for sucking. Their feet have sticky pads with tiny claws that allow them to walk on smooth surfaces. They can even walk upside down. Most flies have a large head and compound eyes, each with as many as 4,000 lenses. This gives them excellent vision.

Aquatic larva (wriggler)   Adult

House mosquito
Culex pipiens
Male feeds on nectar, but the female needs protein from a vertebrate's blood for her eggs to develop.

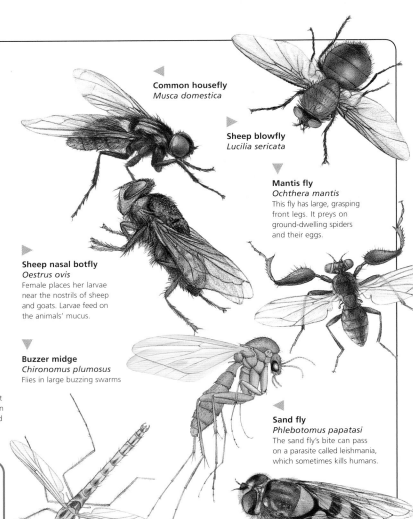

Common housefly
Musca domestica

Sheep blowfly
Lucilia sericata

Mantis fly
Ochthera mantis
This fly has large, grasping front legs. It preys on ground-dwelling spiders and their eggs.

Sheep nasal botfly
Oestrus ovis
Female places her larvae near the nostrils of sheep and goats. Larvae feed on the animals' mucus.

Buzzer midge
Chironomus plumosus
Flies in large buzzing swarms

Sand fly
Phlebotomus papatasi
The sand fly's bite can pass on a parasite called leishmania, which sometimes kills humans.

Hover fly
Syrphus ribesii

Greater bee fly
Bombylius major
Adults look like bees; larvae are parasites in some bee species.

Robber fly
Laphria flava
Preys on other insects: It injects them with paralyzing saliva, then sucks out their body fluids.

Stalk-eyed fly
Diopsis tenuipes
Its eyes and small antennae are carried on long stalks. This probably improves vision.

Horsefly
Tabanus bovinus
Females are bloodsuckers that find mammals to feed on by tracking the carbon dioxide in their breath.

LIFTOFF!

To fly, the deerfly tilts its wings and beats them. This pushes air backward, giving it the thrust it needs for liftoff. It adjusts the angle of its wings' front edges to change the thrust. The more they dip, the stronger the thrust, and the faster the deerfly travels.

The front edges are raised at the top of the upstroke.

At the start of the downstroke, the front edges begin to dip.

The powerful downstroke pushes air backward, thrusting the deerfly forward and up.

5 CLASSES • 36 ORDERS • 145 FAMILIES • 6,000 SPECIES

Sea Stars

Sea stars are echinoderms. This phylum also contains sea urchins, brittle stars, feather stars, and sea cucumbers. As adults, these animals have unusual body shapes. Instead of having two sides that look the same, their bodies are usually arranged into five equal parts around a central axis. This is called radial symmetry. Most of the body's organs are organized in this pattern. Sea stars and their relatives have an internal skeleton of plates made from calcium. These often have spines or small lumps. All echinoderms live in marine environments. Most can move across sediment; however, sea lilies are fixed to the seafloor by a long stalk, and some sea cucumbers float in the open ocean. The larvae of many echinoderms look nothing like their parents until they settle onto the seafloor to change into their adult form.

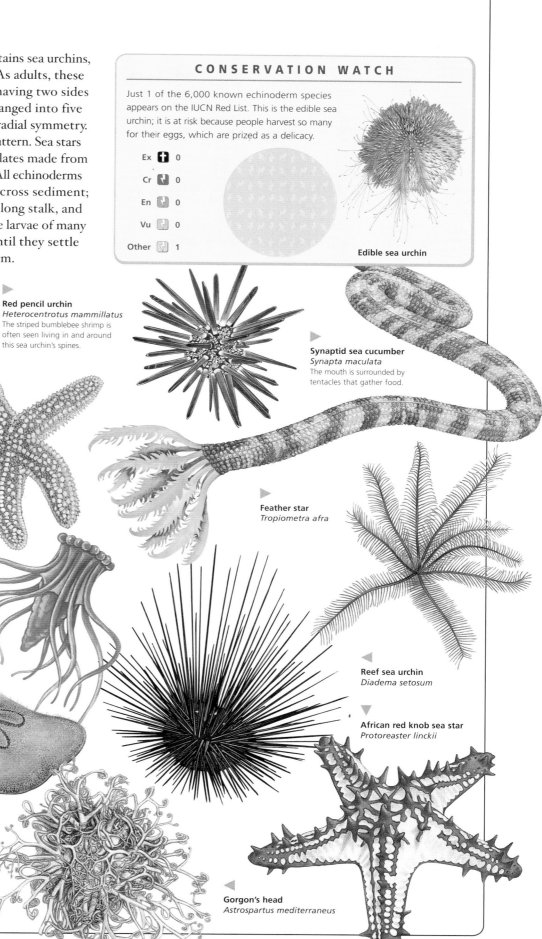

CONSERVATION WATCH

Just 1 of the 6,000 known echinoderm species appears on the IUCN Red List. This is the edible sea urchin; it is at risk because people harvest so many for their eggs, which are prized as a delicacy.

Ex 🕆 0
Cr 📋 0
En 📋 0
Vu 📋 0
Other 📋 1

Edible sea urchin

Red pencil urchin
Heterocentrotus mammillatus
The striped bumblebee shrimp is often seen living in and around this sea urchin's spines.

Synaptid sea cucumber
Synapta maculata
The mouth is surrounded by tentacles that gather food.

Feather star
Tropiometra afra

Common starfish
Asterias rubens

Sea apple
Pseudocolochirus violaceus
This filter feeder defends itself by releasing a poison that can kill other sea animals.

Black brittle star
Ophiocomina nigra
Brittle stars have hardened arms that can be snapped off easily, which gives them their name.

Pelagic sea cucumber
Pelagothuria natatrix

Reef sea urchin
Diadema setosum

African red knob sea star
Protoreaster linckii

Sand dollar (sea biscuit)
Clypeaster humilis

Gorgon's head
Astrospartus mediterraneus

Glossary

Abdomen A section of the body where food is usually digested; also the rear section of insects and other arthropods

Albumen Clear, jelly-like fluid between the shell and yolk of an egg; it provides the developing embryo with protection as well as water and nutrition.

Anatomy Structure of an animal; also science concerned with animal structure

Ancestor A related animal that lived in the past

Antenna An insect head organ used to sense information about the surrounding environment (pl. antennae)

Antlers Bony head growths on deer

Aquatic Living in water

Australasia Region consisting of Australia, New Zealand, and Melanesia, a group of Pacific islands

Bacteria Microscopic life-forms that are usually just a single cell. Their simple structure is so different from any other living cells that they belong to their own kingdom: Protista. (sing. bacterium)

Barbels Thin, fleshy growths around an animal's mouth, used to find food; they are common in some fish groups.

Binocular vision Using two eyes at the same time to see; this helps judge how far away an object is.

Bioluminescence Light produced by living organisms

Blubber A thick layer of fat beneath the skin of some mammals helps keep them warm. It is well developed in marine mammals such as whales and seals.

Camouflage Colors and patterns on an animal's outer cover that help it blend into its surrounding environment

Canines Sharp pointed teeth in mammals; they are used for tearing food.

Carapace A hard outer covering, such as a turtle's shell; this provides protection for an animal's body.

Carnassials Special cheek teeth with scissor-like edges in mammal carnivores; they are used to cut through flesh.

Carnivore An animal that eats mostly other animals; it is also an order of mammals.

Cartilage A tough type of body tissue, softer, more elastic, and lighter than bone; it forms the skeletons of cartilaginous fish such as sharks and rays.

Caudal Located on or near the tail or rear of an animal; the caudal peduncle, for

example, is the narrowest part of a fish's body, before it fans into the tail.

Class One of the highest groups into which scientists sort living things; there are one or more classes in a phylum and each class contains one or more orders. Classes can be divided into subclasses.

Cloaca The opening in most vertebrates through which body wastes pass out. Eggs or young leave the body from this opening in females. In males, it is the passageway for sperm.

Cold-blooded See ectothermic

Colony Members of the same species that live together; they may do so to breed or for protection from predators.

Compound eye An eye that is made up of many smaller eyes, found in many insects and some crustaceans; each of these has its own lens and cells that are sensitive to light and can form a weak image.

Courtship Behavior involving males and females of the same species that helps them select or attract a mate

Crop Expanded part of the digestive tract used to store food; it is found in many birds and some insects.

Dermis The second layer of the skin of animals, located beneath the epidermis; it contains nerves, sweat glands, and blood vessels.

Digestion Processes that occur inside an animal to break down food into substances the body can use for energy, growth, or to repair itself

Diurnal Active during the day

Domestication The process of taming and breeding an animal for use by humans; domesticated animals include pets as well as animals used for sport, food, or work.

Dominance The status of certain animals within a group that are treated with more respect and caution than others; this often determines mating rights.

Dormant To be in a sleeplike state, often because of environmental conditions; the body's activity slows for this period.

Dorsal Located on or toward the back of an animal

Dung Hard waste from an animal; this usually refers to mammal waste.

Echolocation A system used by some animals to sense nearby objects and thus find their way and search for food; it relies on sound rather than sight or touch.

Ectothermic Having a body temperature that adjusts to that of the surrounding

environment; fish, reptiles, amphibians, and invertebrates are ectothermic. Also known as cold-blooded

Eggs Reproductive cells of female animals

Embryo The early stage of an animal's development that begins just after an egg has been fertilized

Endothermic Having a body temperature independent to that of the surrounding environment, which is kept stable by sweating to cool down and shivering to warm up; vertebrates such as birds and mammals are endothermic. Also known as warm-blooded

Epidermis The thin, outermost skin layer in animals; it does not contain any blood vessels but provides a barrier to protect the body against diseases.

Equator This imaginary line runs around the center of Earth, separating it into two equal parts—the Northern and Southern Hemispheres.

Estuary Where a river mouth meets the sea or ocean and fresh water mixes with salt water to produce brackish water; at this point the river is under the influence of the tides.

Eurasia Landmass that consists of the continents of Europe and Asia

Evolve To develop gradually over time as a species; this is often in response to changes in the environment.

Exoskeleton A structure located outside an animal that provides support for the soft body tissues inside; it is found on arachnids, insects, crustaceans, and many other invertebrates.

External fertilization Sperm and egg unite to create an embryo outside a female animal's body.

Extinction The death of a species

Family A term used in classifying animals; there are one or more families in an order, and each family contains one or more genera.

Feces Hard waste from an animal

Feral Domesticated animals, such as cats and dogs, that have returned to live in the wild

Fertilization Occurs when a sperm enters an egg successfully to create an embryo

Fetus In mammals, an embryo that has developed its basic structure and major body organs

Food chain A feeding pattern in which energy from food moves in a sequence from one level to the next

Forage To search for and eat food

Fungi Life-forms, such as mushrooms and molds; they are so different from any other living things they belong to their own kingdom: Fungi.

Genus The second lowest group into which scientists sort living things. Animals in the same genus are closely related and share many characteristics. There is at least one genus in each family, and each genus contains one or more species. (pl. genera)

Gestation Length of a pregnancy; this is the time it takes from the moment fertilization occurs to an animal's birth.

Gills Organs used by water-living animals, such as fish and crustaceans, for breathing; they absorb oxygen from water into an animal's bloodstream and give off carbon dioxide as waste.

Glands Special tissues in an animal that secrete substances, such as hormones, tears, or mucus, used by the body

Habitat The natural environment where an animal lives, including plant life, climate, and geology

Harem A group of same-species female animals that breed with a single male

Herbivore An animal that eats mainly plant material

Hermaphrodite An animal that has both male and female sex organs during its life; this can occur at the same time, or at different times in its life cycle.

Hibernate To spend the winter in a kind of deep sleep; in this state, an animal becomes inactive, its breathing rate and body temperature drops, and it lives off fat reserves. It is common among insects, reptiles, and some mammals.

Hormone A chemical produced in one part of an animal's body that is carried by the blood to another part where it causes a response

Incisors The front teeth in either or both the top and bottom jaws of a mammal

Incubate To keep eggs or embryos in the best environment for their development: Birds usually sit on their eggs; crocodiles bury eggs in a protected chamber.

Indigenous people The original human inhabitants of a region or country

Insectivores Animals that eat mainly insects

Internal fertilization This occurs when sperm and egg unite inside a female animal's body to create an embryo.

Introduced Species that do not occur naturally in a place or a region, but

rather arrive by either the accidental or the deliberate actions of humans

Invertebrates Animals without a backbone, such as worms, mollusks, and insects; most animals on Earth are invertebrates.

Jacobson's organ Small pits in the top of the mouth in snakes, lizards, and mammals; these analyze scents picked up by the tongue.

Keratin A lightweight, but tough, colorless protein: This makes up mammal hair, nails, and horns; bird beaks and feathers; and the filter-feeding plates of baleen whales.

Kingdom The highest group into which scientists sort living things; five separate kingdoms are recognized. The Kingdom Animalia contains all animals. Kingdoms are comprised of phyla.

Larva The young of certain animals that hatch from eggs, such as insects and other invertebrates, fish, and amphibians; they usually look different from their adult form and include grubs, caterpillars, and maggots in insects, and tadpoles in frogs and toads. (pl. larvae)

Lateral line System of sensory canals that runs along the sides of fish; it registers movement by detecting pressure changes in the surrounding water.

Marine The ocean environment

Membrane Soft, thin tissue or cell layer in an animal

Metamorphosis The sometimes dramatic transformation that can occur as a young animal becomes an adult; invertebrates, such as insects, spend time as larvae or nymphs before becoming adults. For vertebrates, metamorphosis from a larva to an adult is widespread in amphibians and common in fish.

Micro-organisms Tiny life-forms, such as bacteria, that can be seen only with a microscope

Migration Regular journeys made by animals from one habitat to another; they are usually made with the seasons and for the purpose of finding food, mates, or a place to produce young.

Molars Teeth in the sides of a mammal's mouth used for crushing and grinding

Molt To shed the body's outer layer, such as hair, scales, feathers, or exoskeleton

Monsoon A seasonal wind that brings heavy rain to parts of the world; it is most common in tropical southern and Southeast Asia.

Mucus Thick, slimy substance produced by some parts of animals' bodies; it provides protection and moisture.

New World North, South, and Central America and nearby islands

Nictitating membrane Thin, usually see-through, protective "third eyelid," found in reptiles, birds, and some mammals; it moves across the eye, not up and down.

Nocturnal Active at night

Northern Hemisphere The northern half of Earth; it includes all of North and Central America, the top part of South America, all of Europe, much of Africa, and all but a small portion of Asia.

Notochord A stiff rod of tissue along the back of some animals, including vertebrate embryos; it is replaced by the backbone in vertebrates as they mature.

Nutrients Substances, usually found in food, that are needed for an animal to grow and function

Nymph A juvenile stage in some insect species; a nymph looks much like the adult it gradually will become but is usually wingless and cannot breed.

Old World Europe, Asia, and Africa

Olfactory An animal's sense of smell

Omnivore An animal that eats both plant and animal material

Opposable thumbs Thumbs that can reach around and touch all of the fingers on the same hand; this allows an animal to hold objects.

Order One of the major groups into which scientists sort living things; there are one or more orders in a class and each order contains one or more families. Orders can be divided into suborders.

Organ A group of tissues that comprises a body part with a specific role inside an animal, such as the brain, skin, and heart

Patagium A skin flap forming a winglike structure that is used for flying or gliding in mammals such as bats and squirrels

Pelt The skin and fur of a mammal

Pelvis A structure of basin-shaped bones that joins the spine with the back legs

Pheromone A chemical produced by an animal; pheromones send signals to and influence the behavior of other members of the same species.

Phylum The second highest group into which scientists sort living things; it falls below the kingdom level. Each phylum contains one or more classes. (pl. phyla)

Pigment The chemical substance in cells that gives color to an animal's skin, eyes, hair, fur, or feathers

Plankton Tiny plants and animals floating in oceans, seas, and lakes; they are filtered from the water by large animals as food, and eaten directly by small animals.

Plumage The feathers of a bird

Poach To hunt or capture animals illegally

Predator An animal that hunts, kills, and eats other animals

Prehensile Able to grasp or grip

Prey An animal that is hunted, killed, and eaten by other animals

Primitive A simple or early form of an animal; having features that are ancient

Pupa A stage of development in insects that does not move or feed; it occurs after the larva and before the adult. (pl. pupae)

Quill Long, sharp, stiffened hair of an echidna, porcupine, or anteater; this is used for defense against predators.

Reproduction The process of creating offspring: Sexual reproduction involves sperm from a male joining with the egg of a female; asexual reproduction does not involve sperm or eggs.

Rookery A regular breeding site used by many animals, particularly seabirds

Roost A safe place used by some animals, such as birds or bats, to sleep in groups

Ruminants Hoofed animals, such as cattle, that have a stomach with four chambers; one chamber, the rumen, contains micro-organisms that help to break down the tough walls of plant cells.

Savanna Open grassland with some trees

Sediment The soil, sand, or gravel that covers the bottom of water bodies; this includes rivers, ponds, oceans, and lakes.

Simple eye An eye that can detect light and dark but cannot form an image; they are found in many invertebrate animals, such as worms and snails.

Snout Front, often elongated, part of an animal's head that includes the nose area

Social Animals that live with others of the same species; they may live with a mate, in a family group, or in a herd or colony with thousands of others.

Sonar A system of locating objects by transmitting and detecting sound waves underwater, used by dolphins and whales

Southern Hemisphere The southern half of Earth; this includes all of Australasia and Antarctica, most of South America, part of Africa, and a small portion of Asia.

Species Animals with the same physical and behavioral features that are able to breed with each other to create young that can also breed

Sperm The reproductive cells of some male animals

Spine The backbone of an adult vertebrate animal; it is also a stiff, rodlike extension from the body of an animal that is used for defense against predators.

Symmetrical To be arranged with all sides having the same appearance and structure; bilaterally symmetrical means to have two equal sides.

Syrinx The special organ in the throat of perching birds used to produce songs and other sounds for communication

Talons The sharp claws of birds of prey, such as owls and eagles; they are used to capture, hold, and kill prey.

Territory An area that an animal defends against intruders from its own or other species; it can be permanent, to control food or other resources, or it may be temporary, to breed.

Tissue A group of cells inside an animal's body; they are located together, have the same or a similar structure, and act together to perform the same function.

Torpor A sleeplike state entered by some animals, particularly small mammals and birds, to survive difficult conditions such as cold weather or food shortages; the body's processes are slowed down greatly.

Troop A group of animals, particularly primates such as monkeys or baboons

Umbilical cord The ropelike structure that connects a developing mammal embryo or fetus with its mother's placenta during pregnancy; it carries nutrients and oxygen to the baby and removes waste products such as carbon dioxide.

Urine Liquid waste from an animal's body produced from the blood by the kidneys

Venom Poison injected by an animal into a predator or prey through fangs, spines, or similar structures

Vertebrate Any animal with a backbone, including all mammals, birds, reptiles, amphibians, and fish

Vibrissae Special hairs that are sensitive to touch; they are often present on the face of mammals and are called whiskers.

Warm-blooded See endothermic

Zooplankton Tiny animals that drift on or near the surface of the ocean; they are an important source of food for some whales, fish, and seabirds.

Animal Sizes

Animals come in an amazing variety of sizes and shapes. Every species featured in this book is listed below in its group by common name. Beside every name is the size of that animal. All of the measurements represent the largest size a normal animal in this species can reach. How each animal is measured—whether by height, length, wingspan, or width—is indicated by an icon at the top of each group, or next to each animal's name. A key on page 185 explains what each icon represents.

Mammals

Monotremes		
Long-nosed echidna	31¼ in (80 cm)	2 in (5 cm)
Platypus	16 in (41 cm)	6 in (15 cm)
Short-nosed echidna	14 in (36 cm)	4 in (10 cm)

Marsupials		
Bilby	21½ in (55 cm)	11⅓ in (29 cm)
Brushtail possum	22⅔ in (58 cm)	15⅔ in (40 cm)
Common opossum	16¾ in (43 cm)	17½ in (45 cm)
Common ringtail possum	14¾ in (38 cm)	10½ in (27 cm)
Common wombat	4 ft (1.2 m)	1¼ in (3 cm)
Ecuadorean shrew-opossum	5⅓ in (13.5 cm)	⅛ in (4 mm)
Fat-tailed dunnart	3½ in (9 cm)	2¾ in (7 cm)
Feathertail glider	2½ in (6.5 cm)	3 in (7.5 cm)
Goodfellow's tree kangaroo	24½ in (63 cm)	29⅔ in (76 cm)
Herbert River ringtail possum	15⅔ in (40 cm)	18¾ in (48 cm)
Koala	32 in (82 cm)	None
Leadbeater's possum	6¼ in (16 cm)	7 in (18 cm)
Little water opossum	15⅔ in (40 cm)	12 in (31 cm)
Monito del monte	5 in (13 cm)	5 in (13 cm)
Mountain pygmy-possum	4⅔ in (12 cm)	6 in (15 cm)
Mulgara	7¾ in (20 cm)	4¼ in (11 cm)
Musky rat-kangaroo	11 in (28 cm)	6⅔ in (17 cm)
Numbat	10¾ in (27.5 cm)	8¼ in (21 cm)
Patagonian opossum	5½ in (14 cm)	4 in (10 cm)
Red kangaroo	4½ ft (1.4 m)	38⅔ in (99 cm)
Robinson's mouse opossum	6½ in (16.5 cm)	8¼ in (21 cm)
Rufous bettong	20¼ in (52 cm)	15⅔ in (40 cm)
Scaly-tailed possum	15¼ in (39 cm)	11⅔ in (30 cm)
Southern brown bandicoot	14 in (36 cm)	5½ in (14 cm)
Southern marsupial mole	6¼ in (16 cm)	1 in (2.5 cm)
Southern short-tailed opossum	6 in (15 cm)	3 in (8 cm)
Spotted cuscus	22⅔ in (58 cm)	17½ in (45 cm)
Spotted-tailed quoll	29¼ in (75 cm)	21¾ in (56 cm)
Striped bandicoot	11⅔ in (30 cm)	10 in (26 cm)
Striped possum	11 in (28 cm)	15¼ in (39 cm)
Sugar glider	12½ in (32 cm)	18¾ in (48 cm)
Tasmanian devil	25⅓ in (65 cm)	10 in (26 cm)
Thylacine	4½ ft (1.4 m)	25⅓ in (65 cm)
Western gray kangaroo	4 ft (1.2 m)	3¼ ft (1 m)
Yapok	15⅔ in (40 cm)	16¾ in (43 cm)
Yellow-footed antechinus	6¼ in (16 cm)	5½ in (14 cm)
Yellow-footed rock wallaby	25⅓ in (65 cm)	27⅓ in (70 cm)

Anteaters & pangolins		
Collared anteater	34⅓ in (88 cm)	23 in (59 cm)
Giant anteater	6½ ft (2 m)	35 in (90 cm)
Giant ground pangolin	3¼ ft (1 m)	27⅓ in (70 cm)
Larger hairy armadillo	15⅔ in (40 cm)	6⅔ in (17 cm)
Maned three-toed sloth	19½ in (50 cm)	2 in (5 cm)
Pale-throated three-toed sloth	29⅔ in (76 cm)	2¾ in (7 cm)
Southern three-banded armadillo	10½ in (27 cm)	3 in (8 cm)

Insect-eating mammals		
Cuban solenodon	15¼ in (39 cm)	9⅓ in (24 cm)
Elegant water shrew	5 in (13 cm)	4¼ in (11 cm)
Eurasian common shrew	3 in (8 cm)	1¾ in (4.5 cm)
European mole	6¼ in (16 cm)	¾ in (2 cm)
Giant otter shrew	13¾ in (35 cm)	11⅓ in (29 cm)
Himalayan water shrew	5 in (13 cm)	4⅔ in (12 cm)
Hottentot golden mole	5½ in (14 cm)	None
Mindanao moonrat	6 in (15 cm)	2¾ in (7 cm)
Western European hedgehog	10 in (26 cm)	1¼ in (3 cm)

Flying lemurs & tree shrews		
Common tree shrew	7⅔ in (19.5 cm)	6½ in (16.5 cm)
Large tree shrew	12½ in (32 cm)	9¾ in (25 cm)
Malayan flying lemur	16½ in (42 cm)	10½ in (27 cm)
Pen-tailed tree shrew	5½ in (14 cm)	7½ in (19 cm)

Bats		
American false vampire bat	6 in (15 cm)	None
Common pipistrelle	1¾ in (4.5 cm)	1⅓ in (3.5 cm)
Common vampire bat	3½ in (9 cm)	None
Diadem leaf-nosed bat	4 in (10 cm)	2⅓ in (6 cm)
Eastern tube-nosed bat	4¼ in (11 cm)	¾ in (2 cm)
Egyptian fruit bat	5½ in (14 cm)	¾ in (2 cm)
Gambian epauletted fruit bat	9¾ in (25 cm)	None
Greater bulldog bat	5 in (13 cm)	1½ in (4 cm)
Greater mouse-tailed bat	3 in (8 cm)	2⅓ in (6 cm)
Hammer-headed fruit bat	11⅔ in (30 cm)	¾ in (2 cm)
Indian flying fox	11 in (28 cm)	None
Least blossom bat	2¾ in (7 cm)	⅓ in (1 cm)
Mauritian tomb bat	3¾ in (9.5 cm)	1¼ in (3 cm)
New Zealand lesser short-tailed bat	2¾ in (7 cm)	⅓ in (1 cm)
Noctule	3 in (8 cm)	2¼ in (5.5 cm)
Particolored bat	2½ in (6.5 cm)	1¾ in (4.5 cm)
Pocketed free-tailed bat	4¼ in (11 cm)	2 in (5 cm)
Serotine	3 in (8 cm)	2⅓ in (6 cm)
Straw-colored fruit bat	8½ in (22 cm)	¾ in (2 cm)
Sucker-footed bat	2⅓ in (6 cm)	2 in (5 cm)
Western barbastelle	2⅓ in (6 cm)	1½ in (4 cm)
Wrinkle-faced bat	2¾ in (7 cm)	None
Yellow-winged bat	3 in (8 cm)	None

Primates		
Allen's swamp monkey	19½ in (50 cm)	21½ in (55 cm)
Angwantibo	10 in (26 cm)	⅓ in (1 cm)
Aye-aye	15⅔ in (40 cm)	15⅔ in (40 cm)
Barbary ape	27⅓ in (70 cm)	None
Bear macaque	25⅓ in (65 cm)	3 in (8 cm)
Black gibbon	25⅓ in (65 cm)	None
Black howler	26 in (67 cm)	26 in (67 cm)
Black-headed uakari	19½ in (50 cm)	8¼ in (21 cm)
Bonobo	32⅓ in (83 cm)	None
Brown capuchin	18¾ in (48 cm)	18¾ in (48 cm)
Chimpanzee	36¼ in (93 cm)	None
Chinese snub-nosed monkey	27⅔ in (71 cm)	29⅔ in (76 cm)
Common marmoset	6 in (15 cm)	13¾ in (35 cm)
Common squirrel monkey	12½ in (32 cm)	16¾ in (43 cm)
Common woolly monkey	22⅔ in (58 cm)	31¼ in (80 cm)
Demidoff's galago	6 in (15 cm)	8¼ in (21 cm)
Diadem sifaka	21½ in (55 cm)	21¾ in (56 cm)
Douc langur	29⅔ in (76 cm)	29⅔ in (76 cm)
Dusky titi	14 in (36 cm)	18 in (46 cm)
Eastern needle-clawed bushbaby	7¾ in (20 cm)	10 in (26 cm)
Gelada	35 in (90 cm)	19½ in (50 cm)
Geoffroy's tamarin	11⅔ in (30 cm)	16½ in (42 cm)
Golden lion tamarin	11 in (28 cm)	15⅔ in (40 cm)
Hamadryas baboon	35 in (90 cm)	27⅓ in (70 cm)
Hanuman langur	30½ in (78 cm)	3¼ ft (1 m)
Hoolock	25⅓ in (65 cm)	None
Indri	35 in (90 cm)	15⅔ in (40 cm)
King colobus	28 in (72 cm)	3¼ ft (1 m)
Kloss's gibbon	25⅓ in (65 cm)	None
Lar gibbon	25⅓ in (65 cm)	None
Long-haired spider monkey	22⅔ in (58 cm)	35 in (90 cm)
Mandrill	31¼ in (80 cm)	4 in (10 cm)
Mantled howler	22⅔ in (58 cm)	26 in (67 cm)
Mountain gorilla	6¼ ft (1.9 m)	None
Northern night monkey	18⅓ in (47 cm)	16 in (41 cm)
Orangutan	5 ft (1.5 m)	None
Proboscis monkey	29⅔ in (76 cm)	29⅔ in (76 cm)
Pygmy marmoset	6 in (15 cm)	8¼ in (21 cm)
Red colobus	26 in (67 cm)	31¼ in (80 cm)
Redtail monkey	23½ in (60 cm)	35 in (90 cm)
Ruffed lemur	21½ in (55 cm)	4 ft (1.2 m)
Siamang	35 in (90 cm)	None
Slender loris	10 in (26 cm)	None
Spectral tarsier	6 in (15 cm)	10½ in (27 cm)
Sykes's monkey	26 in (67 cm)	33 in (85 cm)
Vervet monkey	24¼ in (62 cm)	28 in (72 cm)
Weasel sportive lemur	14 in (36 cm)	11⅔ in (30 cm)
Western gorilla	6 ft (1.8 m)	None
White-cheeked mangabey	28 in (72 cm)	3¼ ft (1 m)
White-faced saki	18¾ in (48 cm)	17½ in (45 cm)
Woolly spider monkey	24½ in (63 cm)	31¼ in (80 cm)

Carnivores		
Aardwolf	26 in (67 cm)	9⅓ in (24 cm)
African golden cat	3¼ ft (1 m)	18 in (46 cm)
African weasel	13¾ in (35 cm)	9 in (23 cm)
American badger	28 in (72 cm)	6 in (15 cm)
American black bear	7 ft (2.1 m)	7 in (18 cm)
American mink	19½ in (50 cm)	7¾ in (20 cm)
Andean cat	33 in (85 cm)	19 in (49 cm)
Andean hog-nosed skunk	13 in (33 cm)	7¾ in (20 cm)
Angolan genet	19½ in (50 cm)	20⅔ in (53 cm)
Arctic fox	27⅓ in (70 cm)	15⅔ in (40 cm)
Asiatic black bear	6¼ ft (1.9 m)	4 in (10 cm)
Asiatic golden cat	3¼ ft (1 m)	21¾ in (56 cm)
Baikal seal	4½ ft (1.4 m)	
Banded linsang	17½ in (45 cm)	16⅔ in (40 cm)
Banded mongoose	17½ in (45 cm)	11⅔ in (30 cm)
Banded palm civet	24½ in (62 cm)	14¾ in (38 cm)
Black-backed jackal	35 in (90 cm)	15⅔ in (40 cm)
Bobcat	3¼ ft (1 m)	7¾ in (20 cm)
Bush dog	29¼ in (75 cm)	5 in (13 cm)
California sea lion	8 ft (2.4 m)	
Canada lynx	3¼ ft (1 m)	5½ in (14 cm)
Cape clawless otter	37 in (95 cm)	26 in (67 cm)
Cape wild dog	35 in (90 cm)	15⅔ in (40 cm)
Caracal	36 in (92 cm)	12 in (31 cm)
Cheetah	4½ ft (1.4 m)	31¼ in (80 cm)
Chinese ferret badger	9⅓ in (24 cm)	7½ in (19 cm)
Common palm civet	27⅔ in (71 cm)	25¾ in (66 cm)
Coyote	37¾ in (97 cm)	14¾ in (38 cm)
Dingo	3¼ ft (1 m)	14 in (36 cm)
Ethiopian wolf	3¼ ft (1 m)	11⅔ in (30 cm)
Eurasian badger	35 in (90 cm)	7¾ in (20 cm)
Eurasian lynx	4¼ ft (1.3 m)	9⅓ in (24 cm)
European brown bear	9 ft (2.8 m)	8¼ in (21 cm)
European mink	16¾ in (43 cm)	7½ in (19 cm)
European otter	27⅓ in (70 cm)	15⅔ in (40 cm)
Falanouc	25⅓ in (65 cm)	9¾ in (25 cm)
Fanaloka	17½ in (45 cm)	8¼ in (21 cm)
Fisher	30¾ in (79 cm)	16 in (41 cm)
Fishing cat	33½ in (86 cm)	13 in (33 cm)
Fishing genet	17½ in (45 cm)	13¼ in (34 cm)
Fossa	29⅔ in (76 cm)	27⅓ in (70 cm)
Giant otter	4 ft (1.2 m)	27⅓ in (70 cm)
Giant panda	5 ft (1.5 m)	4 in (10 cm)
Gray wolf (Alaskan)	5 ft (1.5 m)	20 in (51 cm)
Gray wolf (Scandinavian)	5 ft (1.5 m)	20 in (51 cm)
Grison	21½ in (55 cm)	7¾ in (20 cm)
Harp seal	6½ ft (2 m)	
Himalayan brown bear	9 ft (2.8 m)	8¼ in (21 cm)
Hog badger	27⅓ in (70 cm)	6⅔ in (17 cm)
Hooded seal	8¾ ft (2.7 m)	
Hose's palm civet	21 in (54 cm)	13¼ in (34 cm)
Iberian lynx	3⅔ ft (1.1 m)	5 in (13 cm)
Jaguar	6¼ ft (1.9 m)	23½ in (60 cm)
Jaguarundi	25⅓ in (65 cm)	23¾ in (61 cm)
Japanese marten	21½ in (55 cm)	8½ in (22 cm)
Jungle cat	36⅔ in (94 cm)	12 in (31 cm)
Kinkajou	21½ in (55 cm)	22¼ in (57 cm)
Kit fox	20¼ in (52 cm)	12½ in (32 cm)
Kodiak bear	9 ft (2.8 m)	8¼ in (21 cm)
Kodkod	20 in (51 cm)	9¾ in (25 cm)
Leopard	7 ft (2.1 m)	3⅔ ft (1.1 m)
Leopard cat	23½ in (60 cm)	11⅔ in (30 cm)
Leopard seal	10½ ft (3.2 m)	
Lion	7½ ft (2.3 m)	3¼ ft (1 m)
Long-tailed weasel	10 in (26 cm)	6 in (15 cm)
Maned wolf	3¼ ft (1 m)	15⅔ in (40 cm)
Marbled cat	20⅔ in (53 cm)	21½ in (55 cm)
Marbled polecat	13¾ in (35 cm)	8½ in (22 cm)
Margay	30¾ in (79 cm)	20 in (51 cm)
Masked palm civet	29⅔ in (76 cm)	25 in (64 cm)
Mediterranean monk seal	9 ft (2.8 m)	
New Zealand fur seal	5¼ ft (1.6 m)	

Northern fur seal	7 ft (2.1 m)	
Ocelot	18⅓ in (47 cm)	16 in (41 cm)
Owston's palm civet	28 in (72 cm)	18⅓ in (47 cm)
Polar bear	8 ft (2.4 m)	5 in (13 cm)
Polecat	20 in (51 cm)	7½ in (19 cm)
Puma	5 ft (1.5 m)	37½ in (96 cm)
Raccoon	21½ in (55 cm)	16⅔ in (40 cm)
Ratel	30 in (77 cm)	11⅔ in (30 cm)
Red fox (North American)	19½ in (50 cm)	13 in (33 cm)
Red panda	25⅓ in (65 cm)	18¾ in (48 cm)
Red wolf	4 ft (1.2 m)	13¾ in (35 cm)
Ribbon seal	5¼ ft (1.6 m)	
Ringed seal	5 ft (1.5 m)	
Ringtail	16½ in (42 cm)	17 in (44 cm)
Sea otter	4 ft (1.2 m)	14 in (36 cm)
Serval	3¼ ft (1 m)	17½ in (45 cm)
Siberian weasel	25¾ in (66 cm)	9¾ in (25 cm)
Sloth bear	6 ft (1.8 m)	4⅔ in (12 cm)
Snow leopard	4¼ ft (1.3 m)	3¼ ft (1 m)
Southern elephant seal	19⅔ ft (6 m)	
Spectacled bear	6½ ft (2 m)	4⅔ in (12 cm)
Spotted hyena	4¼ ft (1.3 m)	9¾ in (25 cm)
Spotted skunk	13 in (33 cm)	11 in (28 cm)
Steller's sea lion	10¾ ft (3.3 m)	
Stoat	12½ in (32 cm)	5 in (13 cm)
Striped hog-nosed skunk	19½ in (50 cm)	12½ in (32 cm)
Striped hyena	3⅔ ft (1.1 m)	7¾ in (20 cm)
Striped polecat	14¾ in (38 cm)	11⅔ in (30 cm)
Striped skunk	31¼ in (80 cm)	15¼ in (39 cm)
Sun bear	4½ ft (1.4 m)	2¾ in (7 cm)
Suricate	12 in (31 cm)	9⅓ in (24 cm)
Tayra	27⅓ in (70 cm)	17½ in (45 cm)
Three-striped palm civet	20⅔ in (53 cm)	25¾ in (66 cm)
Tiger	12 ft (3.6 m)	3¼ ft (1 m)
Walrus	11½ ft (3.5 m)	
Weddell seal	9½ ft (2.9 m)	
White-nosed coati	27 in (69 cm)	24¼ in (62 cm)
Wildcat	29¼ in (75 cm)	13¾ in (35 cm)
Yellow mongoose	13¾ in (35 cm)	9¾ in (25 cm)
Yellow-throated marten	27⅓ in (70 cm)	17½ in (45 cm)

Hoofed mammals

Aardvark	4 ft (1.2 m)	21½ in (55 cm)
African elephant	24½ ft (7.5 m)	5 ft (1.5 m)
African manatee	13 ft (4 m)	
Alpaca	6½ ft (2 m)	7¾ in (20 cm)
Amazonian manatee	9 ft (2.8 m)	
Arabian tahr	4½ ft (1.4 m)	4⅔ in (12 cm)
Asiatic elephant	21 ft (6.4 m)	5 ft (1.5 m)
Ass (wild)	6½ ft (2 m)	17½ in (45 cm)
Babirusa	3⅔ ft (1.1 m)	12½ in (32 cm)
Bactrian camel	11½ ft (3.5 m)	20⅔ in (53 cm)
Baird's beaked whale	43 ft (13 m)	
Barasingha	6 ft (1.8 m)	7¾ in (20 cm)
Beluga	16½ ft (5 m)	
Bison	11½ ft (3.5 m)	23½ in (60 cm)
Black rhinoceros	12½ ft (3.8 m)	23½ in (60 cm)
Blackbuck	4 ft (1.2 m)	7 in (18 cm)
Blue whale	110 ft (33.5 m)	
Bottle-nosed dolphin	13 ft (4 m)	
Bowhead whale	59 ft (18 m)	
Brazilian tapir	6½ ft (2 m)	3¼ ft (1 m)
Bush pig	4¼ ft (1.3 m)	14¾ in (38 cm)
Caribbean manatee	14¾ ft (4.5 m)	
Caribou	7 ft (2.2 m)	9¾ in (25 cm)
Chaco peccary	3⅔ ft (1.1 m)	4 in (10 cm)
Chamois	4¼ ft (1.3 m)	1½ in (4 cm)
Chinese water deer	3¼ ft (1 m)	3 in (8 cm)
Chiru	4½ ft (1.4 m)	4 in (10 cm)
Collared peccary	3¼ ft (1 m)	2¼ in (5.5 cm)
Common dolphin	8 ft (2.4 m)	
Common hartebeest	6¼ ft (1.9 m)	27⅓ in (70 cm)
Common porpoise	6¼ ft (1.9 m)	
Dromedary	11½ ft (3.5 m)	19½ in (50 cm)
Dugong	13 ft (4 m)	
Fallow deer	6 ft (1.8 m)	9¾ in (25 cm)
False killer whale	19⅔ ft (6 m)	
Fin whale	82 ft (25 m)	
Finless porpoise	6½ ft (2 m)	
Ganges dolphin	10 ft (3 m)	
Gemsbok	5¼ ft (1.6 m)	35 in (90 cm)
Giant hog	7 ft (2.1 m)	17½ in (45 cm)
Giant muntjak	3¼ ft (1 m)	6⅔ in (17 cm)
Gray whale	49 ft (15 m)	
Greater kudu	5 ft (1.5 m)	18¾ in (48 cm)
Guanaco	6½ ft (2 m)	10½ in (27 cm)
Gulf porpoise	5 ft (1.5 m)	
Hippopotamus	13¾ ft (4.2 m)	21¾ in (56 cm)
Horse (wild)	9 ft (2.8 m)	23½ in (60 cm)
Humpback whale	49 ft (15 m)	
Impala	5 ft (1.5 m)	15⅔ in (40 cm)
Indian muntjak	3⅔ ft (1.1 m)	7½ in (19 cm)
Indian rhinoceros	12½ ft (3.8 m)	31¼ in (80 cm)
Irrawaddy dolphin	9 ft (2.8 m)	
Javan rhinoceros	10½ ft (3.2 m)	27⅓ in (70 cm)
Kenyan giraffe	26¼ ft (8 m)	5 ft (1.5 m)
Kiang	8 ft (2.5 m)	19½ in (50 cm)
Klipspringer	35 in (90 cm)	5 in (13 cm)
Lesser Malay chevrotain	18¾ in (48 cm)	2 in (5 cm)
Little red brocket	3¼ ft (1 m)	4 in (10 cm)
Llama	7 ft (2.2 m)	9¾ in (25 cm)
Long-finned pilot whale	28 ft (8.5 m)	
Malayan tapir	4 ft (1.2 m)	4 in (10 cm)
Minke whale	36 ft (11 m)	
Mongolian wild ass	8 ft (2.5 m)	19 in (49 cm)
Moose	11½ ft (3.5 m)	4 in (10 cm)
Mountain anoa	5 ft (1.5 m)	9⅓ in (24 cm)
Mountain zebra	8½ ft (2.6 m)	15⅔ in (40 cm)
Narwhal	19⅔ ft (6 m)	
Northern right whale	59 ft (18 m)	
Nubian giraffe	15½ ft (4.7 m)	3¼ ft (1 m)
Okapi	6½ ft (2 m)	16½ in (42 cm)
Onager	4½ ft (1.4 m)	19½ in (50 cm)
Orca	32 ft (9.8 m)	
Pampas deer	4¼ ft (1.3 m)	6 in (15 cm)
Peruvian guemal	5½ ft (1.7 m)	5 in (13 cm)
Pronghorn	5 ft (1.5 m)	7 in (18 cm)
Pygmy hippopotamus	6½ ft (2 m)	6 in (15 cm)
Pygmy hog	27⅔ in (71 cm)	1¼ in (3 cm)
Pygmy sperm whale	10 ft (3 m)	
Red river hog	5 ft (1.5 m)	16¾ in (43 cm)
Reticulated giraffe	15½ ft (4.7 m)	3¼ ft (1 m)
Risso's dolphin	12½ ft (3.8 m)	
Rock hyrax	22⅔ in (58 cm)	12 in (31 cm)
Roosevelt elk	8 ft (2.4 m)	6⅔ in (17 cm)
Rusa	3⅔ ft (1.1 m)	9¾ in (25 cm)
Saiga	4½ ft (1.4 m)	4⅔ in (12 cm)
Saola	6½ ft (2 m)	5 in (13 cm)
Serow	6 ft (1.8 m)	6¼ in (16 cm)
Southern giraffe	15½ ft (4.7 m)	3¼ ft (1 m)
Southern pudu	32⅓ in (83 cm)	2 in (5 cm)
Southern tree hyrax	27⅓ in (70 cm)	1¼ in (3 cm)
Spanish ibex	4½ ft (1.4 m)	6 in (15 cm)
Spectacled porpoise	7 ft (2.1 m)	
Sperm whale	60⅔ ft (18.5 m)	
Springbok	4½ ft (1.4 m)	11⅔ in (30 cm)
Sumatran rhinoceros	10½ ft (3.2 m)	25⅓ in (65 cm)
Thomson's gazelle	3⅔ ft (1.1 m)	7¾ in (20 cm)
Tufted deer	5¼ ft (1.6 m)	6¼ in (16 cm)
Vicuña	6¼ ft (1.9 m)	9¾ in (25 cm)
Warthog	5 ft (1.5 m)	19½ in (50 cm)
Water chevrotain	37 in (95 cm)	5½ in (14 cm)
White rhinoceros	13¾ ft (4.2 m)	27⅓ in (70 cm)
White-beaked dolphin	9 ft (2.8 m)	
White-lipped peccary	3¼ ft (1 m)	2⅓ in (6 cm)
White-tailed deer	8 ft (2.4 m)	11⅔ in (30 cm)
Wild boar	6 ft (1.8 m)	11⅔ in (30 cm)
Wildebeest	7½ ft (2.3 m)	21¾ in (56 cm)
Yak	10¾ ft (3.3 m)	23½ in (60 cm)
Yellow-spotted hyrax	14¾ in (38 cm)	None
Zebra (northern)	8 ft (2.5 m)	21¾ in (56 cm)

Rodents

Black rat	9⅓ in (24 cm)	10 in (26 cm)
Black-tailed prairie dog	13¼ in (34 cm)	3½ in (9 cm)
Brazilian porcupine	20¼ in (52 cm)	20¼ in (52 cm)
Capybara	4½ ft (1.4 m)	¾ in (2 cm)
Chinchilla	9 in (23 cm)	6 in (15 cm)
Coypu	25 in (64 cm)	16½ in (42 cm)
Dassie rat	8¼ in (21 cm)	6 in (15 cm)
Demarest's hutia	23½ in (60 cm)	11⅔ in (30 cm)
Desert kangaroo rat	6 in (15 cm)	7¾ in (20 cm)
Eastern chipmunk	6⅔ in (17 cm)	4⅔ in (12 cm)
Eurasian beaver	31¼ in (80 cm)	17½ in (45 cm)
Eurasian red squirrel	11 in (28 cm)	9⅓ in (24 cm)
European hamster	12½ in (32 cm)	2⅓ in (6 cm)
European souslik	8½ in (22 cm)	3 in (7 cm)
Fawn hopping mouse	4⅔ in (12 cm)	6¼ in (16 cm)
Garden dormouse	6⅔ in (17 cm)	5 in (13 cm)
Gray agouti	29⅔ in (76 cm)	1½ in (4 cm)
Great gerbil	7¾ in (20 cm)	6¼ in (16 cm)
Greater bandicoot rat	14 in (36 cm)	11 in (28 cm)
Greater stick-nest rat	10 in (26 cm)	7 in (18 cm)
Gundi	7¾ in (20 cm)	1 in (2.5 cm)
Harvest mouse	3 in (7.5 cm)	3 in (7.5 cm)
Hoary marmot	22¼ in (57 cm)	9¾ in (25 cm)
Large bamboo rat	18¾ in (48 cm)	7¾ in (20 cm)
Malayan porcupine	28½ in (73 cm)	4¼ in (11 cm)
Muskrat	13 in (33 cm)	11⅔ in (30 cm)
Northern three-toed jerboa	6¼ in (16 cm)	7½ in (19 cm)
Paca	30½ in (78 cm)	1¼ in (3 cm)
Pacarana	30¾ in (79 cm)	7½ in (19 cm)
Plains viscacha	25¾ in (66 cm)	7¾ in (20 cm)
Prevost's squirrel	11 in (28 cm)	10 in (26 cm)
Siberian collared lemming	6 in (15 cm)	⅓ in (1 cm)
Southern flying squirrel	5½ in (14 cm)	4⅔ in (12 cm)
Springhare	16¾ in (43 cm)	18⅓ in (47 cm)

Rabbits & elephant shrews

American pika	8½ in (22 cm)	None
Arctic hare	23½ in (60 cm)	3 in (8 cm)
Asiatic brown hare	26½ in (68 cm)	4 in (10 cm)
Black-tailed jackrabbit	24½ in (63 cm)	4¼ in (11 cm)
Brown hare	26½ in (68 cm)	4 in (10 cm)
Central African hare	17½ in (45 cm)	2 in (5 cm)
Checkered elephant shrew	12½ in (32 cm)	10 in (26 cm)
Daurian pika	7¾ in (20 cm)	None
Eastern cottontail	19½ in (50 cm)	2⅓ in (6 cm)
European rabbit	18 in (46 cm)	3 in (8 cm)
Forest rabbit	15⅔ in (40 cm)	1½ in (4 cm)
Four-toed elephant shrew	9 in (23 cm)	6⅔ in (17 cm)
Golden-rumped elephant shrew	11 in (28 cm)	9⅓ in (24 cm)
Hispid hare	19½ in (50 cm)	1½ in (4 cm)
Northern pika	7¾ in (20 cm)	None
Pygmy rabbit	11 in (28 cm)	¾ in (2 cm)
Royle's pika	7¾ in (20 cm)	None
Rufous elephant shrew	6 in (15 cm)	6¼ in (16 cm)
Snowshoe hare	18⅓ in (47 cm)	2 in (5 cm)
Sumatran rabbit	15⅔ in (40 cm)	⅗ in (1.5 cm)
Volcano rabbit	12½ in (32 cm)	1¼ in (3 cm)

Key

These icons show at a glance how each animal is measured. When every animal within a group is measured the same way, the icon is placed at the top of the group's measurement column. Invertebrates are so diverse that even within the same group they are often measured differently. In these cases, a smaller icon appears next to each measurement.

Mammals

Length The mammal's head and body length is measured, excluding its tail. Aquatic mammals are measured from the head to the tip of the tail.

Tail The length of the mammal's tail is measured. Some mammals do not have tails: This is indicated by the word "None."

Birds

Length Most birds are measured by length, from the tip of the bill to the tip of the tail feathers.

Height Some flightless birds, including ostriches and penguins, are measured by height, from head to foot.

Reptiles

Length Turtles and tortoises can pull their heads back into their shells. The length of the shell is measured.

Length All other groups of reptiles are measured from the head to the tip of the tail.

Amphibians

Length The head and body length is measured. For species with tails, the tail is included.

Fish

Length The fish's head and body length is measured, from the head to the tip of the tail fin.

Invertebrates

Length Most invertebrates are measured by head and body length, excluding antennae.

Height Some invertebrates grow upward. These species are measured by their height.

Width Some invertebrates have shells or bodies that are measured across rather than lengthwise.

Wingspan Butterflies and moths are measured from wing tip to wing tip, at the widest point.

Birds

Ratites & tinamous

Elegant crested tinamou	16 in (41 cm)
Emu	6½ ft (2 m)
Great tinamou	18 in (46 cm)
Greater rhea	5¼ ft (1.6 m)
Little spotted kiwi	17½ in (45 cm)
Ostrich	9½ ft (2.9 m)
Southern cassowary	6½ ft (2 m)
Variegated tinamou	13 in (33 cm)

Gamebirds

California quail	11 in (28 cm)
Gray-striped francolin	13 in (33 cm)
Great argus	6½ ft (2 m)
Great curassow	36 in (92 cm)
Indian peafowl	7 ft (2.1 m)
Koklass pheasant	25 in (64 cm)
Mikado pheasant	33½ in (86 cm)
Ocellated turkey	4 ft (1.2 m)
Red junglefowl	29¼ in (75 cm)
Red spurfowl	14 in (36 cm)
Red-legged partridge	14¾ in (38 cm)
Reeves's pheasant	7 ft (2.1 m)
Rock ptarmigan	14¾ in (38 cm)
Vulturine guineafowl	23½ in (60 cm)
White-crested guan	32⅓ in (83 cm)

Waterfowl

Bean goose	34⅓ in (88 cm)
Black-necked swan	3⅔ ft (1.1 m)
Canada goose	3⅔ ft (1.1 m)
Comb duck	29⅔ in (76 cm)
Common eider	27 in (69 cm)
Common pochard	17½ in (45 cm)
Common shelduck	25⅓ in (65 cm)
Coscoroba swan	3¾ ft (1.1 m)
Freckled duck	23 in (59 cm)
Magpie goose	35 in (90 cm)
Mallard	25⅓ in (65 cm)
Muscovy duck	32¾ in (84 cm)
Mute swan	5 ft (1.5 m)
Northern shoveler	18¾ in (48 cm)
Oldsquaw	16½ in (42 cm)
Orinoco goose	25¾ in (66 cm)
Red-breasted goose	21½ in (55 cm)
Red-crested pochard	22⅔ in (58 cm)
Snow goose	31¼ in (80 cm)
Southern screamer	37 in (95 cm)
Torrent duck	18 in (46 cm)
White-faced whistling-duck	19½ in (50 cm)
Whooper swan	5 ft (1.5 m)
Wood duck	20 in (51 cm)

Albatrosses & grebes

Arctic loon	26½ in (68 cm)
Band-rumped storm-petrel	9 in (23 cm)
Cape petrel	15¼ in (39 cm)
Common diving-petrel	9¾ in (25 cm)
Common loon	35 in (90 cm)
Eared grebe	13 in (33 cm)
Gray petrel	19½ in (50 cm)
Great crested grebe	25 in (64 cm)
Great grebe	30½ in (78 cm)
Hooded grebe	13¼ in (34 cm)
Jouanin's petrel	12½ in (32 cm)
Little grebe	11 in (28 cm)
New Zealand grebe	11⅔ in (30 cm)
Northern fulmar	19½ in (50 cm)
Red-throated loon	27⅓ in (70 cm)
Royal albatross	4 ft (1.2 m)
Wedge-tailed shearwater	18 in (46 cm)
Western grebe	29⅔ in (76 cm)
Wilson's storm-petrel	7½ in (19 cm)
Yellow-billed loon	35 in (90 cm)
Yellow-nosed albatross	29⅔ in (76 cm)

Herons & flamingos

Andean flamingo	3⅔ ft (1.1 m)
Boat-billed heron	20 in (51 cm)
Cattle egret	20 in (51 cm)
Great blue heron	4½ ft (1.4 m)
Greater flamingo	4¾ ft (1.45 m)
Hamerkop	21¾ in (56 cm)
Sacred ibis	35 in (90 cm)
Whistling heron	23¾ in (61 cm)
White-crested bittern	31¼ in (80 cm)
Wood stork	3¼ ft (1 m)

Pelicans

Anhinga	35 in (90 cm)
Dalmatian pelican	5½ ft (1.7 m)
Darter	37¾ in (97 cm)
Double-crested cormorant	35½ in (91 cm)
European shag	30¾ in (79 cm)
Great cormorant	3¼ ft (1 m)
Great white pelican	5¾ ft (1.75 m)
Lesser frigatebird	31⅓ in (81 cm)
Northern gannet	36 in (92 cm)
Pelagic cormorant	28¾ in (74 cm)
Peruvian booby	3¼ ft (1 m)
Red-tailed tropicbird	19½ in (50 cm)

Birds of prey

African cuckoo-hawk	15⅔ in (40 cm)
Andean condor	4¼ ft (1.3 m)
Bald eagle	3⅔ ft (1.1 m)
Black baza	13¾ in (35 cm)
Black harrier	19½ in (50 cm)
Black kite	21½ in (55 cm)
Cinereous vulture	3¼ ft (1 m)
Collared falconet	7 in (18 cm)
Common kestrel	14½ in (37 cm)
Crested serpent-eagle	29⅔ in (76 cm)
Crowned eagle	33 in (85 cm)
Eurasian griffon	3⅔ ft (1.1 m)
European honey-buzzard	22⅔ in (58 cm)
Harris's hawk	22⅔ in (58 cm)
Javan hawk-eagle	23¾ in (61 cm)
Osprey	22⅔ in (58 cm)
Secretary bird	5 ft (1.5 m)
Yellow-headed caracara	16¾ in (43 cm)

Penguins

Adelie penguin	23¾ in (61 cm)
Emperor penguin	4 ft (1.2 m)
Jackass penguin	3¼ ft (1 m)
King penguin	3¼ ft (1 m)
Little penguin	17½ in (45 cm)
Royal penguin	27⅓ in (70 cm)
Snares penguin	23½ in (60 cm)
Yellow-eyed penguin	23½ in (60 cm)

Cranes

African finfoot	23 in (59 cm)
Barred buttonquail	6⅔ in (17 cm)
Black crowned crane	3¼ ft (1 m)
Corncrake	11⅔ in (30 cm)
Demoiselle crane	35 in (90 cm)
Denham's bustard	3¼ ft (1 m)
Hoatzin	27⅓ in (70 cm)
Horned coot	20⅔ in (53 cm)
Lesser florican	20 in (51 cm)
Limpkin	27⅓ in (70 cm)
Sunbittern	18¾ in (48 cm)
White-breasted mesite	4 ft (1.2 m)

Waders & shorebirds

Atlantic puffin	14 in (36 cm)
Beach stone curlew	21¾ in (56 cm)
Black skimmer	18 in (46 cm)
Black-faced sheathbill	16 in (41 cm)
Black-tailed godwit	16½ in (42 cm)
Black-winged stilt	15⅔ in (40 cm)
Collared pratincole	9¾ in (25 cm)
Common redshank	11 in (28 cm)
Common snipe	10½ in (27 cm)
Common tern	14¾ in (38 cm)
Crested auklet	10½ in (27 cm)
Curlew sandpiper	8½ in (22 cm)
Fairy tern	10½ in (27 cm)
Great black-backed gull	29⅔ in (76 cm)
Herring gull	25¾ in (66 cm)
Ibisbill	16 in (41 cm)
Pied avocet	16¾ in (43 cm)
Red-necked phalarope	7¾ in (20 cm)
Ruff	12½ in (32 cm)
Southern lapwing	14¾ in (38 cm)
Tufted puffin	14¾ in (38 cm)

Pigeons & sandgrouse

Banded fruit dove	13¼ in (34 cm)
Chestnut-bellied sandgrouse	13 in (33 cm)
Emerald dove	10½ in (27 cm)
Pallas's sandgrouse	15⅔ in (40 cm)
Pied imperial pigeon	16 in (41 cm)
Rock dove	13 in (33 cm)
Seychelles blue pigeon	9⅓ in (24 cm)
Victoria crowned pigeon	29⅔ in (76 cm)
Zebra dove	8¼ in (21 cm)

Cuckoos & turacos

Common cuckoo	13 in (33 cm)
Dideric cuckoo	7 in (18 cm)
Great blue turaco	29¼ in (75 cm)
Greater coucal	20¼ in (52 cm)
Greater roadrunner	21¾ in (56 cm)
Hartlaub's turaco	16¾ in (43 cm)
Jacobin cuckoo	13¼ in (34 cm)
Rufous-vented ground cuckoo	17½ in (45 cm)
Smooth-billed ani	14½ in (37 cm)
Violet turaco	19½ in (50 cm)

Parrots

Blue-fronted parrot	14½ in (37 cm)
Buff-faced pygmy parrot	4 in (10 cm)
Burrowing parakeet	18 in (46 cm)
Eclectus parrot	14 in (36 cm)
Fischer's lovebird	6¼ in (16 cm)
Galah	13¾ in (35 cm)
Ground parrot	11⅔ in (30 cm)
Hyacinth macaw	3¼ ft (1 m)
Kakapo	25 in (64 cm)
Kea	18¾ in (48 cm)
Maroon-faced parakeet	9 in (23 cm)
Military macaw	27⅓ in (70 cm)
Plum-headed parakeet	13 in (33 cm)
Rainbow lorikeet	10 in (26 cm)
Scarlet macaw	34¾ in (89 cm)
Senegal parrot	9¾ in (25 cm)
Swift parrot	9¾ in (25 cm)
White-crowned parrot	9⅓ in (24 cm)
Yellow-collared lovebird	5⅔ in (14.5 cm)

Nightjars & owls

Barn owl	17 in (44 cm)
Barred owl	20⅔ in (53 cm)
Black-banded owl	17½ in (45 cm)
Boreal owl	9¾ in (25 cm)
Burrowing owl	9⅓ in (24 cm)
Common pauraque	11 in (28 cm)
Common poorwill	7¾ in (20 cm)
Common potoo	14¾ in (38 cm)
Elf owl	6 in (15 cm)
Eurasian pygmy owl	6⅔ in (17 cm)
European nightjar	11 in (28 cm)
Great horned owl	21½ in (55 cm)
Long-eared owl	14¾ in (38 cm)
Northern saw-whet owl	7¾ in (20 cm)
Oilbird	19½ in (50 cm)
Snowy owl	23 in (59 cm)
Spectacled owl	18 in (46 cm)
Spotted nightjar	11⅔ in (30 cm)
Tawny frogmouth	20⅔ in (53 cm)
Tropical screech owl	9⅓ in (24 cm)
Ural owl	24¼ in (62 cm)
Verreaux's eagle-owl	25⅓ in (65 cm)

Hummingbirds & swifts

Alpine swift	8½ in (22 cm)
Asian palm swift	5 in (13 cm)
Collared Inca	5⅔ in (14.5 cm)
Festive coquette	3⅓ in (8.5 cm)
Fiery-tailed awlbill	4 in (10 cm)
Giant hummingbird	9 in (23 cm)
Gray-rumped treeswift	9 in (23 cm)
Purple-throated carib	4⅔ in (12 cm)
Ruby topaz	2 in (5 cm)
Sword-billed hummingbird	9 in (23 cm)

Kingfishers

African pygmy kingfisher	4⅔ in (12 cm)
Banded kingfisher	7¾ in (20 cm)
Belted kingfisher	13 in (33 cm)
Carmine bee-eater	10½ in (27 cm)
Common hoopoe	12½ in (32 cm)
Common kingfisher	6¼ in (16 cm)
Cuban tody	4¼ in (11 cm)
Cuckoo-roller	19½ in (50 cm)
Dollarbird	12½ in (32 cm)
European roller	11⅔ in (30 cm)
Great hornbill	3⅔ ft (1.1 m)
Green kingfisher	8½ in (22 cm)
Hook-billed kingfisher	10½ in (27 cm)
Laughing kookaburra	16¾ in (43 cm)
Lilac-cheeked kingfisher	11 in (28 cm)
Narina's trogon	12½ in (32 cm)
Pied kingfisher	11 in (28 cm)
Red-headed trogon	13¾ in (35 cm)
Resplendent quetzal	15⅔ in (40 cm)
Speckled mousebird	15⅔ in (40 cm)
White-headed mousebird	13¾ in (35 cm)
White-tailed trogon	11 in (28 cm)

Woodpeckers

Acorn woodpecker	9 in (23 cm)
Black-rumped woodpecker	11⅓ in (29 cm)
Blue-throated barbet	9 in (23 cm)
Channel-billed toucan	21¾ in (56 cm)
Curl-crested aracari	18 in (46 cm)
Emerald toucanet	14½ in (37 cm)
Golden-tailed woodpecker	9 in (23 cm)
Gray woodpecker	7¾ in (20 cm)
Gray-breasted mountain toucan	18¾ in (48 cm)
Greater honeyguide	7¾ in (20 cm)
Green woodpecker	13 in (33 cm)
Ground woodpecker	11⅔ in (30 cm)
Northern wryneck	6¼ in (16 cm)
Paradise jacamar	13¼ in (34 cm)
Pileated woodpecker	18 in (46 cm)
Red-and-yellow barbet	9 in (23 cm)
Rufous woodpecker	9¾ in (25 cm)
Spotted puffbird	7 in (18 cm)
Yellow-bellied sapsucker	8¼ in (21 cm)

Perching birds

American goldfinch	5 in (13 cm)
American robin	19¾ in (25 cm)
Asian paradise-flycatcher	19½ in (50 cm)
Bananaquit	4 in (10 cm)
Barred antshrike	6¼ in (16 cm)
Black phoebe	7½ in (19 cm)
Black-bellied gnateater	6¼ in (16 cm)
Black-capped vireo	4¼ in (11 cm)
Black-thighed grosbeak	7¾ in (20 cm)
Black-throated accentor	6 in (15 cm)
Black-throated huet-huet	9 in (23 cm)
Black-throated thrush	10½ in (27 cm)
Blue-crowned manakin	3½ in (9 cm)
Blue-faced parrotfinch	5 in (13 cm)
Bluethroat	5½ in (14 cm)
Brown-throated sunbird	5½ in (14 cm)
Cape sugarbird	18 in (46 cm)
Chestnut-crowned babbler	8½ in (22 cm)
Collared redstart	5 in (12.5 cm)
Crimson chat	4⅔ in (12 cm)
Eastern paradise whydah	13 in (33 cm)
Eastern whipbird	10⅓ in (26.5 cm)
Eurasian golden oriole	8½ in (22 cm)
Fairy gerygone	4¼ in (11 cm)
Fluffy-backed tit-babbler	6¼ in (16 cm)
Goldcrest	3½ in (9 cm)
Golden bowerbird	9¾ in (25 cm)
Golden-headed manakin	3½ in (9 cm)
Gouldian finch	5½ in (14 cm)
Greater short-toed lark	6 in (15 cm)
Icterine warbler	5⅓ in (13.5 cm)
Madagascan wagtail	7½ in (19 cm)
Marsh wren	5 in (13 cm)
Northern scrub robin	8½ in (22 cm)
Orange-bellied leafbird	7½ in (19 cm)
Oriental white-eye	4¼ in (11 cm)
Penduline tit	4¼ in (11 cm)
Red-backed shrike	7 in (18 cm)
Red-bellied pitta	6¼ in (16 cm)
Red-billed blue magpie	27⅓ in (70 cm)
Red-billed buffalo weaver	9 in (23 cm)
Red-billed scythebill	10½ in (27 cm)
Red-browed treecreeper	6¼ in (16 cm)
Red-headed honeyeater	4⅔ in (12 cm)
Red-throated pipit	6¼ in (16 cm)
Red-whiskered bulbul	7¾ in (20 cm)
Red-winged blackbird	8½ in (22 cm)
Ruddy treerunner	6¼ in (16 cm)
Scarlet minivet	9 in (23 cm)
Scarlet tanager	6⅔ in (17 cm)
Shining starling	8½ in (22 cm)
Snow bunting	6⅔ in (17 cm)

Southern red bishop	4⅔ in (12 cm)
Streak-chested antpitta	5½ in (14 cm)
Superb lyrebird	35 in (90 cm)
Three-wattled bellbird	11⅔ in (30 cm)
Tropical gnatcatcher	3½ in (9 cm)
Tufted flycatcher	5⅓ in (13.5 cm)
Turquoise cotinga	7¼ in (18.5 cm)
Variegated fairy-wren	6 in (15 cm)
Western parotia	13 in (33 cm)
White-banded swallow	6 in (15 cm)
White-browed shortwing	5 in (13 cm)
White-browed woodswallow	7¾ in (20 cm)
White-capped dipper	6½ in (16.5 cm)
White-necked picathartes	15⅔ in (40 cm)
White-necked raven	21½ in (55 cm)
Yellow-bellied fantail	4⅔ in (12 cm)

Reptiles

Crocodilians & tuatara

African dwarf crocodile	6¼ ft (1.9 m)
American alligator	14¾ ft (4.5 m)
American crocodile	16½ ft (5 m)
Black caiman	13 ft (4 m)
Chinese alligator	6½ ft (2 m)
False gharial	16½ ft (5 m)
Gharial	23 ft (7 m)
Mugger	13 ft (4 m)
Nile crocodile	19⅔ ft (6 m)
Orinoco crocodile	16½ ft (5 m)
Saltwater crocodile	23 ft (7 m)
Siamese crocodile	13 ft (4 m)
Spectacled caiman	8½ ft (2.6 m)
Tuatara	23½ in (60 cm)

Turtles & tortoises

Alligator snapping turtle	31½ in (80 cm)
Australian pig-nosed turtle	29⅔ in (76 cm)
Bell's hinge-back tortoise	8½ in (22 cm)
Black-breasted leaf turtle	4½ in (11.5 cm)
Central American river turtle	25¾ in (66 cm)
European pond turtle	7¾ in (20 cm)
Fitzroy turtle	10 in (26 cm)
Flatback turtle	37½ in (96 cm)
Gopher tortoise	10½ in (27 cm)
Green turtle	5 ft (1.5 m)
Hawksbill turtle	35½ in (91 cm)
Hilaire's toadhead turtle	15⅔ in (40 cm)
Indian softshell turtle	27⅓ in (70 cm)
Leatherback turtle	7 ft (2.1 m)
Loggerhead	4 ft (1.2 m)
Malayan snail-eating turtle	7¾ in (20 cm)
Nile softshell turtle	37 in (95 cm)
Painted terrapin	23½ in (60 cm)
Painted turtle	9¾ in (25 cm)
Ringed sawback	8¼ in (21 cm)
River terrapin	23½ in (60 cm)
Smooth softshell turtle	13¾ in (35 cm)
Twist-necked turtle	6⅔ in (17 cm)
Victoria short-necked turtle	10 in (26 cm)

Lizards

Banded galliwasp	7¾ in (20 cm)
Banded tree anole	3½ in (9 cm)
Black iguana	3¼ ft (1 m)
Borneo earless monitor	18 in (46 cm)
Burton's snake-lizard	23¾ in (61 cm)
Chinese crocodile lizard	18 in (46 cm)
Chinese water dragon	29⅔ in (76 cm)
Chuckwalla	16½ in (42 cm)
Collared lizard	14 in (36 cm)
Common agama	9¾ in (25 cm)
Common leopard gecko	9¾ in (25 cm)
Common wall gecko	6 in (15 cm)
Crocodile monitor	9 ft (2.8 m)
Desert rainbow skink	9 in (23 cm)
Desert spiny lizard	11⅔ in (30 cm)
Eastern bearded dragon	19½ in (50 cm)
Emerald skink	9¾ in (25 cm)
Five-lined flying dragon	10½ in (27 cm)
Frilled lizard	29¼ in (75 cm)
Gallot's lizard	12½ in (32 cm)
Green basilisk lizard	29¼ in (75 cm)
Green iguana	6½ ft (2 m)
Green thornytail iguana	7 in (18 cm)
Horned leaf chameleon	3½ in (9 cm)
Indo-Chinese forest lizard	15⅔ in (40 cm)
Jackson's chameleon	11⅔ in (30 cm)
Karoo girdled lizard	7 in (18 cm)
Knysna dwarf chameleon	6 in (15 cm)
Komodo dragon	10 ft (3 m)
Kuhl's flying gecko	6 in (15 cm)
Leopard lizard	11⅔ in (30 cm)
Lesser chameleon	11⅔ in (30 cm)
Madagascar day gecko	11⅔ in (30 cm)
Menorca wall lizard	7 in (18 cm)
Merrem's Madagascar swift	7¾ in (20 cm)
Mexican beaded lizard	3¼ ft (1 m)
Milo's wall lizard	7 in (18 cm)
Northern leaf-tailed gecko	13¾ in (35 cm)
Northwestern sandslider	4 in (10 cm)
Ocellated tegu	25⅓ in (65 cm)
Otago skink	11⅔ in (30 cm)
Parson's chameleon	23½ in (60 cm)
Rainbow lizard	9⅓ in (24 cm)
Rhinoceros iguana	4 ft (1.2 m)
Rough-scaled plated lizard	18¾ in (48 cm)
Sawtail lizard	5 in (12.5 cm)
Snake-eyed lizard	7¾ in (20 cm)
Spiny-tailed monitor	25¾ in (66 cm)
Sumatra nose-horned lizard	8½ in (22 cm)
Tiger lizard	9¾ in (25 cm)
West Indian iguana	3½ ft (1.05 m)

Snakes

Adder	27⅓ in (70 cm)
Aesculapian snake	7 ft (2.2 m)
Amazon false fer-de-lance	4 ft (1.2 m)
Anaconda	21⅔ ft (6.6 m)
Arafura file snake	6 ft (1.8 m)
Arizona coral snake	20⅔ in (53 cm)
Black mamba	9 ft (2.8 m)
Black-headed python	9 ft (2.8 m)
Black-tailed rattlesnake	4¼ ft (1.3 m)
Blood python	10 ft (3 m)
Blue-lipped sea krait	3¼ ft (1 m)
Boomslang	5¼ ft (1.6 m)
Bushmaster	14 ft (4.3 m)
Cantil	3¼ ft (1 m)
Chinese rat snake	8½ ft (2.6 m)
Common boa constrictor	10 ft (3 m)
Common bronze-back snake	3¼ ft (1 m)
Common death adder	29⅔ in (76 cm)
Copperhead	4 ft (1.2 m)
Coral cylinder snake	36 in (92 cm)
Drummond Hay's earth snake	13 in (33 cm)
Eastern coral snake	29⅔ in (76 cm)
Emerald tree boa	5 ft (1.5 m)
European grass snake	6½ ft (2 m)
False water cobra	9 ft (2.8 m)
Fea viper	29⅔ in (76 cm)
Forest flame snake	3¼ ft (1 m)
Green whip snake	6½ ft (2 m)
Isthmian dwarf boa	3¼ ft (1 m)
Jararacussu	7 ft (2.2 m)
King cobra	16½ ft (5 m)
Lichtenstein's night adder	3¼ ft (1 m)
Mangrove snake	8 ft (2.5 m)
Masked water snake	4 ft (1.2 m)
Massasauga	29⅔ in (76 cm)
Mexican burrowing python	4½ ft (1.4 m)
Milk snake	35 in (90 cm)
Mojave rattlesnake	4 ft (1.2 m)
Monocled cobra	6 ft (1.8 m)
Mulga snake	9 ft (2.8 m)
Natal black snake	3¼ ft (1 m)
Northern water snake	3½ ft (1.05 m)
Red cylinder snake	3¼ ft (1 m)
Rhombic egg-eating snake	12 in (31 cm)
Ringed hognose snake	23½ in (60 cm)
Ring-neck snake	25¾ in (66 cm)
Schokari sand racer	5¼ ft (1.6 m)
Striped kukri snake	25¾ in (66 cm)
Sunbeam snake	5 ft (1.5 m)
Taipan	9 ft (2.8 m)
Tatar sand boa	4 ft (1.2 m)
Tiger snake	8 ft (2.4 m)
Turtle-headed sea snake	4 ft (1.2 m)
Western brown snake	6 ft (1.8 m)
Western diamondback rattlesnake	6 ft (1.8 m)
Wood snake	3¼ ft (1 m)
Yellow-blotched palm pit viper	9¾ in (25 cm)

Amphibians

Salamanders & caecilians

Blue-spotted salamander	5 in (13 cm)
California giant salamander	14 in (36 cm)
Chinese giant salamander	4½ ft (1.4 m)
Chinese salamander	4 in (10 cm)
Common newt	4½ in (11.5 cm)
European fire salamander	9¾ in (25 cm)
Fischer's clawed salamander	5 in (13 cm)
Four-toed salamander	4 in (10 cm)
Hellbender	20⅔ in (53 cm)
Jackson's mushroomtongue salamander	3 in (7.5 cm)
Japanese firebelly newt	5 in (13 cm)
Lesser siren	19½ in (50 cm)
Mengla County caecilian	16½ in (42 cm)
Mudpuppy	13¾ in (35 cm)
Red-backed salamander	5 in (13 cm)
Siberian salamander	9¾ in (25 cm)
Slimy salamander	6¼ in (16 cm)
Tiger salamander	9¾ in (25 cm)
Two-toed amphiuma	29⅔ in (76 cm)
Vietnam warty newt	7¾ in (20 cm)

Frogs & toads

Barking tree frog	2¾ in (7 cm)
Blue poison frog	2 in (5 cm)
Brown New Zealand frog	2 in (5 cm)
Bullfrog	7¾ in (20 cm)
Cane toad	9⅓ in (24 cm)
Common parsley frog	2 in (5 cm)
Coqui	2¼ in (5.5 cm)
Crucifix toad	2¼ in (5.5 cm)
Dahaoping sucker frog	4 in (10 cm)
Dainty green tree frog	1¾ in (4.5 cm)
Everett's Asian tree toad	11⅔ in (30 cm)
Giant banjo frog	3½ in (9 cm)
Hairy frog	4¼ in (11 cm)
Harlequin frog	2 in (5 cm)
Horned toad	3 in (8 cm)
Java flying frog	3½ in (9 cm)
Madagascar reed frog	1½ in (4 cm)
Malayan horned frog	5 in (12.5 cm)
Marsupial frog	2¾ in (7 cm)
Mexican burrowing toad	3½ in (9 cm)
Nicaragua giant glass frog	1 in (2.5 cm)
Oriental firebelly toad	2⅓ in (6 cm)
Ornate horned toad	7¾ in (20 cm)
Painted frog	3 in (8 cm)
Red rain frog	1½ in (4 cm)
Red toad	5 in (13 cm)
Red-eyed tree frog	3 in (7.5 cm)
Schmidt's forest frog	4 in (10 cm)
Shovel-headed tree frog	3 in (7.5 cm)
Singapore wart frog	4 in (10 cm)
Southern bell frog	4 in (10 cm)
Spotted snout-burrower	2⅓ in (6 cm)
Strawberry poison frog	1 in (2.5 cm)
Surinam toad	7¾ in (20 cm)
Syrian spadefoot toad	3 in (8 cm)
Tailed frog	2 in (5 cm)
Tulear golden frog	1¼ in (3.2 cm)
Turtle frog	2⅓ in (6 cm)
Vizcacheras's white-lipped frog	4 in (10 cm)
Weal's running frog	1¾ in (4.5 cm)

Fish

Jawless fish

Atlantic hagfish	23¾ in (61 cm)
European river lamprey	19 in (49 cm)
Pacific lamprey	29⅔ in (76 cm)
Pouched lamprey	24¼ in (62 cm)
Sea lamprey	35 in (90 cm)

Cartilaginous fish

Angel shark	8 ft (2.4 m)
Atlantic guitarfish	29⅔ in (76 cm)
Blue shark	13 ft (4 m)
Blue-spotted ribbontail ray	27⅓ in (70 cm)
Bramble shark	10¼ ft (3.1 m)
Bull shark	11½ ft (3.5 m)
Common stingray	4½ ft (1.4 m)
Cownose ray	7 ft (2.1 m)
Devil fish	13 ft (4 m)
Great white shark	23⅔ ft (7.2 m)
Japanese butterfly ray	3¼ ft (1 m)
Largetooth sawfish	16½ ft (5 m)
Longnose sawshark	4½ ft (1.4 m)
Manta	22 ft (6.7 m)
Marbled electric ray	3¼ ft (1 m)
Nurse shark	14 ft (4.3 m)
Ocellate river stingray	3¼ ft (1 m)
Sharpnose sevengill shark	4½ ft (1.4 m)
Shortfin mako	13 ft (4 m)
Smooth hammerhead	16½ ft (5 m)
Soupfin shark	6⅓ ft (1.95 m)
Spiny dogfish	5¼ ft (1.6 m)
Spotted eagle ray	9 ft (2.8 m)
Spotted ratfish	37 in (95 cm)
Thornback ray	4 ft (1.2 m)
Tiger shark	24¼ ft (7.4 m)
Whale shark	59 ft (18 m)

Bony fish

Alaska blackfish	13 in (33 cm)
American anglerfish	4 ft (1.2 m)
American shad	29⅔ in (76 cm)
Angel squeaker	21½ in (55 cm)
Atlantic cod	5 ft (1.5 m)
Atlantic herring	16¾ in (43 cm)
Atlantic salmon	5 ft (1.5 m)
Ayu	27⅓ in (70 cm)
Beluga	13 ft (4 m)
Bitterling	4¼ in (11 cm)
Blackfin wolf-herring	3¼ ft (1 m)
Blunt-jaw elephantnose	15⅔ in (40 cm)
Bonefish	3¼ ft (1 m)
Bowfin	3⅔ ft (1.1 m)
Burbot	5 ft (1.5 m)
California slickhead	23¾ in (61 cm)
Capelin	7¾ in (20 cm)
Chain pickerel	38⅔ in (99 cm)
Cherry salmon	27⅔ in (71 cm)
Chinese sucker	23½ in (60 cm)
Chinese swordfish	10 ft (3 m)
Cisco	22¼ in (57 cm)
Coelacanth	6½ ft (2 m)
Common carp	4 ft (1.2 m)
Conger eel	8¾ ft (2.7 m)
Cutthroat trout	38⅔ in (99 cm)
Electric catfish	4 ft (1.2 m)
Electric eel	8 ft (2.4 m)
Emperor tetra	2¼ in (5.5 cm)
European eel	3¼ ft (1 m)
European hake	4½ ft (1.4 m)
European pilchard	9¾ in (25 cm)
European smelt	11⅔ in (30 cm)
European sprat	6¼ in (16 cm)
European sturgeon	11½ ft (3.5 m)
Freshwater butterflyfish	4⅔ in (12 cm)
Geometric moray	25⅓ in (65 cm)
Gizzard shad	22¼ in (57 cm)
Glass catfish	6 in (15 cm)
Golden trout	27⅔ in (71 cm)
Grayling	23½ in (60 cm)
Haddock	35 in (90 cm)
Harlequin rasbora	1¾ in (4.5 cm)
Hatchetfish	3½ in (9 cm)
Huchen	5 ft (1.5 m)
Laced moray	10 ft (3 m)
Lake trout	4 ft (1.2 m)
Longnose gar	6 ft (1.8 m)
Marbled hatchetfish	1⅓ in (3.5 cm)
Metallic lanternfish	3 in (8 cm)
Milk fish	6 ft (1.8 m)
Mottled bichir	21 in (54 cm)
Mudminnow	5 in (13 cm)
Northern pearleye	9⅓ in (24 cm)
Northern pike	4½ ft (1.4 m)
Oarfish	26¼ ft (8 m)
Onion-eye grenadier	3¼ ft (1 m)
Oxeye	5 ft (1.5 m)
Pacific viperfish	9¾ in (25 cm)
Peruvian anchoveta	7¾ in (20 cm)
Pink salmon	29⅔ in (76 cm)
Rainbow trout	3¾ ft (1.15 m)
Redeye piranha	16½ in (42 cm)
Round herring	9¾ in (25 cm)

Sea trout	4½ ft (1.4 m)
Sockeye salmon	32¾ in (84 cm)
Spanish sardine	12 in (31 cm)
Spanner barb	7 in (18 cm)
Spotted garden eel	14 in (36 cm)
Starry handfish	11⅔ in (30 cm)
Stone loach	8¼ in (21 cm)
Stout beardfish	18¾ in (48 cm)
Striped eel-catfish	13 in (33 cm)
Swallower	5¼ ft (1.6 m)
Tarpon	8 ft (2.4 m)
Trout perch	7¾ in (20 cm)
Wels catfish	10 ft (3 m)
West African lungfish	3¼ ft (1 m)

Spiny-rayed fish

Amazon leaffish	3 in (7.5 cm)
Archerfish	11⅔ in (30 cm)
Atlantic halibut	8 ft (2.5 m)
Atlantic mudskipper	9¾ in (25 cm)
Balloonfish	19½ in (50 cm)
Barramundi perch	6 ft (1.8 m)
Blue marlin	15 ft (4.6 m)
Brill	29¼ in (75 cm)
Brook silverside	5 in (13 cm)
Clown anemonefish	4 in (10 cm)
Clown triggerfish	19½ in (50 cm)
Clown wrasse	4 ft (1.2 m)
Crown squirrelfish	6⅔ in (17 cm)
Emperor angelfish	15⅔ in (40 cm)
Emperor snapper	3¼ ft (1 m)
Eurasian perch	20 in (51 cm)
False cleanerfish	4½ in (11.5 cm)
Flat needlefish	4½ ft (1.4 m)
Forktail rainbowfish	2 in (5 cm)
Freshwater pufferfish	26 in (67 cm)
Golden pheasant panchax	3 in (7.5 cm)
Goldribbon soapfish	15⅔ in (40 cm)
Gourami	27⅓ in (70 cm)
Guineafowl puffer	19½ in (50 cm)
Guppy	2 in (5 cm)
Indo-Pacific sailfish	11½ ft (3.5 m)
Jack-knifefish	9¾ in (25 cm)
John Dory	25¾ in (66 cm)
Kissing gourami	11⅔ in (30 cm)
Largemouth bass	37¾ in (97 cm)
Leafy seadragon	15⅔ in (40 cm)
Moorish idol	9 in (23 cm)
Ocean sunfish	10¾ ft (3.3 m)
Pearl gourami	4⅔ in (12 cm)
Pineconefish	6⅔ in (17 cm)
Prickly leatherjacket	12 in (31 cm)
Radial firefish	9⅓ in (24 cm)
Red mullet	15⅔ in (40 cm)
Redtail surgeonfish	9⅓ in (24 cm)
Ringed pipefish	7½ in (19 cm)
Saberfin killie	1½ in (4 cm)
Sea goldie	6 in (15 cm)
Sharpchin flyingfish	9⅓ in (24 cm)
Shrimpfish	6 in (15 cm)
Siamese fighting fish	2½ in (6.5 cm)
Skipjack tuna	3⅔ ft (1.1 m)
Splitfin flashlightfish	13¾ in (35 cm)
Stonefish	14 in (36 cm)
Stripey	6¼ in (16 cm)
Summer flounder	36⅔ in (94 cm)
Swamp eel	18 in (46 cm)
Swordfish	16 ft (4.9 m)
Thornback cowfish	9 in (23 cm)
Threadfin rainbowfish	1⅓ in (3.5 cm)
Three-spined stickleback	2¾ in (7 cm)
Velvet whalefish	14 in (36 cm)
Viviparous blenny	20¼ in (52 cm)
Yellowback fusilier	15⅔ in (40 cm)

Invertebrates

Sponges & squirts

Acorn worm	11⅔ in (30 cm)
Arrow worm	⅛ in (4 mm)
Colonial sea squirt	4 in (10 cm)
Common lancelet	2 in (5 cm)
Glove sponge	23½ in (60 cm)
Gold sponge	2⅓ in (6 cm)
Ink-pot sea squirt	6 in (15 cm)
Lightbulb sea squirt	¾ in (2 cm)
Melon jellyfish	6 in (15 cm)
Neptune's cup	29¼ in (75 cm)
Purse sponge	2 in (5 cm)
Sea potato	4 in (10 cm)
Venus's flower basket	11⅔ in (30 cm)

Worms

Caenorhabditis elegans	1/25 in (1 mm)
Gastrotrich	⅛ in (3 mm)
Goblet worm	⅕ in (5 mm)
Human whipworm	2 in (5 cm)
Intestinal roundworm	15⅔ in (40 cm)
Medicinal leech	4 in (10 cm)
Night crawler	9¾ in (25 cm)
Palolo worm	23½ in (60 cm)
Polystoma integerrimum	1/25 in (1 mm)
Ragworm	7¾ in (20 cm)
Rotifer	1/100 in (0.4 mm)
Shovel-headed garden worm	11⅔ in (30 cm)
Spiny-crown worm	1/25 in (1 mm)
Velvet worm	2¾ in (7 cm)
Water bear	1/25 in (1 mm)

Corals & jellyfish

Beadlet anemone	3 in (8 cm)
Brachiopod	1⅓ in (3.5 cm)
Daisy anemone	6 in (15 cm)
Fire coral	27⅓ in (70 cm)
Formosan soft coral	3¼ ft (1 m)
Freshwater bryozoan	7¾ in (20 cm)
Green hydra	1/25 in (1 mm)
Lion's mane jellyfish	6½ ft (2 m)
Organ-pipe coral	3¼ ft (1 m)
Portuguese man-of-war (float)	4⅔ in (12 cm)
(tentacles)	33 ft (10 m)
Red brain coral	15⅔ in (40 cm)
West Indian sea fan	36 in (92 cm)
Yellow feathers	6 in (15 cm)

Mollusks

Atlantic thorny oyster	5½ in (14 cm)
Blue sea slug	1½ in (4 cm)
Blue-ringed octopus	7¾ in (20 cm)
Chocolate arion	6 in (15 cm)
Common cuttlefish	23½ in (60 cm)
Common egg cowrie	5 in (13 cm)
Common limpet	2⅓ in (6 cm)
Common nautilus	7¾ in (20 cm)
Common octopus	3¼ ft (1 m)
Deep-sea vampire squid	11 in (28 cm)
Elephant tusk	6 in (15 cm)
Escargot	2 in (5 cm)
European edible abalone	3½ in (9 cm)
Flat oyster	3 in (8 cm)
Flying squid	3¼ ft (1 m)
Freshwater pearl mussel	4 in (10 cm)
Giant squid	60 ft (18.3 m)
Giant tiger snail	12 in (31 cm)
Glistenworm	½ in (1.2 cm)
Gray garden slug	2 in (5 cm)
Lesser cuttlefish	2⅓ in (6 cm)
Long-finned squid	19½ in (50 cm)
Musky octopus	21½ in (55 cm)
Nudibranch	2 in (5 cm)
Nut shell	⅓ in (1 cm)
Paper nautilus	11⅔ in (30 cm)
Pen shell	3¼ ft (1 m)
Queen conch	11⅔ in (30 cm)
Spiny cockle	4½ in (11.5 cm)
Trumpet triton	17½ in (45 cm)
West Indian green chiton	3 in (8 cm)

Arachnids

Black widow	⅓ in (1 cm)
Book scorpion	⅛ in (4 mm)
Bristly millipede	⅛ in (3 mm)
European garden spider	¾ in (2 cm)
Fat-tailed scorpion	4⅔ in (12 cm)
Giant desert centipede	3 in (8 cm)
Golden orb weaver	2 in (5 cm)
Goldenrod spider	⅓ in (1 cm)
Gracile sea spider	⅓ in (1 cm)
Harvest bug	⅕ in (5 mm)
Hooded tick spider	⅓ in (1 cm)
Horseshoe crab	23½ in (60 cm)
House spider	⅓ in (1 cm)
Ladybird spider	⅕ in (5 mm)
Malaysian trapdoor spider	4 in (10 cm)
Mombasa golden starburst tarantula	2 in (5 cm)
Money spider	⅕ in (5 mm)
Orb weaver	¼ in (6 mm)
Pear bud mite	<1/100 in (0.2 mm)
Scabies mite	1/100 in (0.4 mm)
Sheep tick	⅗ in (1.5 cm)
Short-tailed whip-scorpion	⅛ in (3 mm)
Thorn spider	⅗ in (1.5 cm)
Tropical tentweb spider	1 in (2.5 cm)
Varroa mite	1/25 in (1 mm)
Wasp spider	⅔ in (1.7 cm)
Whip-scorpion	11⅔ in (30 cm)
Whip-spider	¾ in (2 cm)
Zebra jumping spider	¼ in (7 mm)

Crabs & crayfish

Acorn barnacle	1¼ in (3 cm)
Amphipod (*Caprella* sp.)	¼ in (7 mm)
Amphipod (*Gammarus* sp.)	⅔ in (1.8 cm)
Atlantic lobster	11⅔ in (30 cm)
Black tiger prawn	13 in (33 cm)
Cephalocarid	1⅓ in (3.5 cm)
Chinese mitten crab	3 in (8 cm)
Cleaner shrimp	2 in (5 cm)
Common pill wood louse	⅔ in (1.7 cm)
Copepod	1/50 in (0.5 mm)
European green crab	3 in (8 cm)
Freshwater fish louse	¼ in (7 mm)
Giant water flea	⅔ in (1.8 cm)
Horn-eyed ghost crab	3 in (8 cm)
Mantis shrimp	4 in (10 cm)
Mystarocarid	1/100 in (0.4 mm)
Ostracod	1/50 in (0.6 mm)
Spiny lobster	23½ in (60 cm)
Spinycheek crayfish	6¼ in (16 cm)
Tadpole shrimp	4 in (10 cm)
Tasmanian mountain shrimp	2 in (5 cm)

Dragonflies, mantids, cockroaches, termites & crickets

Beautiful demoiselle	2 in (5 cm)
Blue dasher	1¾ in (4.5 cm)
Blue-winged grasshopper	4 in (10 cm)
Common praying mantis	2½ in (6.5 cm)
Dawn dropwing	1½ in (4 cm)
Dipluran	⅕ in (5 mm)
German cockroach	⅔ in (1.6 cm)
Giant cockroach	3 in (8 cm)
Green banana roach	¾ in (2 cm)
Large fungus-growing termite	⅔ in (1.8 cm)
Migratory locust	2½ in (6.5 cm)
Orchid mantis	2 in (5 cm)
Proturan	1/12 in (2 mm)
Spinifex termite	¼ in (6 mm)
Springtail	1/10 in (2.5 mm)
Tropical leaf katydid	11⅔ in (30 cm)

Bugs

Assassin bug	¾ in (2 cm)
Cotton stainer bug	⅖ in (1.1 cm)
Green shield bug	½ in (1.4 cm)
Lace bug	1/10 in (2.5 mm)
Long-tailed mealy bug	⅛ in (3 mm)
Nettle ensign scale	⅙ in (4 mm)
Peanut-headed lanternfly	3½ in (9 cm)
Red and black froghopper	⅓ in (1 cm)
Red cicada	2 in (5 cm)
Spined stink bug	½ in (1.4 cm)
Treehopper	½ in (1.2 cm)
Water bug	1 in (2.5 cm)
Water measurer	⅓ in (1 cm)
Woolly apple aphid	1/12 in (2 mm)

Beetles

Ant-nest beetle	⅗ in (1.5 cm)
Bess beetle	2½ in (6.5 cm)
Bombardier beetle	1¼ in (3 cm)
Cigarette beetle	⅙ in (4 mm)
Colorado potato beetle	⅓ in (1 cm)
European burying beetle	¾ in (2 cm)
European splendor beetle	⅓ in (8 mm)
Fire beetle	1¾ in (4.5 cm)
Glow worm	¾ in (2 cm)
Golden rove beetle	¾ in (2 cm)
Goliath beetle	4⅔ in (12 cm)
Harlequin beetle	3 in (8 cm)
Hercules beetle	7 in (18 cm)
Java fiddle beetle	4 in (10 cm)
King weevil	1 in (2.5 cm)
Seven-spotted lady beetle	⅓ in (8 mm)
Spanish fly	¾ in (2 cm)
Stag beetle	3 in (8 cm)
Tiger beetle	¾ in (2 cm)

Butterflies & moths

African giant swallowtail	9¾ in (25 cm)
African monarch	2⅓ in (6 cm)
Bent-wing ghost moth	9¾ in (25 cm)
Bird-cherry ermine	1 in (2.5 cm)
Bogong moth	2 in (5 cm)
Carpet moth	1 in (2.5 cm)
Dead leaf butterfly	2¾ in (7 cm)
Eliena skipper	1⅓ in (3.5 cm)
European pine shoot moth	1 in (2.5 cm)
Eyed hawk moth	3 in (8 cm)
Giant atlas moth	11⅔ in (30 cm)
Helena butterfly	6 in (15 cm)
Hornet clearwing	1½ in (4 cm)
Large blue	1½ in (4 cm)
Mimic	2⅓ in (6 cm)
Mottled umber	1¾ in (4.5 cm)
Northern jungle queen butterfly	5 in (13 cm)
Orange-barred sulphur	2¾ in (7 cm)
Postman, the	3 in (8 cm)
Silver-washed fritillary	2¾ in (7 cm)

Bees, wasps & ants

Bull ant	¾ in (2 cm)
Common wasp	1¾ in (4.5 cm)
Currant sawfly	⅓ in (7.5 mm)
Ensign wasp	⅗ in (1.5 cm)
Giant hunting ant	1¼ in (3 cm)
Honey ant	⅓ in (9 mm)
Oak apple gall wasp	1/10 in (2.5 mm)
Paper wasp	⅔ in (1.6 cm)
Potter wasp	¾ in (1.9 cm)
Red-tailed bumblebee	1¼ in (3 cm)
Rose sawfly	⅓ in (1 cm)
Ruby-tailed wasp	½ in (1.2 cm)
Sand digger wasp	1 in (2.5 cm)
Sirex parasite	1½ in (4 cm)
Slave-making ant	¼ in (7 mm)
Torymid wasp	⅛ in (4 mm)
Velvet wasp	1⅓ in (3.5 cm)
Weaver ant	¼ in (7 mm)

Flies

Buzzer midge	⅓ in (1 cm)
Common housefly	¼ in (6 mm)
Greater bee fly	½ in (1.2 cm)
Horsefly	1 in (2.5 cm)
House mosquito	⅕ in (5 mm)
Hover fly	½ in (1.2 cm)
Mantis fly	⅕ in (5 mm)
Robber fly	1 in (2.5 cm)
Sand fly	⅛ in (3 mm)
Sheep blowfly	⅓ in (1 cm)
Sheep nasal botfly	½ in (1.4 cm)
Stalk-eyed fly	¼ in (6 mm)

Sea stars

Black brittle star	9¾ in (25 cm)
Common starfish	19½ in (50 cm)
Feather star	9¾ in (25 cm)
Gorgon's head	15⅔ in (40 cm)
Pelagic sea cucumber	3 in (8 cm)
Red pencil urchin	11 in (28 cm)
Reef sea urchin	27⅓ in (70 cm)
Sand dollar	2½ in (6.5 cm)
Sea apple	7 in (18 cm)
Synaptid sea cucumber	10 ft (3 m)

Index

Credits

Key t=top; l=left; r=right; tl=top left; tcl=top center left; tc=top center; tcr=top center right; tr=top right; cl=center left; c=center; cr=center right; b=bottom; bl=bottom left; bcl=bottom center left; bc=bottom center; bcr=bottom center right; br=bottom right

AAP = Australian Associated Press; AFP = Agence France-Presse; APL = Australian Picture Library; APL/CBT = Australian Picture Library/Corbis ; APL/MP = Australian Picture Library/Minden Pictures; AUS = Auscape International; DV = Digital Vision; GI = Getty Images; PL = photolibrary.com; WA = Wildlife Art Ltd

Front cover c Randy Wells, bl NHPA, bcl bcr br GI, bc COR **Spine** David Kirshner **Back cover** MagicGroup s.r.o. **Endpapers** Stuart Armstrong

Photographs 1bc, bl, c GI br DV cl APL cr APL/MP **10t** APL/CBT **11b** APL/CBT bc GI br APL/CBT **12br** APL t APL/CBT **13bl** GI **26t** AAP **34t** APL **48t** GI **63**bl PL t AUS **70br** APL/MP t GI **71bl** GI **93br**, cl APL/MP **98t** APL/CBT **104cr** APL/CBT t APL/MP **105bl** APL/CBT **111t** APL/MP **117t** APL/MP **122cr** AUS **124br** APL/CBT t GI **125bl**, br APL/MP **129t**l APL/MP **132c** PL tl GI **133bc** AFP bl, br APL/MP **135t** GI **140t** AUS **149**cl PL tl AUS **150t** PL **156br** APL/CBT t APL/MP **157bl** DV **164t** APL/CBT **170t** DV

Illustrations All illustrations © MagicGroup s.r.o. (Czech Republic)—www.magicgroup.cz— except for the following:

Alistair Barnard 129b, 147br; **Bernard Thornton Artists UK/John Francis** 116bl; **Bernard Thornton Artists UK/Tim Hayward** 55br; **Andre Boos** 43br; **Martin Camm** 47bcr br, 139b; **Creative Communications** 10br; **Simone End** 39br, 51bl, 156cl, 160tr, 175bc bl br; **Christer Eriksson** 5c, 16bl, 45br, 53br, 164bl, 166bl; **Folio/John Mac** 23c cl cr, 56cl bcl bl tl 57br; **Lloyd Foye** 93c, 156c;

Illustration Ltd/Mike Atkinson 72bl; **Jon Gittoes** 29tl, 40cr, 50bl; **Ray Grinaway** 143bc, 156br, 164cr, 165bc bcl, 170bcr; **Robert Hynes** 178bl; **David Kirshner** 17br, 25br, 26br, 27tr, 35tr, 37r bl, 47tc, 48bc bcr br, 53tr, 55cl, 60tr, 65br, 70c bl, 82cr, 84bl, 86bl, 91bc, 104bcl bcr bl br, 105br, 107b, 108bl, 122l, 125cr, 132bcl bcr bl br, 141tr, 142tr, 150cr, 151br, 155br, 164r; **Frank Knight** 23t, 34br, 36bcl bl, 37br, 45bl cl cr t tl tr, 46br c cl cr tc tcr tl, 47bc b c cl l r tcl tcr tl tr, 49b, 120bl, 129b; **James McKinnon** 106tr; **Rob Mancini** 3c, 63c, 70bc, 91br, 97tr, 164bc, 167br, 177bc bcr; **Peter Bull Art Studio** 13br, 158bl; **Tony Pyrzakowski** 62bl, 106bl; **Barbara Rodanska** 44br; **Trevor Ruth** 2l, 119br, 149b, 169br; **Marco Sparaciari** 161bcl; **Kevin Stead** 14cl, 156bc, 164br, 170bcl, 173b tr, 177bl, 179br; **Roger Swainston** 156bl, 170br; **Thomas Trojer** 143bcr; **Guy Troughton** 11cr tl, 14br cl cr tr, 15br, 16bc c cl, 18cl, 21bl c cl cr ctl tr, 23b tl, 24bl br, 29bc br, 31br, 32c cl cr tr, 33bc bl br tr, 45bcl, 49tr, 55tl, 58bl, 59bcl bcr bl br c cl tr, 61br, 69br, 103br; **WA/Dan Cole** 75b, 77br; **WA/Mark Dando** 136b; **WA/Sandra Doyle** 89br, 157br, 180l c cl; **WA/Ian Jackson** 156c, 170bl, 177br; **WA/Ken Oliver** 123br, 127tl; **WA/Steve Roberts** 174bl, 176bl; **WA/Peter Schouten** 32bl, 114bl; **WA/P. Scott** 71bc br; **WA/Chris Shields** 156cl, 165bl, 172tr; **WA/Chris Turnbull** 138bl; **Trevor Weekes** 90bl, 95r; **Ann Winterbotham** 143br

Montages Created by Domenika Markovtzev and John Bull. All images by artists listed above.

Maps/Graphics All pie charts by Domenika Markovtzev. All maps by Domenika Markovtzev and Map Illustrations.

The publishers wish to thank Helen Flint, Jennifer Losco, and Dr. Richard Schodde for their assistance in the preparation of this volume.

One of the world's largest nonprofit scientific and educational organizations, the National Geographic Society was founded in 1888 "for the increase and diffusion of geographic knowledge." Fulfilling this mission, the Society educates and inspires millions every day through its magazines, books, television programs, videos, maps and atlases, research grants, the National Geographic Bee, teacher workshops, and innovative classroom materials. The Society is supported through membership dues, charitable gifts, and income from the sale of its educational products. This support is vital to National Geographic's mission to increase global understanding and promote conservation of our planet through exploration, research, and education.

For more information, please call 1-800-NGS LINE (647-5463) or write to the following address:

National Geographic Society
1145 17th Street N.W.
Washington, D.C. 20036-4688 U.S.A.

Visit the Society's Web site at www.nationalgeographic.com.